CAMPBELL'S
2501 QUIZ QUESTIONS

A gift from the Hopkinton PTA.

By John P. Campbell

Campbell's High School/College Quiz Book (Revised Edition)

Campbell's Potpourri I of Quiz Bowl Questions

Campbell's Potpourri II of Quiz Bowl Questions (Revised Edition)

Campbell's Middle School Quiz Book #1 (Revised Edition)

Campbell's Potpourri III of Quiz Bowl Questions

Campbell's Middle School Quiz Book #2

Campbell's Elementary School Quiz Book #1

Campbell's 2001 Quiz Questions

Campbell's Potpourri IV of Quiz Bowl Questions

Campbell's Middle School Quiz Book #3

The 500 Famous Quotations Quiz Book

Campbell's 2002 Quiz Questions

Campbell's 210 Lightning Rounds

Campbell's 175 Lightning Rounds

Campbell's 2003 Quiz Questions

Campbell's 211 Lightning Rounds

Omniscience™: *The Basic Game of Knowledge in Book Form*

Campbell's 2004 Quiz Questions

Campbell's 212 Lightning Rounds

Campbell's Elementary School Quiz Book #2

Campbell's 176 Lightning Rounds

Campbell's 213 Lightning Rounds

Campbell's Potpourri V of Quiz Bowl Questions

Campbell's Mastering the Myths Quiz Book

Campbell's 3001 Quiz Questions

Campbell's 2701 Quiz Questions

Campbell's Quiz Book on Explorations and U.S. History to 1865

Campbell's Accent Cubed: Humanities, Math, and Science

Campbell's Accent on the Alphabet Quiz Book

CAMPBELL'S
2501 QUIZ QUESTIONS

by Rinda Brewbaker

PATRICK'S PRESS

Columbus, Georgia

Printed in the United States of America

CIP data suggested by the author

Brewbaker, Rinda, 1940-
Campbell's 2501 Quiz Questions

    Includes index.
    Summary: Questions and answers on a wide-range of topics, such as history, literature, geography, sports, the Bible, science, art, mythology, and religion, are arranged into fifty chapters.
    1. Questions and answers. [1. Questions and answers]
I. Title II. Title: Campbell's 2501 Quiz Questions
III. Title: 2501 Quiz Questions
IV. Title: Two Thousand Five Hundred and One Quiz Questions
AG195.C299b   2002   031'.02

ISBN (International Standard Book Number): 0-944322-26-3

First Edition
First Printing, September 1999
Second Printing, September, 2002

ACKNOWLEDGMENTS

I appreciate the help of Georgia Allison, John Campbell, Jo Fike, and David Taggart.

I would also like to thank Connie Erb for indexing the book.

I also thank Jackie Taylor for her typesetting capabilities.

TO

Office staff members Rubye Bruce, Connie Erb, and Carolyn Griffin, and office manager Saundra Voter, whose good humor and good will have created an atmosphere conducive to the preparation of this book, and to Patrick's Press owner and president John Campbell for his perseverance in making this a successful business venture.

PREFACE

This book is intended as quiz bowl material not only for the coach of an **elementary school** Academic Bowl team to use in conducting practices but also for team members to use as study material. The complete index complements this intention as the users of this book are able to find quickly material they wish to review.

In general, the 50 questions in each round are focused according to the ending digit as follows:

Numbers ending in 1: General, any subject

Numbers ending in 2: U.S. History

Numbers ending in 3: Geography

Numbers ending in 4 and #9, #29, #49: Math

Numbers ending in 5: Current events

Numbers ending in 6 and #19, #39: Science

Numbers ending in 7: Literature or language

Numbers ending in 8: Fine arts, Bible, religion, mythology, or sports

Numbers ending in 9: Math or science, as noted above

Numbers ending in 0: World History

Your suggestions and comments will be appreciated. Please send them to Rinda Brewbaker care of PATRICK'S PRESS, Box 5189, Columbus, Georgia, 31906.

CONTENTS

Round One 1
Round Two 6
Round Three 11
Round Four 16
Round Five..21
Round Six..26
Round Seven 31
Round Eight...36
Round Nine...42
Round Ten...48
Round Eleven 54
Round Twelve 59
Round Thirteen 64
Round Fourteen 69
Round Fifteen 74
Round Sixteen 79
Round Seventeen..84
Round Eighteen 89
Round Nineteen 94
Round Twenty..99
Round Twenty-One..104
Round Twenty-Two...109
Round Twenty-Three..114
Round Twenty-Four..119
Round Twenty-Five 124
Round Twenty-Six..129
Round Twenty-Seven 134
Round Twenty-Eight 139
Round Twenty-Nine 144
Round Thirty 150
Round Thirty-One 155
Round Thirty-Two 161
Round Thirty-Three 167
Round Thirty-Four 172
Round Thirty-Five...177
Round Thirty-Six..182
Round Thirty-Seven 187
Round Thirty-Eight...192
Round Thirty-Nine 197
Round Forty..202
Round Forty-One..207
Round Forty-Two..212

Round Forty-Three...217
Round Forty-Four...222
Round Forty-Five 227
Round Forty-Six 233
Round Forty-Seven...239
Round Forty-Eight 245
Round Forty-Nine..251
Round Fifty...256
Index 261

ELEMENTARY SCHOOL QUIZ BOOK - 1

1) Give the full name of either the FBI or the CIA.
   Answer: Federal Bureau of Investigation or Central Intelligence Agency.

2) Which Atlantic Coast city did James Oglethorpe establish as the first European settlement in Georgia on February, 12, 1733? Its name designates "a flat, treeless plain."
   Answer: Savannah (Oglethorpe served as its governor from 1733- 1743).

3) In the early 1990s, a record 32 people reached the summit of the world's tallest mountain. Name this mountain.
   Answer: Mount Everest (at 29,108 feet, located in Nepal and Tibet).

4) What percent of NCAA tournament games has a coach won with a record of 33 wins and 7 losses?
   Answer: 82.5%.

5) In which city in Spain was a torch ignited by an archer's flaming arrow to signal the beginning of the 1992 Summer Olympic Games?
   Answer: Barcelona.

6) According to Alaskan scientists, 1991 was the best year in centuries to view the northern lights. What is the Latin name for this colorful display in Arctic skies?
   Answer: *Aurora borealis*.

7) Name Arthur Conan Doyle's fictional British detective who always outsmarts Scotland Yard.
   Answer: Sherlock Holmes (introduced in 1887).

8) In 1999, the Smithsonian Institution unveiled a $40.6 million expansion that added a 6-story sky-lighted central area with a theater, cafe, and shops. What word rooted in Latin and beginning with *A* names such a high open area in the center of a modern building?
   Answer: Atrium.

9) What is the sum of the prime factors of 42?
   Answer: 12 (2 + 3 + 7).

10) PLO leader Yasir Arafat walked away unharmed from an airplane crash that killed 3 other people during a desert sandstorm in Libya. Name the Holy Land for which the *P* in PLO stands.
Answer: Palestine (Palestine Liberation Organization).

11) William Shakespeare was born in the 4th year of the 6th decade of the 16th century. Give this year.
Answer: 1564.

12) According to the Warren Commission's final report on September 27, 1964, who "acted alone" in killing President Kennedy.
Answer: Lee Harvey Oswald.

13) Name the nation on the Jutland Peninsula whose capital is Copenhagen.
Answer: Denmark.

14) When the New York Mets paid $13 million to Bobby Bonilla, Vince Coleman, and Howard Johnson, was this about 10%, 20%, 30%, or 40% of the team's $44 million in salaries?
Answer: 30%.

15) Complete the name of the nation's oldest environmental group, _____ Club, by completing the name of the California mountains, the _____ Nevada.
Answer: Sierra (Club; Sierra Nevada).

16) Scientists point to a 111-mile-wide crater in Mexico as evidence that a giant meteorite was responsible for the extinction of dinosaurs. Spell *dinosaurs*.
Answer: D-I-N-O-S-A-U-R-S.

17) Name Daniel Defoe's character who was stranded on an island for 24 years following a shipwreck.
Answer: Robinson Crusoe.

18) American Bobby Fischer once competed against Boris Spassky in Yugoslavia in which game played on a board with such pieces as pawns, knights, and rooks?
Answer: Chess.

19) Of the three kinds of rock, to which class does coal, which is often referred to as a fossil fuel, belong?
Answer: Sedimentary rock.

20) Name the Caribbean island where work on the country's largest industrial project, a Soviet-designed nuclear power plant, was halted in 1992 by its Communist president, Fidel Castro, because of rising costs.
Answer: Cuba.

21) Which color completes the following? *The government reported a $124.6 billion budget surplus in April 1998, ensuring that the year would finish in the _____ for the first time since 1969.*
Answer: Black (the U.S.'s fiscal, or financial year, ends September 30).

22) Thomas Jefferson faced considerable Congressional opposition to which 1803 land purchase that virtually doubled the size of the U.S.?
Answer: Louisiana Purchase (of 828,000 square miles for about $15 million).

23) Which South American country is the largest on the continent?
Answer: Brazil.

24) Drug lord Manuel Noriega was once convicted on 8 of 10 drug charges. In lowest terms, for what fraction of charges was he acquitted?
Answer: One-fifth.

25) According to a London newspaper, a man on his death bed confessed to using a toy submarine to help stage the famous 1934 photograph of the Loch Ness monster rising out of a lake in which United Kingdom division north of England?
Answer: Scotland.

26) Where do aquatic animals spend most of their time?
Answer: In the water.

27) Of these awards—Oscar, Pulitzer, Grammy, or Cy Young—which designates the American prize for literature and journalism first presented in 1917?
Answer: Pulitzer Prize.

28) Name the only black man to win Wimbledon and the U.S. Open tennis championships. He announced in 1992 that he had AIDS.
Answer: Arthur Ashe (he died in 1993).

29) If a square yard of fabric costs 90 cents, how much will a square foot cost?
Answer: 10 cents.

30) Name England's basic unit of money, which has the same name as a unit of weight.
Answer: Pound.

31) The Russian Church's Julian calendar trails our Gregorian calendar by 13 days. How many days are in our calendar year?
Answer: 365 days.

32) Oliver North's convictions in the Iran-*contra* scandal were reversed on appeal and his case dismissed when the highest court in the land refused to review it. Name this court.
Answer: Supreme Court.

33) Identify the bay for which the British named the mercantile company they founded on May 2, 1670, to establish a fur trade in what is now Canada.
Answer: Hudson Bay (the company was named the Hudson's Bay Company).

34) If a boy can walk a mile in 20 minutes, how far can he walk in 2 hours and 40 minutes at the same rate?
Answer: 8 miles.

35) Name the President from Texas under whom the Voting Rights Act of 1965 was passed to ensure voting rights for blacks.
Answer: Lyndon Johnson.

36) The low temperatures of 1992 may have resulted from the eruption of Mount Pinatubo. In which Pacific island country is this volcano located?
Answer: Philippines.

37) Robert Kennedy was assassinated in Los Angeles while campaigning for the Democratic presidential nomination in 1968. Spell *campaigning*.
Answer: C-A-M-P-A-I-G-N-I-N-G.

38) Engineer Henry Bessemer filed for the legal right to his process for making steel from molten pig iron on October 17, 1855. What term designates a government paper giving an inventor, and no one else, the right to make and sell an invention?
Answer: Patent.

39) In 1731, British scientist Henry Cavendish first recognized hydrogen gas as a distinct substance. How many atoms of hydrogen are in each molecule of water?
Answer: 2 (H_2O).

40) In which country did the Allied Expeditionary Force make its D-Day landing on June 6, 1944? This country is known for its Eiffel Tower.
Answer: France (in the province of Normandy).

41) Which structure featured in a children's song was transported from England and dedicated as a tourist attraction at Lake Havasu City, Arizona, on October 7, 1971?
Answer: **London Bridge (now Arizona's 2nd-biggest tourist attraction).**

42) Name the civil rights leader who was a candidate for the Democratic presidential nomination in 1984 and 1988.
Answer: **Jesse Jackson.**

43) Henry Clay first said in a Senate speech on February 7, 1839, "I'd rather be right than be president." Name the "Bluegrass State" which he represented.
Answer: **Kentucky.**

44) In 1992, California Governor Pete Wilson ended a 63-day deadlock, during which the state issued IOUs to employees, when he signed a $57-billion budget. Is 63 days about 1/8, 1/6, 1/4, or 1/3 of a year?
Answer: **1/6 (a few days more than 2 months).**

45) A flotilla of British warships and commercial vessels headed to French beaches to mark the 50th anniversary of the D-Day invasion. Which of the following words describes such an invasion using naval and land forces: *amphibious, amplified, ballistic,* or *supersonic?*
Answer: **Amphibious (D-Day was June 6, 1944).**

46) In the 1990s, medical scientists recommended that a morning oral temperature reading of up to 99 degrees and an evening reading of up to 100 degrees be considered normal. What had been accepted as the normal temperature since 1868?
Answer: **98.6.**

47) How many *l*'s and how many *p*'s are in the name *Philippines?*
Answer: **One *l* and 3 *p*'s.**

48) Political candidates sometimes court "blue-collar Americans," or those engaged in manual labor. What kind of collar represents professionals like attorneys and doctors?
Answer: **White collar.**

49) If the dollar value is quoted at 4.8 French francs, how much would one pay in dollars and cents for an object costing 25 francs in Paris?
Answer: **$5.20 (accept $5.21).**

50) Name the first U.S. President to visit Hawaii. He did so in 1934.
Answer: **Franklin Roosevelt.**

ELEMENTARY SCHOOL QUIZ BOOK - 2

1) In 1975, Elizabeth Seton became the first native-born American to be canonized by the head of the Roman Catholic Church. What title is given to a person who has been *canonized*, or glorified, by the Catholic Church?
   Answer: Saint.

2) On which day in June 1777, now known as Flag Day, did John Adams introduce the resolution that gave the U.S. flag 13 stripes and 13 stars?
   Answer: June 14.

3) Is Africa the 1st, 2nd, 3rd, or 4th largest continent in area?
   Answer: Second largest.

4) Expressed in fractional form, what is the average of 1/5 and 1/7?
   Answer: 6/35.

5) King Tut's tomb was discovered in 1922. Is a person who studies the past by digging up ancient civilizations an *archaeologist*, *lexicographer*, *orthodontist*, or *physicist*?
   Answer: Archaeologist.

6) Name the "Wizard of Menlo Park," who in 1868 filed for his first invention, an electric vote recorder designed to tabulate Congressional votes.
   Answer: Thomas Edison.

7) Harvard College held its first commencement exercises on September 23, 1642. Does *to commence* mean to begin, to end, to march, or to honor?
   Answer: To begin.

8) The epitaph for architect Christopher Wren, who is buried in St. Paul's Cathedral, reads, "If you would see his monument, look about you." Spell *architect*.
   Answer: A-R-C-H-I-T-E-C-T.

9) What is the average of 76, 81, and 95?
   Answer: 84.

10) Which French leader was defeated at Waterloo on June 18, 1815? His name also identifies a cream-filled pastry.
   Answer: Napoleon.

11) A truce signed at Panmunjom on July 27, 1953, ended which war involving the U.S. and resulting in an Asian country divided into North and South?
Answer: Korean War.

12) Over which U.S. state was the U.S. flag formally raised in October 1867, following its purchase from Russia by Secretary of State William H. Seward?
Answer: Alaska.

13) Identify the Middle Eastern country where King Hussein reigned for 47 years. It shares its name with a river of biblical fame.
Answer: Jordan (Hussein died in 1999 and was succeeded by his son Abdullah).

14) What is a 15% tip on a bill of $14.80?
Answer: $2.22.

15) Of the 197 countries in the 1996 Summer Olympics, which one was admitted with the understanding that the song it considers its national anthem would not be played to honor its gold medalists since China considers it a renegade province? Taipei is its capital city.
Answer: Taiwan (or Chinese Taipei, the name it had to use to compete since China considers it a province).

16) Into how many time zones is the earth divided?
Answer: 24 (it takes the sun an hour to cross each zone).

17) Boris Yeltsin was inaugurated as the first popularly elected president of Russia in July 1991. Spell *inaugurated*.
Answer: I-N-A-U-G-U-R-A-T-E-D.

18) In which of the following fields did Hungarian Franz Liszt become famous: music, architecture, medicine, or politics?
Answer: Music (Liszt was a composer and pianist).

19) There is a difference of 4 hours between the time in New York City and in Alaska. When it is midnight in New York, what time is it in Anchorage?
Answer: 8:00 p.m.

20) From which country did Costa Rica, El Salvador, Guatemala, Honduras, and Nicaragua gain independence in September 1821?
Answer: Spain.

21) Any year that is evenly divisible by 4, with exception of years ending in -00, is a leap year. Which of the following is *not* a leap year: 1992, 1960, 1926, or 1944?
Answer: **1926.**

22) Four U.S. states' names begin with the word *New*. In which of these states is Carlsbad Caverns National Park?
Answer: **New Mexico.**

23) An ozone "hole" over Antarctica has been detected. Spell *Antarctica*.
Answer: **A-N-T-A-R-C-T-I-C-A.**

24) President William Taft served on the U.S. Supreme Court after his term of office. How many justices make up this court, or how many months is 3/4 of a year?
Answer: **9.**

25) Which word, meaning "100th anniversary," names the Atlanta park where a bomb exploded during the 1996 Olympic Games, killing one person and injuring about 100?
Answer: **Centennial (Olympic) Park.**

26) According to researchers, milk often lacks the claimed amount of which vitamin found in fish-liver oils and formed in the skin when the body is exposed to sunlight?
Answer: **Vitamin D (called the "sunshine vitamin").**

27) To reduce the flood of refugees, Germany signed an accord with Romania to return citizens with inadequate identity papers. Spell *refugees*.
Answer: **R-E-F-U-G-E-E-S.**

28) Beethoven's *Fidelio*, a play in which the lines are sung, was performed at the opening of a Vienna theater on November 6, 1955. Which term designates a play set to music?
Answer: **Opera.**

29) The "Elvis Collection" of 660 cards when released sold in sets of 12 for $1.49 per set. How much did 48 cards cost?
Answer: **$5.96.**

30) The Korean War ended with an armistice signed in July 1953, eight years after the end of WWII. In which year did WWII end?
Answer: **1945.**

31) Name the first U.S. President to ride in an auto (1902), go underwater in a submarine (1905), and fly in an airplane (1910). A WWII President shares his surname.
Answer: **Theodore Roosevelt.**

32) The Great Seal of the United States was first used on a document in 1782. What animal is pictured on this seal?
Answer: American eagle.

33) Name the "Green Mountain" state, the birthplace of U.S. President Chester A. Arthur. It is the 8th smallest state.
Answer: Vermont.

34) What integer is the square of three squared?
Answer: 81.

35) Name the island divided by a border since 1920 where in May 1998 residents on both sides of the border voted approval of a peace settlement to end 30 years of bloodshed. Its northern area is part of the United Kingdom.
Answer: Ireland (consisting of Ireland and Northern Ireland, of the United Kingdom).

36) Name the element once found in the water system of Charleston, South Carolina, at levels 14 times higher than the allowable level. Absorption of this element, whose name is a homograph for the verb meaning "to show the way," can cause brain disorders and retardation, and its symbol is Pb.
Answer: Lead.

37) With Jocelyn Burdick's succession to her late husband's North Dakota seat in 1992, the U.S. Senate had 3 female members for the first time. Spell *succession*.
Answer: S-U-C-C-E-S-S-I-O-N.

38) Which prefix for "loving" completes ___*harmonic* to name the oldest U.S. symphony?
Answer: *Phil-* (New York Philharmonic, which opened its 157th season in 1999).

39) According to a medical journal report, 1,470 children died of Reyes Syndrome because of a nearly 5-year government delay in requiring warnings on bottles of which common fever medication?
Answer: Aspirin.

40) In 1513, which explorer became the first European to see the eastern shore of the Pacific Ocean? The second syllable of his surname identifies a large snake.
Answer: Vasco Núñez de Balboa.

41) What term designates a man-made water channel used to connect 2 existing bodies of water, such as the one first used for passage between the Atlantic and Pacific in 1914?
Answer: Canal.

42) On October 22, 1962, which U.S. President imposed a "quarantine" or naval blockade and demanded that the Soviet Union remove its missiles from Cuba?
Answer: John F. Kennedy.

43) Which of the following words identifies a flat-topped hill with steeply sloping sides: *mesa, oasis, plain,* or *delta*?
Answer: Mesa.

44) In a class of 32 students, there are 3 times as many brown-eyed students as blue-eyed ones. How many students have blue eyes?
Answer: 8.

45) In which state were NASA scientists at the U.S. Space and Rocket Center in Huntsville assigned the task of designing a space station? George Wallace was formerly governor of this state.
Answer: Alabama.

46) What term designates a line along which the earth's plates shift, such as the one under Parkfield, California, for which a U.S. agency once issued its first-ever earthquake warning?
Answer: Fault (San Andreas Fault in this case).

47) Name the adverb in the following sentence: "Former Alabama Governor George Wallace, partially paralyzed when shot during a presidential campaign stop in 1972, underwent emergency surgery in 1992."
Answer: Partially.

48) Archaeologists have found that a site near Nazareth is Israel's richest site for finding ancient mosaics. Spell *archaeologists*.
Answer: A-R-C-H-A-E-O-L-O-G-I-S-T-S.

49) How many prime numbers are there between 30 and 40?
Answer: 2 (31 and 37).

50) Several countries have pushed for change in the makeup of the U.N. Security Council. Name 3 of the 5 countries that are permanent members of this council.
Answer: Britain, China, France, Russia, and U.S.

1) The U.N. took $1 billion from Iraq to compensate victims in Kuwait, pay for U.N. weapons inspections, and give aid to dissident Kurds and Shiites. Spell *seizure*, meaning "the act of taking possession."
Answer: **S-E-I-Z-U-R-E.**

2) Name the two 1960 presidential candidates who held 4 debates. One was assassinated in 1963, and the other resigned the presidency in 1974.
Answer: **John Kennedy and Richard Nixon.**

3) Which U.S. state borders 4 of the 5 Great Lakes?
Answer: **Michigan.**

4) The U.S. Olympic basketball "Dream Team" won its last game of the 1992 qualifying tournament by 47 points, scoring a total of 80 points. How many points did the U.S. score in the game?
Answer: **127 points.**

5) In which city is there a 4-story-tall movie theater built below the Mississippi River's water table at the site of the Gateway Arch?
Answer: **St. Louis.**

6) Which astronomer predicted that the great comet he observed in 1682 would reappear 76 years later? This comet is now named for him.
Answer: **Edmund Halley.**

7) James Brady, who was gravely injured in the assassination attempt on President Reagan, campaigned for a handgun control bill in 1992. Spell *assassination*.
Answer: **A-S-S-A-S-S-I-N-A-T-I-O-N.**

8) Which British author wrote the line "Once upon a time there were four little Rabbits, and their names were Flopsy, Mopsy, Cottontail, and Peter"?
Answer: **(Helen) Beatrix Potter.**

9) U.S. swimmer Summer Sanders won a gold for the 200-meter butterfly. Is 200 meters approximately 400, 600, 800, or 1,000 feet?
Answer: **600 feet.**

10) Which country exploded its first atomic bomb in September 1949?
Answer: **Soviet Union.**

11) Which American League team took the World Series to Canada for the first time in 1992 in a matchup with the National League's champion Atlanta Braves?
Answer: **Toronto Blue Jays.**

12) President George Washington said in his Farewell Address, "'Tis our true policy to steer clear of permanent alliances with any portion of the foreign world." In which century did he make this speech?
Answer: **18th century (in September 1796).**

13) In which city was Faneuil Hall the site of protests by colonists before the American Revolution? It is often called the "Cradle of Liberty."
Answer: **Boston.**

14) According to U.S. National Tick Collection records, the average tick travels 60 feet an hour. At this rate, how many yards does a tick travel in 2½ hours?
Answer: **50 yards.**

15) Japanese leader Akihito once expressed regret but did not formally apologize for war atrocities in China during WWII. Is his title *president, king, emperor,* or *czar*?
Answer: **Emperor (he is the first Japanese emperor to visit China).**

16) Which disease is the result of a lack of insulin, the hormone discovered by Canadian physician Frederick Grant Banting that lowers the level of sugar in the blood?
Answer: **Diabetes.**

17) Vice President Quayle misspelled *potato* by adding an *e* to a student's writing of the word. Which of these plurals does not end in *-es*: *vetoes, heroes, echoes,* or *studios*?
Answer: **Studios.**

18) Identify the person into whose garden Peter is warned not to go in *The Tale of Peter Rabbit.*
Answer: **Mr. McGregor.**

19) Which word beginning with the letter *a* designates "any mixture of metals, such as brass, a mixture of copper and zinc"?
Answer: **Alloy.**

20) President Anwar el-Sadat was assassinated on October 6, 1981, while reviewing a military parade commemorating his country's 1973 war with Israel. Name this African country whose capital is Cairo.
Answer: **Egypt.**

21) Which presidential candidate did 11-year-old Grace Bedell persuade to grow a beard, telling him she would then encourage her brothers to vote for him in the 1860 election?
Answer: Abraham Lincoln.

22) In which year was the first permanent English settlement in the New World established near the James River in Virginia, 169 years before the colonies declared independence?
Answer: 1607.

23) Name 3 of the 5 Great Lakes.
Answer: Ontario, Erie, Huron, Michigan, and Superior.

24) President Bush once proposed cutting the pay of top federal officials, including himself, by 10%. What would he have made with a cut of 10% of his salary of $200,000?
Answer: $180,000.

25) Name the Eurasian country whose ship was once accidentally struck by a U.S. missile during NATO war games in the Aegean Sea. Its capital is Ankara, and its name also identifies a kind of poultry.
Answer: Turkey (missiles fired from *USS Saratoga*).

26) Which word beginning with the letter *A* designates the "smallest part of an element with all the characteristics of that element"?
Answer: Atom.

27) President Lincoln issued his preliminary Emancipation Proclamation in September 1862. Spell the verb from which *proclamation* comes.
Answer: P-R-O-C-L-A-I-M.

28) Are those who follow Mohammed's teachings called Buddhists, Muslims, Jews, or Mormons?
Answer: Muslims.

29) If you misspell 20 words from a list of 80, what percentage of the words did you spell correctly?
Answer: 75%.

30) In which city does the United Nations open its annual regular sessions of the General Assembly on the third Tuesday of September?
Answer: New York.

31) President Bush chose Democrat Robert S. Strauss to represent the U.S. in Moscow. What is the term for the highest ranking person sent by a government to represent it in another country?
Answer: Ambassador.

32) In 1996, the Crown Prince of the Netherlands helped dedicate a new recreation center for people with disabilities at a reha- bilitation institute founded by which U.S. President in Warm Springs, Georgia, in 1927? His wife's name was Eleanor.
Answer: Franklin D. Roosevelt (he underwent treat- ment for polio in its warm waters).

33) On which of the Great Lakes does the state of Michigan not border?
Answer: Lake Ontario.

34) If the perimeter of a rectangle is 90 cm and its length is 30, what is its width?
Answer: 15 cm.

35) President Bush once approved an amendment to compensate spouses and parents of Japanese-Americans interned during WWII with $20,000 each. Does *interned* mean "fined," "executed," "imprisoned," or "assigned to hard labor"?
Answer: Imprisoned (especially during wartime).

36) Which 2-word term beginning with the letter *B* designates "the temperature at which a liquid becomes a gas"?
Answer: Boiling point.

37) What word designates a widespread shortage of food: *famine, fast, plague,* or *holocaust*?
Answer: Famine.

38) Composer George Gershwin is known for his opera *Porgy and Bess* and for such songs as "Funny Face," and "I Got Rhythm." Spell *rhythm*.
Answer: R-H-Y-T-H-M.

39) Which word beginning with the letter *C* designates the temper- ature scale on which the melting point of ice is 0%?
Answer: Centigrade.

40) Name the Icelandic-born Norse explorer credited with the dis- covery of North America on October 9 in A.D. 1000.
Answer: Leif Eriksson (Eiriksson; Erikson; Ericson; Ericsson).

41) Except for the peace prize, the Nobel prizes established by Alfred Nobel, the inventer of dynamite, are awarded in Stock- holm, the capital of his native land. Name this land.
Answer: Sweden.

42) Charleston, South Carolina, was hit by Hurricane Hugo in 1989. Name the state whose capital city is called Charleston.
Answer: West Virginia (Columbia is the capital of South Carolina).

43) In which Maryland city did the U.S. Naval Academy open in October 1845?
Answer: Annapolis.

44) In lowest terms, what is the mixed number for 24 over 9?
Answer: 2 2/3.

45) For the first time in 17 years, to which planet was an American spacecraft sent in 1992 on an 11-month, $980 million trip? It is known as the Red Planet.
Answer: Mars (*Mars Observer*).

46) A human has 4 flat-edged teeth in front on both the top and bottom used specifically for biting food. Name these teeth.
Answer: Incisors.

47) The space shuttle *Atlantis* had to abandon a historic experiment to generate electricity with a tethered satellite after the cord snagged repeatedly. Spell *satellite*.
Answer: S-A-T-E-L-L-I-T-E.

48) Name the native country of pianist Ignace Paderewski, who abandoned his musical career to fight for his country's freedom in WWI. Its capital is Warsaw.
Answer: Poland.

49) In how many minutes can an automobile travelling at 30 miles per hour make a 30-mile trip without stopping?
Answer: 60 minutes (accept one hour).

50) Which European country was formally divided into 2 parts in September 1949 and reunited in 1990, following the opening of the Berlin Wall a year earlier?
Answer: Germany.

ELEMENTARY SCHOOL QUIZ BOOK - 4

1) How many years are in a U.S. senator's term, or how many inches are in 1/6 of a yard?
Answer: 6.

2) Name the hero of the Battle of San Jacinto who was inaugurated as the first president of the Republic of Texas on October 22, 1836. The largest city in Texas is named for him.
Answer: Sam Houston.

3) What ranks as Arizona's most popular tourist attraction, ahead of London Bridge?
Answer: Grand Canyon.

4) Find the area of a rectangle 42 inches by 15 inches.
Answer: 630 square inches.

5) In 1995, Mohican Indians protested a proposal to build a Wal-Mart at a New York site at the foot of which of the following mountains: Blue Ridge, Ozark, Catskill, or Green?
Answer: Catskill.

6) The Canadian flag was once mistakenly flown upside down at a World Series game. What kind of leaf is pictured on the Canadian flag?
Answer: Maple leaf.

7) In 1998, Queen Elizabeth followed tradition by traveling from her palace to Parliament in a carriage escorted by a unit of guards on horseback. Spell the word beginning with C that names such guards or soldiers, especially U.S. troops who defended settlers in the U.S. West.
Answer: C-A-V-A-L-R-Y.

8) English poet Alfred, Lord Tennyson became England's state poet in 1850. What title designates the official poet of a country?
Answer: Poet laureate.

9) A survey said that about 80% of airline passengers sleep on long flights. On this basis, how many of 240 passengers sleep?
Answer: 192.

10) On September 18, 1961, U.N. Secretary General Dag Hammarskjöld was killed in a plane crash while trying to arrange a cease-fire in the Congo. Spell the word *cease-fire*.
Answer: C-E-A-S-E hyphen F-I-R-E (or C-E-A-S-E-F-I-R-E, without hyphen).

11) In which century did British Admiral Horatio Nelson defeat the French and Spanish in October 1805, off of Spain's Cape Trafalgar at the Battle of Trafalgar?
Answer: 19th century.

12) Which religious group did Brigham Young lead in their migration west from Nauvoo, Illinois, to a new "promised land" in Utah in 1846?
Answer: Mormons (departed Nauvoo on February 10, 1846).

13) The shape of the state of Georgia resembles most closely which of the following: Colorado, Idaho, Missouri, or West Virginia?
Answer: Missouri.

14) Find the number of seconds in 2.5 hours.
Answer: 9,000 seconds.

15) Which European country developed the $4 million satellite placed aboard *Columbia* that studied the movement of the Earth's crust? It is known for its Apennine Mountains and its Po and Tiber rivers.
Answer: Italy.

16) Which word beginning with the letter *D* designates the hardest substance in nature, a form of carbon?
Answer: Diamond.

17) Identify the noun *officers* as a subject, direct object, or object of a preposition in the following: Joseph Stalin ordered the execution of 14,700 Polish officers during WWII according to a signature on a document.
Answer: Object of a preposition.

18) Name the secretary of state who became White House chief of staff in charge of President Bush's re-election campaign, or complete the rhyme: "Three men in a tub./ The butcher, the _____, the candlestick maker."
Answer: James A. Baker III.

19) Which disease, known by an acronym, took the lives of the more than 20,000 people memorialized by a 15-acre quilt that was displayed at the base of the Washington Monument in 1992?
Answer: AIDS.

20) Name the Canadian city on the St. Lawrence River where the French lost a disastrous battle to the British and then surrendered on September 18, 1759.
Answer: Quebec.

21) Which Venus-orbiting spaceship, meant to last 243 days, began a slow plunge into the planet's atmosphere in 1992 after 14 years? Its name means "one who opens up new areas."
Answer: *Pioneer 12* (accept *Pioneer*).

22) In 1991, House members spent $44 million using their privilege of franking, or sending mail free. Spell *privilege*.
Answer: P-R-I-V-I-L-E-G-E.

23) Between which 2 seas does Turkey lie? One of them has a colorful name.
Answer: Mediterranean Sea and Black Sea.

24) Congress once rejected the President's veto of a bill requiring the FCC to set basic cable TV rates. For the House to override the veto, how many votes were needed to make the required 2/3 majority of the 422 members present?
Answer: 282 (House voted 308-14; Senate, 74-25; after a string of 35 successful vetoes).

25) Guerilla leader Abimael Guzman has been sentenced to life in prison without parole in Peru's military trial of a rebel leader. On which body of water is Peru located?
Answer: Pacific Ocean.

26) In 1999, President Clinton and his family were among the 1,300 people attending Renaissance Weekend with its 365 off-the-record panels at Hilton Head, South Carolina. Spell *renaissance*, meaning "rebirth or renewal."
Answer: R-E-N-A-I-S-S-A-N-C-E.

27) Give the verb in the following: The London Zoo has been saved from extinction by popular appeal and a $2 million check from Kuwait.
Answer: Has been saved (present perfect tense, passive voice).

28) Name the Pennsylvania-born composer and band conductor often called the "March King" and known for "The Stars and Stripes Forever."
Answer: John Philip Sousa.

29) What is the average age of the following: John, 83; Bill, 75; Mary, 72; Betty, 68; and Harold, 22?
Answer: 64.

30) In October 1989, Hungary declared itself independent, 33 years after Soviet troops crushed a revolt against Communist rule. On which continent is Hungary located?
Answer: Europe.

31) After picking the correct winner in the prior 9 presidential elections, which news publication for students announced George Bush as the 1992 winner of its poll?
Answer: *Weekly Reader.*

32) Who wrote the book *My Story* to tell of her refusal to give her seat on a bus to a white man in Montgomery, Alabama, in 1955?
Answer: **Rosa Parks.**

33) In a 31-nation study of basic reading skills in the 1990s, which Scandinavian country, whose capital is Helsinki, finished first?
Answer: **Finland.**

34) Japanese children attend school 240 days a year, compared with about 180 days in the U.S. What percent of 240 days is 180 days?
Answer: **75%.**

35) Steven McAuliffe, husband of the teacher killed in a spacecraft explosion, was once nominated to be a U.S. judge. Name the space shuttle in which his wife Christa died.
Answer: *Challenger.*

36) What is the common seasoning represented by the chemical formula NaCl or known as the compound *sodium chloride*?
Answer: **(Table) salt.**

37) On September 28, 1542, explorer Juan Cabrillo sailed into San Diego harbor, an action that qualifies him as the European discoverer of California. Spell *discoverer*.
Answer: **D-I-S-C-O-V-E-R-E-R.**

38) Which term designates a person who is holding an office, particularly at the time the officeholder is running for re-election: *recluse, incumbent, precursor*, or *lame duck*?
Answer: **Incumbent.**

39) Name the internal combustion engine that uses oil instead of gasoline. This engine, named for its German inventor, is used in heavy trucks and buses, and in some cars.
Answer: **Diesel engine (named for R. Diesel).**

40) Norman leader William the Conqueror landed in England with his army on September 28, 1066. What language did he bring with him?
Answer: **French.**

41) Name the city in whose harbor the "Star-Spangled Banner" was written and in which it was sung for the first time in 1814. It is Maryland's largest city.
Answer: Baltimore.

42) Which Virginia city, the first permanent English settlement in the New World, was burned in September 1676 during a popular uprising led by Nathaniel Bacon?
Answer: Jamestown.

43) In which Western U.S. city known as the "Mile High City" was a Columbus Day parade canceled in 1992 to avoid a clash with hundreds of American Indian activists?
Answer: Denver.

44) What amount, represented by the Roman numeral M, is the most an individual can give to a U.S. presidential campaign?
Answer: $1,000.

45) In 1996, President Clinton ordered sanctions against companies that invest in "two of the world's most dangerous supporters of terrorism." Name either of these 2 African nations, whose capitals are Tripoli and Teheran.
Answer: Libya or Iran, respectively.

46) The Mesabi Range is famous for its iron deposits discovered in 1844? What 3-letter word, a homonym for a conjunction, designates rock or earth with silver, iron, or other metals in it?
Answer: Ore.

47) Margaret Thatcher, former British prime minister, once denounced the Maastricht European unity treaty and criticized her successor, John Major. Spell *successor*.
Answer: S-U-C-C-E-S-S-O-R.

48) The 1929 Lateran Treaty signed by Cardinal Gasparri and Benito Mussolini on February 11 guaranteed an independent state for the Catholic Church headquarters. Name it.
Answer: The Vatican.

49) If a Russian has 10,000 rubles, or $50, how many rubles equal one dollar?
Answer: 200 rubles.

50) In September 1946, an international military court found 22 top WWII German leaders guilty of war crimes. Name the German political party to which they belonged.
Answer: Nazi Party.

1) Traditionally, how many people are on a trial jury in the U.S., or how many labors did the mythological Hercules perform?
Answer: **12 (some states have only 6 people on a trial jury).**

2) Which U.S. President was killed in 1881? His surname identifies a comic strip cat.
Answer: **James Garfield.**

3) The U.S. dependency of Guam was declared a disaster area after Typhoon Omar caused major damage. In which ocean is Guam located?
Answer: **Pacific Ocean.**

4) Alaska's government once gave all Alaskans $915.84 as a dividend from a fund set up from the state's oil wealth. With this dividend, how much did a family of 4 receive?
Answer: **$3,663.36.**

5) Which luxury liner sank in 1912? Its name comes from a mythological family of giants.
Answer: *Titanic.*

6) Name the science that is the study of the moon, sun, stars, and other heavenly bodies.
Answer: **Astronomy.**

7) Give the Greek root for "life" that is used in naming a kind of literature that tells a life story, such as James Boswell's *Life of Samuel Johnson*.
Answer: *Bio-* **(as in** *biography***).**

8) How many keys are on a standard piano keyboard, a number equivalent to 11 octaves?
Answer: **88.**

9) The family suite in the White House consists of 1/11 of its 132 rooms. How many rooms are in this suite?
Answer: **12.**

10) In which country did the Gulf War Allies set the 32nd parallel as the boundary of a "no-fly zone" to protect 7 million Shiites from Saddam Hussein's forces?
Answer: **Iraq.**

11) Helmut Kohl served as Germany's leader for 16 years. As head of its government, was Kohl's title *king, chancellor, president,* or *prime minister?*
Answer: **Chancellor.**

12) British officer Major John André was hanged as a spy in October 1780 after plotting with which American general and traitor to capture West Point?
Answer: **Benedict Arnold.**

13) Russia agreed to withdraw all of its Red Army troops from Lithuania by August, 31, 1993. On which sea is Lithuania located: Red, Baltic, Mediterranean, or Caribbean?
Answer: **Baltic Sea.**

14) An actor sold his 1947 Oscar for $60,500. How much more did another actor pay for the 1986 World Series baseball he purchased for $93,500?
Answer: **$33,000.**

15) Which city, the U.S.'s 6th largest at the time it hosted the 1996 Republican National Convention, offers easy access to the beach, snow-covered mountains, a desert, and Mexico?
Answer: **San Diego.**

16) Which kind of animal scientifically known as *Canis lupus* was spotted in Yellowstone National Park in 1992 for the first time since 1926?
Answer: **Gray wolf (or timber wolf).**

17) In 1991, the Soviet Union dropped charges of treason against author Alexander Solzhenitsyn, who had been in exile for 17 years. What literary prize did he win in 1970?
Answer: **Nobel Prize (in literature).**

18) Spell the word that completes the following phrase from the "Pledge of Allegiance": "...one Nation, under God, _____, with liberty and justice for all."
Answer: **I-N-D-I-V-I-S-I-B-L-E.**

19) What name is given to the path a heavenly body travels around a second larger body?
Answer: **Orbit.**

20) Identify the "Admiral of the Ocean Sea" who set sail from Palos, Spain, on August 2, 1492, for "Cathay," or China.
Answer: **Christopher Columbus.**

21) A drunken driver who killed the daughter of MADD founder Candy Lightner in 1980 was convicted again in 1992 as a first offender. What does the acronym MADD stand for?
Answer: Mothers Against Drunk Driving.

22) In which present-day state did Lord Cornwallis surrender more than 7,000 English and Hessian soldiers to George Washington in Yorktown on October 19, 1781?
Answer: Virginia.

23) In late May 1998, which country joined India in testing nuclear weapons for the first time ever, raising fears of another war between them? Its capital is Islamabad.
Answer: Pakistan.

24) Give the Roman numerals for all of the following: 10, 100, and 1000.
Answer: X, C, and M.

25) In which nation did voters once reject constitutional reforms designed to put an end to 200 years of English-French squabbling and to keep the country's 10 provinces united? This North American country is sometimes called "America's Attic."
Answer: Canada.

26) Which word beginning with the letter E designates the surname of the physicist known for his formula $E=mc^2$?
Answer: (Albert) Einstein.

27) The Hawaiian island of Kauai was once devastated by Hurricane Iniki, this century's most powerful storm. Spell *Hawaiian*.
Answer: H-A-W-A-I-I-A-N.

28) In 1517, a German posted 95 objections to the Catholic Church, starting a movement that led to the founding of Protestantism. Identify this churchman who shares his name with the civil rights winner of the 1964 Nobel Peace Prize.
Answer: Martin Luther (Martin Luther King Jr. was named for him).

29) What is the perimeter of a rectangle with a length of 8 inches and a width of 6 inches?
Answer: 28 inches.

30) In which year were the Japanese cities of Hiroshima and Nagasaki hit by atomic bombs, on August 6 and 9, respectively, to hasten the end of WWII?
Answer: 1945.

31) Frank Sinatra, the singer once featured in a *Life* magazine issue, was nicknamed "Ol' Blue Eyes." Which of the following is a shade of blue: *amber, azure, emerald*, or *ruby*?
Answer: **Azure.**

32) Women were given the right to vote in 1920. Name the city whose residents were given the right to vote in presidential elections by the 23rd Amendment, ratified in 1961.
Answer: **Residents of Washington, D.C.**

33) In which Western state is the U.S. Geological Survey's National Earthquake Information Center located? This state's name comes from the Spanish for "colored red."
Answer: **Colorado.**

34) Following charges of tax evasion, U.S. Vice President Spiro Agnew resigned from office on October 10 in which year designated by the Roman numeral MCMLXXIII?
Answer: **1973.**

35) Arkansas Gov. Bill Clinton defeated George Bush to become the U.S.'s 42nd President. What party did Clinton represent?
Answer: **Democratic Party.**

36) Does the fact that an egg will float in salt water but not in regular water depend on *its shape, its density, its age*, or *its luster*?
Answer: **Its density.**

37) Identify the appositive in the following sentence: "Geraldine Ferraro, Mondale's running mate in the 1984 presidential election, has conceded defeat in a New York Senate primary."
Answer: **Running mate.**

38) Complete the following line from Julia Ward Howe's song "The Battle Hymn of the Republic": "Glory! Glory! Hallelujah! His _____ is marching on."
Answer: **Truth.**

39) Which word beginning with the letter *G* designates the state of matter in which molecules can move freely?
Answer: **Gas.**

40) In which port of the Hawaiian Islands did Japan suddenly attack U.S. forces on December 7, 1941, at 7.55 a.m.?
Answer: **Pearl Harbor (on Oahu).**

41) Identify the 2 tiny reindeer whose names begin with the letter C in Clement Moore's 1823 poem *An Account of a Visit from St. Nicholas*. One is named for a heavenly body, and the other for the Roman god of love.
Answer: Comet and Cupid.

42) What name is given today to the Badge of Military Merit created by George Washington? This award for those wounded or killed in combat bears the name of a color associated with royalty.
Answer: Purple Heart.

43) Thousands of veterans and troops have marched in New York City's Veterans' Day parades on which avenue, site of the traditional Easter Parade?
Answer: 5th Avenue.

44) What percent of 200 is 50?
Answer: 25 percent.

45) In 1990, scientists extracted fragile strands of which kind of substance, often referred to as the genetic code of life, from a magnolia leaf that thrived 17 million years ago?
Answer: DNA.

46) Which chemical compound used to treat water to prevent tooth decay has been linked to increased hip fractures in the elderly?
Answer: Fluoride (accept fluorine, the chemical element).

47) Name the American author whose first published story, "The Celebrated Jumping Frog of Calaveras County," appeared in 1865. His pen name includes a word for "two."
Answer: Mark Twain (Samuel Langhorne Clemens).

48) President Mikhail Gorbachev was once the target of a failed coup. Spell *coup*, a word meaning "a sudden effort to overthrow an existing government."
Answer: C-O-U-P.

49) How many square yards of carpeting are needed to carpet a room 3 feet by 12 feet?
Answer: 4 square yards.

50) Which military term completes *secretary-_____*, the title of Boutros Boutros-Ghali as administrative head of the U.N.?
Answer: (Secretary)-general.

1) Name the book tracing his ancestors for which Alex Haley won the Pulitzer, or name the edible parts of carrot plants.
   Answer: *Roots* **(or roots).**

2) Which U.S. city did British forces invade and burn on August 24-25, 1814?
   Answer: **Washington, D.C.**

3) The Central American country that borders South America declared itself independent from Colombia on November 3, 1903. Name this country.
   Answer: **Panama.**

4) A score is a group of 20 items. How many dozen are there in four score and 4?
   Answer: **7.**

5) Which word meaning "a written agreement" is represented by the *T* in the acronym NATO?
   Answer: **Treaty (NATO is the North Atlantic Treaty Organization).**

6) Which word beginning with the letter *H* designates the image of an object formed by reflected laser light?
   Answer: **Hologram.**

7) Former President Carter wrote 2 poems published in the magazine called *Georgia Journal*. How is the title of a magazine indicated in a handwritten manuscript?
   Answer: **Underlining.**

8) Massachusetts Senator Kennedy once acknowledged "faults in the conduct of my private life" and pledged to confront his faults. Spell *acknowledged*.
   Answer: **A-C-K-N-O-W-L-E-D-G-E-D.**

9) What is the least common denominator for the fractions 1/16 and 1/5?
   Answer: **80.**

10) Complete the full name of the Bedloe Island sculpture _____ *Enlightening the World* with a word meaning "freedom." This statue was dedicated on October 28, 1886.
    Answer: *Liberty* **(Bedloe's Island, now called Liberty Island, is in New York Harbor).**

11) A report on censorship charged Florida groups with making the most attempts at banning books in the 1991-92 school term. Spell *censorship.*
Answer: C-E-N-S-O-R-S-H-I-P.

12) Who led a march on Washington on August 28, 1963, and delivered the famous "I Have a Dream" speech during this protest?
Answer: Martin Luther King Jr.

13) Which national memorial containing sculptures of the heads of 4 U.S. Presidents was completed on October 31, 1941, after 14 years of work?
Answer: Mount Rushmore National Memorial (in South Dakota).

14) Calculate how much Bill Clinton had spent on national TV advertising as of October 31, 1992, based on the facts that President Bush had spent $18 million, Ross Perot had spent $5 million more than Bush, and Clinton had spent $14 million less than Perot.
Answer: $9 million.

15) Name the state whose Everglades National Park lost its last 2 female panthers when they died in August 1991.
Answer: Florida.

16) Which measurement is 1,000 times greater than the watt?
Answer: Kilowatt.

17) Former Louisiana prosecutor Jim Garrison believed the CIA was responsible for killing President Kennedy to keep the U.S. involved in the Vietnam War. Spell *prosecutor*, meaning "one who conducts a law case against a charged criminal."
Answer: P-R-O-S-E-C-U-T-O-R (also called *prosecuting attorney*).

18) Artist Frederic Remington is known for his paintings and sculptures of cowboys and Indians, particularly his statue *Bronco Buster*. Name the brownish alloy of copper and tin of which this statue is made.
Answer: Bronze.

19) Which letter completes the Roman numeral MCM_ for 1950?
Answer: L.

20) Which seaman, the first Englishman to circumnavigate the world, died on his ship off the coast of Panama on January 28, 1596? His surname designates a male duck.
Answer: Sir Francis Drake.

21) Spell both of the following words of French origin: *chalet*, designating a wooden cottage or hut, and *chateau*, designating a castle.
   Answer: C-H-A-L-E-T and C-H-A-T-E-A-U.

22) Name the WWII military leader and president of Columbia University who was elected U.S. President in 1952. After leaving office, he retired to a farm in Gettysburg, Pennsylvania.
   Answer: Dwight David Eisenhower.

23) Name the U.S. state whose panhandle is located between Washington and Montana.
   Answer: Idaho.

24) How much more was 1992's 3.7% Social Security cost-of-living increase than 1987's 1.3%?
   Answer: 2.4%.

25) A federal court panel in Virginia recently gave police in 5 Eastern states the right not to have to inform, or warn, those arrested of their right to remain silent. Of Dred Scott, Miranda, Roe, or Brown, which name identifies this warning used by police since 1966?
   Answer: Miranda (warning; from the *Miranda v. Arizona* case).

26) In a reversal of earlier recommendations, CPR experts have said the best way to save someone's life is to call which telephone number before beginning CPR?
   Answer: 911 (previously, experts said to give 1 minute of CPR before calling 911).

27) Complete the title of the 1943 film _____ *Come Home* with the name of the only animal, a collie, profiled in *Jane and Michael Stern's Encyclopedia of Pop Culture*.
   Answer: Lassie.

28) What part of speech is *spending* in the following? Michael Huffington's campaign for the U.S. House set a spending record with more than $4 million in campaign costs.
   Answer: Adjective (Huffington ran in California).

29) What is the result of replacing the tens digit of 1992 with 3 and the hundreds digit with 4 and doubling the new number?
   Answer: 2,864.

30) Between which 2 countries was a peace treaty signed on September 3, 1783, to end the Revolutionary War?
   Answer: Great Britain and the United States.

31) On October 29, 1940, the first peacetime compulsory service in the U.S. was inaugurated when the secretary of war drew the first draft number. Spell *secretary*.
Answer: S-E-C-R-E-T-A-R-Y (the first number was 158).

32) Which 3 U.S. Presidents besides George Washington are sculpted on Mount Rushmore?
Answer: Thomas Jefferson, Abraham Lincoln, and Theodore Roosevelt.

33) Name the U.S. state whose panhandle is located between Oklahoma and New Mexico.
Answer: Texas.

34) How many degrees are between north and south on a compass?
Answer: 180 degrees.

35) Name the national museum in Washington, D.C., that displays heart-wrenching notes and other mementos left at the Vietnam Veterans Memorial.
Answer: The Smithsonian Institution.

36) Which word beginning with the letter *R* designates "a device whose name stands for radio direction and ranging"?
Answer: Radar.

37) John Kennedy initiated the idea of a Peace Corps in a campaign speech at the University of Michigan in 1960. Spell the word *corps*, meaning "a group of people."
Answer: C-O-R-P-S (Kennedy formally proposed the Peace Corps 19 days later).

38) Professor William Holtz attributes the "Little House" books about prairie life to Rose Wilder Lane, daughter of the author to whom they are credited. Name this author.
Answer: Laura Ingalls Wilder.

39) Which word beginning with the letter *S* designates "the range of colors obtained when light is split up"?
Answer: Spectrum.

40) In which country were 11 members of the Israeli Olympic Team killed in an attack on the Olympic Village in Munich in 1972?
Answer: Germany (West Germany at the time).

41) Orson Welles' October 30, 1938, broadcast of radio drama about an extraterrestrial invasion caused near panic. On which H.G. Wells novel was this drama based?
Answer: *The War of the Worlds.*

42) In 1912, which former U.S. President, nicknamed "Teddy," delivered a campaign speech before seeking medical treatment after being shot by a would-be assassin?
Answer: Theodore Roosevelt.

43) Which state bordering California and Oregon entered the Union on October 31, 1864, as the 36th state?
Answer: Nevada.

44) If Patrick goes to sleep at 9:30 p.m. and sleeps for 8 hours and 30 minutes, what time will he wake up?
Answer: 6:00 a.m.

45) In which African country did President Bush spend New Year's Eve in 1992, praising the 18,000 American troops deployed there? Its capital is Mogadishu.
Answer: Somalia.

46) Which word beginning with the letter *V* designates "an empty space without atoms"?
Answer: Vacuum.

47) The half-hour TV series *Fudge* was based on *Tales of a Fourth Grade Nothing*, *Superfudge*, and *Fudge-A-Mania*. Name the author of these children's books.
Answer: Judy Blume.

48) Alabama-born Jesse Owens won 4 gold medals at the 1936 Olympic Games in Berlin, Germany. Was Owens *a gymnast, a tennis player, a swimmer*, or *a runner*?
Answer: A runner (Owens won one of his golds in the broad jump).

49) Name the Chinese device that is the world's oldest known mechanical computing aid.
Answer: Abacus (used in China as early as the 6th century B.C.).

50) Scientists in Denmark have found a fossilized clam they claim Vikings brought from North America 200 years before Columbus arrived in the Americas. What is the term for a native of Denmark?
Answer: Dane.

1) Identify the organization, founded on March 12, 1912, in Savannah, Georgia, whose motto is "Be Prepared." It was founded as the Girl Guides.
   Answer: Girl Scouts of America.

2) Four of the first 5 U.S. Presidents came from Virginia. Name 3 of these 4 Presidents.
   Answer: George Washington, Thomas Jefferson, James Madison, and James Monroe.

3) Which Southern state in the U.S. is said to be a peninsula?
   Answer: Florida.

4) What fractional part of 2_ hours is 25 minutes?
   Answer: One sixth.

5) Name the arm of the Arabian Sea where a U.S. submarine once kept tabs on Iran's first submarine. A breed of long-haired cat bears the same name.
   Answer: Persian Gulf.

6) In 340 B.C., Greek philosopher Aristotle wrote the book from whose title the more scientific word for "study of the weather" comes. Give this word.
   Answer: Meteorology (from *Meteorologica*).

7) Do equestrian events involve *cycling, horseback riding, skiing,* or *shooting*?
   Answer: Horseback riding.

8) Name the famous book of quotations whose 16th edition includes Cookie Monster's line "Me want cookie!" and the *Star Wars* slogan "May the force be with you."
   Answer: *Bartlett's Familiar Quotations.*

9) The American Farm Bureau once estimated that the cost of a traditional Thanksgiving dinner was about $2.64 per person. On this basis, how much did a dinner for 12 cost?
   Answer: $31.68.

10) On April 25, 1990, the U.S. deployed at Johns Hopkins University its most powerful instrument ever for looking at the stars from afar. What is such an instrument called?
    Answer: Telescope (the Hubble Space Telescope is the U.S.'s most powerful).

11) Complete the title of the book whose 1993 edition prompted a promotional party attended by the world's fastest noodle maker, the world's fastest yo-yoer, and the tallest living lady: *The* _____ *Book of World Records*.
Answer: **Guinness.**

12) William Rehnquist swore in Bill Clinton at his inauguration in 1996. What is his official title as head of the highest court in the United States?
Answer: **Chief Justice (of the United States).**

13) Somalia is bordered by Ethiopia on the west and by which ocean on the east?
Answer: **Indian Ocean.**

14) When the last American service person departed from the Subic Bay base in 1993, the Philippines was free of foreign military forces for the first time since 1543. For how many years were foreign forces on the land?
Answer: **450 years.**

15) In which state was the *Brown v. Board of Education* National Historic Site established in Topeka to memorialize the 1954 Supreme Court ruling that segregated schools are unconstitutional? It is Dorothy's home in *The Wonderful Wizard of Oz*.
Answer: **Kansas.**

16) Which weather phenomenon occurs when the sun shines upon falling rain?
Answer: **Rainbow.**

17) Spell the comparative and superlative of the adjective *dry*.
Answer: **D-R-I-E-R and D-R-I-E-S-T.**

18) In 1992, Independent candidate Ross Perot finished 2nd to President Bush in which Western state with a large Mormon population? It is the site of the Great Salt Lake.
Answer: **Utah (with 29% of the vote).**

19) Does the International Date Line, the imaginary line at which a day's date changes, roughly correspond with *the Equator, the 180th meridian of longitude,* or *the line of latitude at 40° South*?
Answer: **180th meridian of longitude.**

20) Which interrogative pronoun is the acronym for the World Health Organization, the U.N. agency that declared December 1 as World AIDS Day, in 1988?
Answer: **WHO.**

21) Which U.S. President, later assassinated, won the nomination with a record 62.8% voter turnout in 1960?
Answer: John Kennedy (defeated Richard Nixon).

22) Which Atlantic port city was chosen as the seat of government on September 13, 1788, by the Continental Congress? It is now the most populous city in the U.S.
Answer: New York City.

23) Captain Henry Wirz of the Confederate army was executed on November 10, 1865, after being convicted of mistreating soldiers at the Andersonville prison in which state?
Answer: Georgia.

24) Express 45/75 in lowest terms.
Answer: 3/5.

25) The Pope has stated that the Catholic Church erred 4 centuries ago in condemning Galileo for holding that the Earth was not the center of the universe. What is the silent consonant in the word *condemning*?
Answer: N.

26) Many sculpted bronze body parts possibly from a vessel that sank sometime between the 3rd century A.D. and the early Middle Ages were found off the coast of Italy. Complete the word *arti_____* used to designate any manmade object of historical interest.
Answer: (Arti)fact.

27) American teacher Noah Webster published his first dictionary in 1806. Which of the following words would appear first in a dictionary: *episode, epidemic, enlist* or *errand*?
Answer: Enlist.

28) At least 12 people were killed in the French Alps when a huge sliding mass of snow crashed down on some chalets, or mountain cottages, in the village of Le Tour in 1999. Spell the word of French origin used to designate such a wave of snow.
Answer: A-V-A-L-A-N-C-H-E.

29) What fractional part of 1/2 hour is 1/2 minute?
Answer: 1/60.

30) Who crowned himself emperor in the Cathedral of Notre Dame in Paris on December 2, 1804? He was eventually defeated by the British at the Battle of Waterloo.
Answer: Napoleon (I; Bonaparte).

31) Name the dentist who became the first recipient of a permanent artificial heart, in Utah on December 2, 1982. His surname is the same as Superman's first name.
Answer: Dr. Barney Clark (he lived for 112 days; Superman's name is Clark Kent).

32) Charles Mason and Jeremiah Dixon settled the boundary line dispute between Maryland and Pennsylvania with their survey completed in October 1767. Spell *survey*.
Answer: S-U-R-V-E-Y (this boundary became known as the Mason- Dixon Line).

33) Under which river does the Holland Tunnel run between New York City and Jersey City, New Jersey? This 2-tube tunnel was completed on November 13, 1927.
Answer: Hudson River (there are 7 of these tunnels today).

34) What is the product of 20 and 36?
Answer: 720.

35) In which country did the state church, or Anglican Church, shatter 458 years of tradition by agreeing in 1992 to ordain female priests?
Answer: England.

36) At what degrees Celsius does water boil?
Answer: 100 degrees.

37) What is the superlative form of *beautiful*?
Answer: Most beautiful.

38) Identify the large piano with strings set horizontally in a wing-shaped case braced on 3 legs.
Answer: Grand piano.

39) In 1991, the EPA gave 22 states and territories 90 days to set safe waterway standards. Is 90 days approximately 1/5, 1/4, 1/3, or 1/2 of a year?
Answer: 1/4 of a year.

40) In which Asian country did President Dwight Eisenhower land on December 2, 1952, thus keeping a campaign promise to go there to try to end hostilities?
Answer: Korea (he visited troops in South Korea and Syngman Rhee in Seoul).

41) President Polk's confirmation of the discovery of gold in California in a speech to Congress prompted the state's major gold rush. In which 19th century year did this rush occur, a year for which San Francisco's professional football team is nicknamed?
Answer: 1849 (Polk informed Congress of the find on December 5, 1848).

42) Name the famous hunter and woodsman who helped open the Wilderness Road from Virginia to Kentucky through the Appalachian Mountains in 1775.
Answer: Daniel Boone.

43) In 1956, American film star Grace Kelly married Prince Ranier of Monaco, a small country on the Mediterranean Sea. Spell *Mediterranean*.
Answer: M-E-D-I-T-E-R-R-A-N-E-A-N.

44) How much did a minimum-wage worker earn per hour as of September 1, 1997, as a result of the law signed on August 20, 1996, raising the minimum wage of $4.25 by 50 cents on October 1, 1996, and by another 40 cents on September 1, 1997?
Answer: $5.15.

45) Name the parklike area between the Washington, Jefferson, and Lincoln memorials and the U.S. Capitol where space was granted for a WWII memorial in 1996. This word also designates an indoor shopping center.
Answer: The Mall.

46) What is the sum of all colors of the spectrum?
Answer: White.

47) On November 12, 1892, William "Pudge" Hefflinger became the first professional football player. Spell the word *amateur*, which is the antonym of *professional*.
Answer: A-M-A-T-E-U-R.

48) Which Far East country, whose capital is Manila, defeated Long Beach, California, for the 1992 Little League World Series title? The title was later forfeited for having overage players.
Answer: Philippines.

49) At what time will a 3-hour, 21-minute film end if it begins at 2:15 p.m.?
Answer: 5:36 p.m.

50) President-elect Clinton once sought hearings for all refugees from Haiti before deciding whether to send them back home. Which word using the Latin root *port* for "to carry" means "to send back to another country"?
Answer: Deport.

ELEMENTARY SCHOOL QUIZ BOOK - 8

1) What is the primary language spoken in Panama City, Panama?
Answer: **Spanish.**

2) Which 2 explorers sighted the Pacific Ocean for their first time on November 7, 1805, at the mouth of the Columbia River in the Oregon Territory?
Answer: **Meriwether Lewis and William Clark.**

3) In which state, the "Centennial State," did Zebulon Pike sight Pikes Peak on November 15, 1806?
Answer: **Colorado (admitted to the Union in 1876).**

4) What is the quotient when the sum of the number of days in a year, the number of days in February in a leap year, and the number of months with 30 days is divided by 2?
Answer: **199.**

5) In which film does Quasimodo sing "Out There" to describe the world beyond the bell tower where he is forced to live because of his misshapen body?
Answer: ***The Hunchback of Notre Dame.***

6) Which word that begins with *C* names the substance that gives a green plant its color?
Answer: **Chlorophyll.**

7) In which Robert Louis Stevenson book does Bill Bones die of fright after a blind man gives him the black spot, the pirates' death notice?
Answer: ***Treasure Island***.

8) Prior to his entry into politics, was Ohio Senator John Glenn *a movie star, a professional athlete, an astronaut,* or *a college professor*?
Answer: **Astronaut (Glenn was the first American to orbit the earth).**

9) How much will it cost to run a 3-line classified ad for 4 days if the cost per line is 40 cents per day?
Answer: **$4.80.**

10) In which country did the Bolsheviks seize power during the 1917 Great October Revolution? Vladimir Lenin and Leon Trotsky helped plan the revolution.
Answer: **Russia.**

11) The largest group of the 1.9 million American Indians counted by the Census Bureau in 1990 belong to which tribe forced from its home in the 1800's Trail of Tears? A vehicle in the Jeep family bears the same name.
Answer: Cherokee (542 tribes were counted).

12) In which century did 41 Pilgrims sign the Mayflower Compact that became the basis of government for the Massachusetts Bay colony?
Answer: 17th century (on November 11, 1620).

13) Which U.S. state, the 4th largest state in area, entered the Union on November 8, 1889? Its name comes from a Spanish word for "mountainous."
Answer: Montana.

14) What is the product of 5, 4, and 3?
Answer: 60.

15) Which state bordering Canada is the site of Little Bighorn Battlefield National Monument, where Indians in 1992 honored those who defeated General Custer in 1876 and those who persuaded Congress to drop his name from the monument in 1991?
Answer: Montana.

16) Tropical cyclones originating in the Atlantic are called hurricanes. What is a severe tropical storm that originates in the western Pacific Ocean called?
Answer: Typhoon.

17) Which story was Mary Mapes Dodge inspired to write after reading *The Rise of the Dutch Republic*? The subtitle of her work is *The Silver Skates*.
Answer: *Hans Brinker*.

18) In 1823, President Monroe warned European countries not to interfere with the free nations of the Western half of the world. What word designates "half of the globe"?
Answer: Hemisphere (the policy of 12/2/1823 is known as the Monroe Doctrine).

19) In 1992, many distinguished scientists, including 101 Nobel prize winners, appealed to 160 world leaders to take immediate action to reverse trends toward environmental disaster. Spell *environmental*.
Answer: E-N-V-I-R-O-N-M-E-N-T-A-L.

20) Name the British monarch, purportedly the world's richest woman, who volunteered in 1992 to pay taxes on her personal income, said to be $50 million annually.
Answer: Queen Elizabeth II.

21) Complete Bob Dole's former title, Senate _____ Leader, by giving a word that designates those different from the majority.
Answer: Minority (Senate Minority Leader).

22) Name the Confederate General who began his 300-mile march of destruction across Georgia to the sea on November 15, 1864.
Answer: William T. Sherman.

23) In which Western state did Democrat Ben Nighthorse Campbell become the third Native American to win a U.S. Senate seat? Cities in this state are named Fort Collins, Greeley, and Pueblo.
Answer: Colorado.

24) If the hot water tap in Mary's house leaks 8 ounces of water every 20 minutes, how many cups of water are lost in a day?
Answer: 72 cups.

25) In 1992, about 50 students at Greater Hartford Community College once protested the renaming of their school after which writer who lived in Hartford from 1874 to 1891? They questioned his treatment of blacks in novels such as *The Adventures of Huckleberry Finn*.
Answer: Mark Twain (or Samuel Clemens).

26) A probable ancestor of the largest meat-eating dinosaur has been assembled from skeletal parts from a fossil find in Argentina in 1992. Name this largest meat-eater.
Answer: *Tyrannosaurus rex* (the *Herrerasaurus* is the ancestor).

27) Complete the titles of 2 of the following Hans Christian Andersen works: "The Ugly _____," "The Red _____," and "The Princess and the _____."
Answer: "Duckling" / "Shoes" / "Pea."

28) On December 4, 1918, President Wilson set sail for the peace conference at Versailles. Identify one of the 2 different silent consonants in the French name *Versailles*.
Answer: *L* or *S*.

29) In which year, did Joseph Glidden patent barbed wire, the fencing material that made farming possible on the Great Plains? It is expressed as MDCCCLXXIV in Roman numerals.
Answer: 1874 (on November 24).

30) In a slap at the U.S., the U.N. General Assembly once supported a resolution seeking to repeal the U.S. trade embargo against the largest island in the Caribbean. Name it.
Answer: Cuba.

31) Identify the patron saint of little children, whose feast day is still celebrated by many European countries on December 6 as a holiday on which children are given gifts.
Answer: Saint Nicholas.

32) President Bush was the first incumbent to win less than 40% of the popular vote since which President in 1932 received 39.7% of the vote? His initials are H.H.
Answer: Herbert Hoover.

33) Which Southwestern state, shaped like a sauce pan, was admitted to the Union on November 16, 1907? A Broadway musical tells the story of its cattlemen and farmers.
Answer: Oklahoma.

34) What is the average of .4, .04, and .004?
Answer: .148.

35) A fire swept through a wing of the Hofburg Palace in Vienna, Austria, a city known for its Lipizzaner horses, particularly the adult male horses kept for breeding. Is such a horse called *a filly, a foal, a stallion, a dam*, or *a gelding*?
Answer: Stallion.

36) Researchers say that one kind of test for blocked arteries can sometimes be skipped or postponed. Which Greek root meaning "something written or drawn" completes the word *angio*_____ that names this test?
Answer: *-gram* (angiogram).

37) Arturo Toscanini made his U.S. debut on November 16, 1908, conducting *Aïda* at the Met in New York. Spell *debut*, meaning "first appearance."
Answer: D-E-B-U-T.

38) Identify the Arkansas town whose name identifies the one thing left in Pandora's box after its evils were released.
Answer: Hope (some sources say hope was the last thing released from Pandora's box).

39) A robot named Dante once made an unprecedented descent into the 12,350-foot icebound Mount Erebus volcano to prepare for possible Mars missions. On which continent is Mount Erebus located?
Answer: Antarctica.

40) Francis Drake, the first Englishman to circumnavigate the world, died on his ship off Panama on January 28, 1596. What title of address did he acquire when he was made a knight in 1581?
Answer: Sir.

41) What does the *C* in UNICEF, the acronym for the U.N. agency created in 1946, stand for?
Answer: Children's (United Nations International Children's Emergency Fund).

42) A 1991 Oakland-area fire with its estimated more than $5 billion in damage surpassed which city's fire in 1871 as the costliest blaze in U.S. history?
Answer: Chicago's.

43) In 1992, Bill Clinton won the electoral votes in Minnesota (10) and Louisiana (7) and all 3 states in a straight line from north to south between the 2 in the 1992 election. Name 1 of these states.
Answer: Iowa (7), Missouri (10), and Arkansas (6).

44) How wide is a rectangle with a length of 8 cm and a perimeter of 24 cm?
Answer: 4 cm.

45) Name the "Silver State," where nuclear explosions were banned until June 1993 when nuclear labs were allowed 15 safety tests before a 1996 comprehensive test ban. Its capital is Carson City.
Answer: Nevada.

46) Which element, named from the Greek word for "sun," is the 2nd lightest? It is often used to fill scientific balloons.
Answer: Helium (hydrogen is the lightest element).

47) Which author was born in Missouri in 1835, the year Halley's comet arrived, and died in 1910, the year the comet reappeared? He created Becky Thatcher and Tom Sawyer.
Answer: Mark Twain.

48) According to researchers, on which day is the risk of having a heart attack 40% higher than on the other days of the week? According to an old rhyme, the child born on this day is "fair of face."
Answer: Monday (Thursday is the 2nd riskiest day).

49) The House of Representatives had 110 new members, or freshmen, as of the 1992 election. Did these freshmen make up about 15%, 20%, 25%, or 30% of the 435-member body?
Answer: 25% (the largest number since 1948 but smaller than the 120-150 predicted).

50) Which 2 European countries became one on October 3, 1990? The unified country's capital is Berlin.
Answer: East Germany and West Germany.

1) Lucy Stone, who founded the American Woman Suffrage Association, kept the name she had before she was married. What term designates such a name?
Answer: Maiden name (she founded it in 1869).

2) On December 7, 1787, which state, the "First State of the Union," became the first to ratify the proposed U.S. Constitution? Its capital is Dover.
Answer: Delaware.

3) Name the President from whose home, Monticello, the Clintons and Gores embarked on a bus caravan to the White House inaugural festivities in 1993.
Answer: Thomas Jefferson.

4) The Census Bureau predicts that by the year 2050 the percent of non-Hispanic whites in the U.S. will be about a third less than the 75% of today. On this basis, what is the approximate percentage of non-Hispanic whites expected in the year 2050?
Answer: 50% (53% to be exact).

5) Winter snows came late for Muscovites in 1996-1997, after a record for balmy weather was just set. In which world capital do Muscovites live?
Answer: Moscow.

6) How many standard time zones does the contiguous U.S. have?
Answer: 4 (Eastern, Central, Mountain, and Pacific).

7) What word is used in law to mean "without the resources to pay off bills"?
Answer: Bankrupt.

8) Name the sea connected with the Mediterranean by the Suez Canal, which opened in 1869. A biblical story tells of the parting of its waters.
Answer: Red Sea.

9) If 1/2 the sum of 2 numbers is 10 and one of the numbers is 8, what is the other?
Answer: 12.

10) Which U.S. Caribbean commonwealth celebrates Discovery Day on November 19, the day Christopher Columbus discovered it on his 2nd voyage in 1493?
Answer: Puerto Rico.

11) Name the daughter of the President and Mrs. Clinton. Her parents chose her name from a Judy Collins song.
Answer: Chelsea Clinton (from "Chelsea Morning").

12) Name the 2 U.S. Presidents who died on July 4, 1826. They served as the 2nd and 3rd Presidents of the U.S.
Answer: John Adams and Thomas Jefferson.

13) Which mountain system, the highest in the world, extends from Pakistan into India, Tibet, and Nepal: the Andes, Alps, Cascades, or Himalayas?
Answer: Himalayas.

14) What is the average of 90, 98, 92, and 96?
Answer: 94.

15) California was once warned to expect water shortages during a seventh year of drought. Spell *drought*.
Answer: D-R-O-U-G-H-T.

16) Which metal, the only one that is a liquid at room temperature, is used in thermometers? It is named for the messenger of the gods in Roman mythology.
Answer: Mercury.

17) Scottish-born American financier Andrew Carnegie donated funds for the construction of over 2,500 libraries. Spell *libraries*.
Answer: L-I-B-R-A-R-I-E-S.

18) Name the Georgia-born author who was so identified with the character he created that he was nicknamed "Uncle Remus" and even received mail so addressed.
Answer: Joel Chandler Harris.

19) Identify the device invented by Massachusetts-born Eli Whitney for separating fiber of short-staple cotton from the seed.
Answer: Cotton gin.

20) On November 29, 1929, which American commander became the first to fly over the South Pole? His name is a homophone for an animal in the largest group of vertebrates.
Answer: Richard E. Byrd.

21) In which year was George Washington inaugurated on April 30 as the first U.S. President, 13 years after the signing of the Declaration of Independence?
Answer: 1789.

22) Margaret Chase Smith of Maine was the first woman to be elected to both houses of the U.S. Congress. Name these 2 houses.
Answer: House of Representatives and Senate.

23) In which mountains is Bolivia, the South American country named for Simón Bolívar, located: the Ozarks, Appalachians, Cascades, or Andes?
Answer: Andes Mountains.

24) *Home Alone 2* and *Aladdin* led the motion picture industry's richest- ever Thanksgiving weekend at the box office in 1992 with a $135 million overall take. What is the increase from the previous box office high of $114 million in 1989?
Answer: $21 million.

25) Name the Prince and Princess of Wales, the British heir to the throne and his wife who separated 11 years after their 1981 marriage.
Answer: Charles and Diana (they divorced in 1996).

26) Which prefix used with *graph* and *scope* means "far away"?
Answer: *Tele-*.

27) On November 26, 1862, which President on meeting Harriet Beecher Stowe said, "So this is the little lady who made the big war"?
Answer: President Lincoln (in reference to *Uncle Tom's Cabin*).

28) After 26 years Charles Schulz created a follow-up to TV's *A Charlie Brown Christmas*. What word is used to designate "a new story that continues an earlier one"?
Answer: Sequel (the sequel is *It's Christmas Time Again, Charlie Brown*).

29) New food labels are based on a recommended daily diet of how many calories a day, a number equivalent to MM in Roman numerals?
Answer: 2,000 (and 65 grams of fat).

30) Boris Yeltsin once survived a call for his removal from office. What verb means "to accuse a public official, such as a president, of wrongdoing before a group that can remove him from his job"?
Answer: Impeach.

31) The Russians have adopted Western rules of parliamentary procedure for conducting meetings. Spell *procedure*.
Answer: P-R-O-C-E-D-U-R-E.

32) Slavery and involuntary servitude were abolished by which 1865 amendment to the U.S. Constitution? The square of its number is 169.
Answer: 13th.

33) What name is given to the area of the Atlantic Ocean where five airplanes disappeared in 1945 and were erroneously thought to have been discovered in 1991 about 10 miles off Fort Lauderdale, Florida? This name contains the name of a figure or shape.
Answer: Bermuda Triangle.

34) Based on the fact that all or parts of 15 states were carved from the area the U.S. purchased from France on December 20, 1803, what percent of the 50 U.S. states include some of this territory?
Answer: 30% (known as the Louisiana Purchase).

35) Identify the country whose banks agreed to pay Holocaust survivors $1.2 billion to settle claims to assets lost during WWII. It borders France, Italy, Austria, and Germany.
Answer: Switzerland.

36) Which word completes the following: *On October 14, 1947, Charles E. Yeager became the first person to fly faster than the speed of _____ when he flew a jet more than Mach 2.5.?*
Answer: Sound (in 1953 in an army rocket-powered plane; Mach 2.5 is 2½ times the speed of sound).

37) How many prepositions are in the following: *More than 2,000 Mexicans protesting current tariffs on goods imported from the U.S. rampaged at border crossings?*
Answer: 3 (on, from, and at).

38) Which U.S. President was the first American to receive a Nobel Prize? This President, known as a big-game hunter, won the Peace prize on December 10, 1906.
Answer: Theodore Roosevelt (for his efforts to end the Russo- Japanese War).

39) Which prefix used with *organism* and *scope* means "very small"?
Answer: Micro-.

40) Spain ceded the Philippines, Puerto Rico, and Guam to the U.S. on December 10, 1898. Spell *ceded*, meaning "to give up possession of."
Answer: C-E-D-E-D.

41) On May 3, 1979, Margaret Thatcher became Britain's first female head of government. By what title is Britain's head of government known?
Answer: Prime Minister.

42) Name the Abraham Lincoln document that went on display in 1992 in its entirety at the National Archives in Washington for the first time since it was issued on January 1, 1863, to free slaves in Confederate states during the Civil War.
Answer: Emancipation Proclamation.

43) Name any of the 3 Western states in which Yellowstone National Park lies. All are north of Colorado and Utah, and one has a panhandle.
Answer: Wyoming, Montana, or Idaho.

44) A 15-foot-long board can be cut into how many 2 1/2-foot-long pieces?
Answer: 6 pieces.

45) In 1992, NASA's *Galileo* spacecraft passed by Earth for the second time during its 6 year journey to study which planet, the solar system's largest?
Answer: Jupiter.

46) According to a U.S. Surgeon General, hepatitis-B can infect up to 90% of children under 5 annually unless they are vaccinated. Which body organ, the largest gland in the body, does hepatitis attack?
Answer: Liver.

47) Which phrase from the title of a Hans Christian Andersen story today means "an unpromising person who may mature into someone successful and beautiful"? In the Andersen story an unpromising animal becomes a lovely white swan.
Answer: Ugly duckling.

48) On November 11, 1921, President Harding dedicated the Tomb of the Unknown Soldier in Virginia's Arlington National Cemetery. Spell *tomb*.
Answer: T-O-M-B.

49) Cartoon character Dagwood calculated the shaving time he'd save each year by growing a mustache. How many hours per year would he save by saving 10 seconds per day?
Answer: One.

50) El Salvador destroyed weapons as promised in peace accords that ended a 12-year war between opposing forces within the country. What is a war between groups within the same country called?
Answer: Civil war.

1) In 1992, President Bush bestowed his 1,000th Point of Light award in the program he initiated for recognition of community service. Spell *initiated*.
Answer: I-N-I-T-I-A-T-E-D.

2) Surgeon Mary Edwards Walker was awarded the Medal of Honor in 1865 for her treatment of soldiers during which war?
Answer: Civil War.

3) The *Monitor*, a Union ironclad, sank off a narrow strip of land jutting into the sea off the coast of North Carolina in 1862. What word designates both such a piece of land and a garment hung over the shoulders?
Answer: Cape (in this case, Cape Hatteras).

4) Round 5.896 to the nearest hundredth.
Answer: 5.90.

5) Give the acronym for the arms reduction treaty signed in 1993 that is expected to cut the U.S. and Russia's nuclear weapons by two-thirds within 10 years. It is also a verb meaning "to begin."
Answer: START (Strategic Arms Reduction Treaty; signed by President Bush and Boris Yeltsin).

6) Name the "Magnolia State" represented by Congressman Mike Espy, who was named the first black secretary of agriculture.
Answer: Mississippi.

7) Maya Angelou tells of her childhood near Hope, Arkansas, in her book *I Know Why The Caged Bird Sings*. What term designates "a book about one's life written by oneself"?
Answer: Autobiography.

8) Spell *mosque*, the name for a Moslem house of worship.
Answer: M-O-S-Q-U-E.

9) What is the sum of all the whole number factors less than 24 that are factors of 24?
Answer: 36 (1, 2, 3, 4, 6, 8, 12).

10) Ivan the Terrible, or Ivan IV, became the first Russian emperor on January 16, 1547. What is the Russian title for an emperor?
Answer: Czar (tsar or tzar).

11) Which word designating "a plan for expenditures" completes the full name of the OMB, or the Office of Management and _____?
Answer: Budget.

12) Give the full name of the EPA, the agency that attempts to control pollution and protect our natural resources.
Answer: Environmental Protection Agency.

13) Which large one- or two-horned animal is threatened with extinction because several African and Asian countries are ignoring a U.N. ban on the sale of its horns which, by weight, can sell for up to 3 times the price of gold?
Answer: Rhinoceros (*rhino-* is the combining form for "nose").

14) Mathematician/scientist Isaac Newton is known for his 3 laws of motion. Spell *mathematician*.
Answer: M-A-T-H-E-M-A-T-I-C-I-A-N.

15) According to archaeologists, which king of biblical fame owned the luxurious palace discovered in the 1990s with a 115-foot swimming pool on the coast of Israel? The Bible reports that he ordered the deaths of male babies in Bethlehem 2,000 years ago.
Answer: King Herod.

16) Is an amp a unit for measuring humidity, electric current, air pressure, or light intensity? It was named for French physicist André Ampere.
Answer: Electric current.

17) Complete Benjamin Franklin's proverb "Early to bed, early to rise, makes a man _____, _____, and _____," one of many in his *Poor Richard's Almanac*.
Answer: "healthy, wealthy, and wise."

18) Evangelist Billy Graham gave the prayer at the beginning of Bill Clinton's 1993 inaugural ceremony. Is such a prayer called the *prelude, invocation, benediction,* or *grace*?
Answer: Invocation.

19) Transcontinental telephone service was inaugurated in San Francisco in 1915 when the inventor of the telephone said once again, "Watson come here. I want you." Name him.
Answer: Alexander Graham Bell.

20) Name the tiny British colony at the mouth of the Mediterranean whose chief minister in 1998 told the U.N. that it deserves independence, despite Spain's claim of ownership. Its name appears in the simile *as solid as the Rock of* ____.
Answer: Gibraltar (it has been a British possession since 1704).

21) Muslim groups have denounced what they call *Islamophobia*, or dislike for Muslims, in the movie *The Siege*. What term designates a word part such as *-phobia* that is added to the end of another word or root to form a new word?
Answer: Suffix (the suffix *-phobia* means "fear of or dislike of").

22) The long *e* sound in *diesel* is spelled *i-e*. In which of the following are these 2 letters reversed: *believe, seize, thief,* or *relieve*?
Answer: Seize.

23) Name the Boston church where, according to a Longfellow poem, Paul Revere's friend hangs 2 lanterns to signal the arrival of the British by sea. It is named for a direction.
Answer: (Old) North Church.

24) What was the average ticket price for Steven Spielberg's film *Jurassic Park*, which broke the record for the highest-grossing premiere weekend when 10 million tickets were sold for $50.2 million?
Answer: $5.02.

25) In 1992, which city received the official Olympic flag from Barcelona exactly 2 years from the day it was awarded the 1996 Olympics?
Answer: Atlanta (September 18, 1990).

26) What kind of animal was Ling-Ling, who died at the National Zoo in Washington. She was survived by her mate Hsing-Hsing, who arrived with her as a gift from the People's Republic of China after President Nixon's visit in 1972.
Answer: Giant Panda.

27) Which literary work is known for its Yellow Brick Road, wicked witches, and Munchkins?
Answer: *The Wonderful Wizard of Oz* (by L. Frank Baum).

28) The New York immigration center known as Ellis Island opened on January 1, 1892, to process those coming into this country. Spell *immigration*.
Answer: I-M-M-I-G-R-A-T-I-O-N.

29) What time is it at 1.7 hours after 12:15 p.m.?
Answer: 1:57 p.m.

30) On January 8, 1815, General Andrew Jackson defeated enemy forces 2 weeks after the treaty ending the War of 1812. Which country did the U.S. fight in this war?
Answer: Great Britain.

31) The Census Bureau estimated the U.S. population of more than a quarter billion grew by 2.9 million people in 1992. Was the 1992 population about 107 million, 157 million, 200 million or 257 million?
Answer: 257 million (256,561,239 estimated for January 1, 1993 U.S. population).

32) Zoë Baird was President-elect Clinton's first nominee as the first female Justice Department head. What title including a word for "lawyer" and a military term designates this position?
Answer: Attorney general.

33) Name the country on the western coast of the Iberian Peninsula that hosted the 20th century's largest world's fair, Expo 98, in Lisbon.
Answer: Portugal.

34) If cat food sells for 2 cans for 79 cents in one city, how much more will 10 cans of this same food cost in another where the price is 59 cents a can?
Answer: $1.95.

35) In 1992, which country of 15 million people separated into 2 republics, one of which is today called Slovakia? Prague was its capital.
Answer: Czechoslovakia (Prague is now the capital of the Czech republic).

36) Physician and missionary Albert Schweitzer established a hospital in Lambaréné, Gabon, in 1913. Spell *physician*.
Answer: **P-H-Y-S-I-C-I-A-N.**

37) Owl's treehouse and Eeyore's Twig house were part of a New York exhibit to celebrate the 70th anniversary of which character created by author A.A. Milne?
Answer: **Winnie-the-Pooh.**

38) What is the religious tradition of Sidwell Friends School, the exclusive private school that Chelsea Clinton attended in Washington? Members of this religion were active abolitionists and helped slaves to escape via the Underground Railroad.
Answer: **Quaker.**

39) Name the planet in the solar system that is closest to the sun.
Answer: **Mercury.**

40) The French lost a disastrous battle to the British and then surrendered on September 18, 1759, in Quebec. Spell *disastrous*.
Answer: **D-I-S-A-S-T-R-O-U-S.**

41) When it was completed on January 15, 1943, which five-sided office building in Arlington, Virginia, was the world's largest?
Answer: **Pentagon.**

42) Name the Massachusetts town near Concord where Captain John Parker rallied the militia on April 19, 1775, with the words, "Stand your ground! Don't fire unless fired upon, but if they mean to have a war, let it begin here!"
Answer: **Lexington.**

43) On January 17, 1917, the U.S. purchased the territory known as the U.S. Virgin Islands from Denmark. Between which ocean and which sea do these islands lie?
Answer: **Atlantic and Caribbean (purchase price was $25,000,000).**

44) The 1920s-'30s Ringling Brothers and Barnum and Bailey Circus is featured in a miniature model in the Knoxville Museum of Art. If in the model 3/4 inches is equal to one foot, how many inches tall is the scaled representation of a 6-foot clown?
Answer: **4$1/2$ inches.**

45) Name 1 of the 2 bodies of water bordering Saudi Arabia from which Tomahawk missiles were fired from U.S. warships into Iraq in early 1993.
Answer: Persian Gulf or Red Sea.

46) Name the planet in the solar system that is closest to Earth.
Answer: Venus.

47) The house in a neighborhood that inspired a Dr. Seuss book was demolished despite its listing on the National Register of Historic Places. Complete this book's title *And to Think I Saw It on _____.*
Answer: *Mulberry Street.*

48) Nintendo put notices on all its games warning users with epilepsy that the flickering lights and small flashing figures could trigger seizures. Spell *seizures*.
Answer: S-E-I-Z-U-R-E-S.

49) What term designates any closed figure formed by line segments?
Answer: Polygon.

50) On April 20, 1903, Andrew Carnegie gave $1.5 million for the construction of a Peace Palace in a city called The Hague. In which country, once called Holland, is it located?
Answer: The Netherlands.

1) How many years are in a decade?
   Answer: Ten years.

2) Which war was officially ended when the Treaty of Paris was ratified by the Continental Congress on January 14, 1784?
   Answer: American Revolutionary War.

3) America's bloodiest battle was fought in Maryland on September 17, 1862, at Antietam or Sharpsburg. Which bay divides Maryland into 2 parts?
   Answer: Chesapeake Bay.

4) How many vertices does an octagon have?
   Answer: 8.

5) In which small Central American country did the U.S. reduce its military force from 10,000 to 6,000 by 1995 and then remove them all in 1999 when it relinquished control of a major waterway?
   Answer: Panama.

6) Name the force that pulls objects toward each other, such as the force the sun exerts on the planets to keep them in their orbits.
   Answer: Gravity.

7) On January 21, 1993, about 5,000 people gathered in Paris to commemorate the exact moment 200 years ago when Louis XVI was beheaded. Spell *commemorate*.
   Answer: C-O-M-M-E-M-O-R-A-T-E.

8) A radio broadcast of *The War of the Worlds* on October 30, 1938, caused near panic with its story of an invasion by beings from which planet named for the Roman god of war?
   Answer: Mars (actor and director Orson Welles broadcast the story).

9) What percent is equal to 1/8?
   Answer: 12 1/2% (or 12.5%).

10) In 1993, to help the struggling American steel industry, the U.S. imposed heavy taxes on steel from 19 countries. What term designates a tax, or duty, on imported goods?
    Answer: Tariff.

11) In 1993, the U.S. unveiled a plaque at the future site of its embassy beside the Brandenburg Gate in Berlin. Spell *plaque*.
Answer: P-L-A-Q-U-E.

12) In his farewell address on January 17, 1961, which U.S. President, a former general, warned the country about the "military-industrial complex"?
Answer: Dwight Eisenhower.

13) In which Tennessee city did the National Civil Rights Museum open an art exhibit to commemorate the 25th anniversary of the assassination of Dr. Martin Luther King Jr.? This museum was built on the site of the Lorraine Motel, where Dr. King was killed.
Answer: Memphis.

14) How many years are in 3/4 of a century?
Answer: 75.

15) Of *barbaric*, *charismatic*, *geriatric*, or *pacific*, which means "attractively charming" and names the horse that in 1999 won the Kentucky Derby and the Preakness, then broke its leg in the Belmont Stakes?
Answer: Charismatic (ridden by Chris Antley and trained by D. Wayne Lukas).

16) Name the force that causes an object moving around in a circle to be pulled away from the center.
Answer: Centrifugal force.

17) What name is given to two words like *heir*, meaning "one who inherits," and *air*, meaning "atmosphere," which sound alike but have different spellings and meanings?
Answer: Homophones (or homonyms).

18) Rudolf Nureyev, who defected from Russia in 1961, died in 1993 at age 54, reportedly of AIDS. Was Nureyev *a fashion designer, an artist, a cellist,* or *a ballet dancer*?
Answer: Ballet dancer.

19) On February 4, 1901, Major William C. Gorgas of the U.S. Army began a campaign in Cuba to eradicate yellow fever with a program to control which insect?
Answer: Mosquito.

20) Which Mideast country expressed sorrow at President Bush's departure from the White House with a 14-page supplement on his career in a daily newspaper, including the headline "Bush: We Love You"? Iraq invaded this country in 1990.
Answer: Kuwait.

21) President-elect Clinton named Madeleine Albright ambassador to the United Nations in 1993. Spell *ambassador*.
    Answer: A-M-B-A-S-S-A-D-O-R.

22) On which date is Inauguration Day in the U.S.?
    Answer: January 20.

23) Jesse Leroy Brown, the first black American naval pilot, died in combat in 1950. In which country on a peninsula attached to China was he shot down?
    Answer: Korea.

24) If the hands on the clock indicate 9:00, how many degrees are in the smaller angle formed by the hands?
    Answer: 90 degrees.

25) Give the Hawaiian word for "mountain" that completes the name of Hawaii's active volcano _____ *Loa*.
    Answer: Mauna.

26) On December 2, 1982, a Utah-born dentist became the first to receive a permanent artificial heart. Spell *artificial*.
    Answer: A-R-T-I-F-I-C-I-A-L (the dentist lived 112 days after the implant).

27) Name the striped animal friend of A.A. Milne's character Winnie-the-Pooh.
    Answer: Tigger.

28) Which Austrian musician, whose first name is Wolfgang, began performing at age 3 and writing music at age 5? He composed *The Magic Flute*.
    Answer: Wolfgang Amadeus Mozart.

29) How much greater is the tens' digit of 1993 than the hundreds' digit of 1492?
    Answer: 5.

30) From which country did the U.S. acquire the land that became California, Nevada, Utah, and most of Arizona with the 1848 signing of the Treaty of Guadalupe Hidalgo?
    Answer: Mexico (as well as parts of New Mexico, Colorado, and Wyoming, on 2/2/1848).

31) Robert Weaver became the first black Cabinet member as head of the Department of Housing and Urban Development, or HUD. Which word ending in -*nym* identifies a word like HUD made from initials?
    Answer: Acronym.

32) Which word completes the epitaph "_____ at last" on the tomb of Martin Luther King Jr., whose birthday is observed as a federal holiday on the third Monday of January?
Answer: Free.

33) In which state did Negro students occupy lunch counter seats in Greensboro on February 1, 1960, in order to fight discrimination? It is known as the "Tar Heel State."
Answer: North Carolina.

34) A pair of $70 shoes has been discounted 15%. What is the sale price?
Answer: $59.50.

35) If the 3 Baltic republics represented 20% of those formerly in the USSR, how many republics were there before the split?
Answer: 15.

36) Some fossils show that the whale's closest cousins are deer, cows, camels, and other hoofed animals, lending support to the theory that its ancestors, too, once walked on land. To which group of vertebrates do all of these animals belong?
Answer: Mammals.

37) In 1993, negotiations led to the reinstatement of former Haitian leader Jean-Bertrand Aristide in an effort to avoid a new exodus of refugees bound for the U.S. Spell *negotiations*.
Answer: N-E-G-O-T-I-A-T-I-O-N-S.

38) The Folger Library in Washington, D.C., once received a $2.5 million grant to improve the world's largest collection of books and manuscripts by which famous English playwright born in Stratford-upon-Avon?
Answer: William Shakespeare.

39) What name is given to animals that can live both in water and on land? Frogs are an example.
Answer: Amphibians.

40) Name both the capital of Norway and the capital of Sweden, the 2 cities where the Nobel Prizes are awarded annually on December 10.
Answer: Oslo (Norway) and Stockholm (Sweden).

41) Name the statesman who was the first to sign the Declaration of Independence. His name is now often used as a synonym for *signature*.
Answer: John Hancock.

42) Which U.S. senator from Mississippi resigned his office after his state seceded from the Union and later became the president of the Confederacy?
Answer: Jefferson Davis.

43) Which capital city implemented a plan to become the first major western European city to banish all non-vital traffic from its streets? This city is known for its canals and for its museums holding paintings by natives Rembrandt and Van Gogh.
Answer: Amsterdam.

44) Bill Clinton's 1993 inaugural speech was 14 minutes in length. How many words did George Washington average per second with his second inaugural speech of 135 words delivered in 90 seconds, the shortest in history?
Answer: 1.5.

45) Despite protests, in 1993 Gov. Pedro Rosello signed a bill making English the official language in Puerto Rico. What is the predominant language in this U.S. territory?
Answer: Spanish.

46) Name the instrument invented by the French-born "Father of Chest Medicine," Théophile Laënnec, for listening to sounds in patients' chests.
Answer: Stethoscope.

47) Give the direct object of the following sentence: "A $1.3 million congressional investigation found no signs of an alleged Republican deal to delay the release of U.S. hostages in Iran until after the 1980 U.S. election."
Answer: Signs.

48) Englishman Robert Scott reached the South Pole on January 18, 1912, only to find that Roald Amundsen, a Norwegian, had preceded him by about 5 weeks. Spell *preceded*.
Answer: P-R-E-C-E-D-E-D.

49) The average cost of 3 meals and lodging for a U.S. business traveler was highest in New York City and lowest in Macon, Georgia, in 1993. Was the $73 average cost in Macon about 1/3, 1/4, 1/5, or 1/2 the $297 cost in New York?
Answer: 1/4.

50) In which country, South America's second largest, was Juan Perón elected president on February 24, 1946?
Answer: Argentina.

1) In 1830, Massachusetts Senator Daniel Webster said to South Carolina's Senator Robert Hayne, "Liberty and Union, now and forever, one and inseparable." Spell *inseparable*.
   Answer: I-N-S-E-P-A-R-A-B-L-E (on January 26).

2) Name the youngest President to be inaugurated, the President who took office in 1901 and shares his surname with a WWII President.
   Answer: Teddy Roosevelt (he was 42 at the time).

3) Name the river on which George Washington's home, Mount Vernon, is located.
   Answer: Potomac River.

4) Multiply 1/4 by 3/4.
   Answer: 3/16.

5) Former President George Bush's 1995 fund-raising summit in Colorado to discuss the end of the Cold War and its legacy included Mikhail Gorbachev and Margaret Thatcher, the former leaders of which 2 countries?
   Answer: Russia (USSR) and Great Britain.

6) Which planet, named for the Roman god of the underworld, was discovered by an astronomer at the Lowell Observatory in Flagstaff, Arizona, on February 18, 1930?
   Answer: Pluto.

7) Spell *predecessor*, meaning "one who earlier held the office."
   Answer: P-R-E-D-E-C-E-S-S-O-R.

8) In which city is the museum called the Louvre located on the Seine River?
   Answer: Paris.

9) If the average of 3 consecutive whole numbers is 28, what is the largest of these 3 whole numbers?
   Answer: 29.

10) The title Prince of Wales is given to the first male heir to the throne of Great Britain. Spell *heir*, meaning "one who inherits."
    Answer: H-E-I-R.

11) President Clinton uses the same desk as Presidents Kennedy and Reagan. In which White House room named for its shape is this desk located?
    Answer: Oval Office.

12) President Bush was the 4th oldest President to take office in U.S. history. Who was the oldest to be elected U.S. President?
Answer: Ronald Reagan (elected at age 73).

13) Name the Canadian island that is the setting for Lucy Maud Montgomery's *Anne of Green Gables.*
Answer: Prince Edward Island.

14) In lowest terms, what is the ratio of cashew nuts to peanuts in a mixture that contains 3 pounds of cashew nuts to 3 ounces of peanuts?
Answer: 16 to 1.

15) Playwright Vaclav Havel became the first president of the Czech Republic. Spell *playwright.*
Answer: P-L-A-Y-W-R-I-G-H-T (Havel became Czechoslovakia's president in 1989).

16) A federal court once ordered an investigation into allegations that the White House unlawfully influenced the Endangered Species Committee to permit logging on federal land in Oregon inhabited by the northern spotted variety of which nocturnal bird?
Answer: Owl (it was the 2nd exemption to the 1973 Endangered Species Act).

17) What 2-word greeting used before noon completes these lines at the end of Maya Angelou's 1993 inaugural poem: "And say simply / Very simply / With hope / _____ _____"?
Answer: Good morning.

18) Which woodwind instrument did Bill Clinton play at the Arkansas Ball on his first inaugural night to the tune of "Your Mama Don't Dance and Your Daddy Don't Rock 'n' Roll"?
Answer: Saxophone.

19) Luther Burbank, author of *How Plants Are Trained to Work for Man,* developed the Shasta daisy and the Burbank potato. Is a plant breeder or one who works with plants referred to as *a geologist, horticulturist, genealogist,* or *speleologist?*
Answer: Horticulturist.

20) Of which country was Brian Mulroney, President Clinton's first visiting foreign leader in 1993, the Prime Minister? It is the U.S.'s largest trading partner and the world's second largest country in land size.
Answer: Canada.

21) Name the first black U.S. Supreme Court justice, who died in 1993 at age 84.
Answer: Thurgood Marshall.

22) Bill Clinton's 1993 inaugural speech reflected the themes of personal responsibility and service used by which President whom Clinton met in 1963 in the Rose Garden? This President is buried in Arlington National Cemetery.
Answer: John F. Kennedy.

23) Name the granite boulder on which the Pilgrims who settled Massachusetts allegedly landed.
Answer: Plymouth Rock.

24) The sum of the ages of my 3 older siblings is now 46. What was the sum of their ages 4 years ago?
Answer: 34.

25) Give the more common name for the National Railroad Passenger Corporation, which introduced in 1993 in the northeastern U.S. a high-speed passenger train that allows the cars to tilt in order to handle centrifugal force more smoothly.
Answer: Amtrak (from the words *Am*erican, *tra*vel, and trac*k*).

26) Identify the metal whose name completes the phrase "_____ Curtain" that Winston Churchill used to refer to the division between Communist and free countries in Europe. This metal's chemical symbol is Fe.
Answer: "Iron."

27) Name the poet honored in the Richmond, Virginia, museum that features a room with a blood-red floor and walls decorated with illustrations for his poem "The Raven."
Answer: Edgar Allan Poe (the room is called "The Raven Room").

28) More Americans die in January than in other months, perhaps because cold weather makes people more susceptible to infections. Spell *susceptible.*
Answer: S-U-S-C-E-P-T-I-B-L-E.

29) How much more does a German pay for 100 cubic meters of water at an average rate of $1.17 per cubic meter than an American at the average rate of 36 cents per cubic meter?
Answer: $81.00.

30) Ousted President Jean-Bertrand Aristide once denounced the Vatican for recognizing the Haitian government that overthrew him. What is the title of the Vatican's ruler?
Answer: Pope (John Paul II is now pope).

31) In 1807, U.S. Vice President Aaron Burr was acquitted of which crime defined as "levying war against the U.S. or giving aid and comfort to its enemies"?
Answer: Treason.

32) As an NAACP lawyer, Thurgood Marshall argued the 1954 case that made racially segregated schools illegal. Give the surname, a color, that completes the name of this case: _____ *vs. Board of Education.*
Answer: Brown.

33) Name the imaginary line from which longitude east and west is measured.
Answer: Prime meridian.

34) A rectangle is 36 feet long and 4 feet wide. What is the length of a side of a square that has the same area?
Answer: 12 feet.

35) Three U.S. diplomats who were on their way to peace talks in 1995 died when their vehicle fell down a ravine in Bosnia and exploded. What word beginning with *G* designates "a ravine or deep drop-off with steep sides"?
Answer: Gorge.

36) Identify the aquatic animal whose name means "eight feet."
Answer: Octopus.

37) Treasure hunters inspired by legends of wealth buried in ancient times are paying up to $50,000 to dig in Greece. Name the mythical figure to whom they have been compared since he and his Argonauts went on a great quest for the Golden Fleece.
Answer: Jason.

38) Hawaiian Chad Rowan became the first foreigner to win the highest award in Japan's centuries-old sport of sumo wrestling. Spell *wrestling.*
Answer: W-R-E-S-T-L-I-N-G.

39) Which planets are named for the supreme Roman god and his father? They are the 2 largest planets, and a car company owned by GM bears the name of the latter.
Answer: Jupiter (supreme god) and Saturn (father of Jupiter).

40) Which war ended with the Treaty of Paris signed on February 10, 1763? The Revolutionary War ended 20 years later with another Treaty of Paris.
Answer: The French and Indian War.

41) Name the famous American markswoman of Buffalo Bill's Wild West show whose gun was up for auction in 1993.
Answer: Annie Oakley.

42) Name the first President to die in office. His great grandson Benjamin became the 23rd President.
Answer: William Henry Harrison.

43) Name the national park in California and Nevada that includes the Western Hemisphere's lowest point.
Answer: Death Valley.

44) What integer is two-seventeenths of 51?
Answer: 6.

45) Name the author of *Birds of America*, the 1839 book that brought $4 million when auctioned by Christie's in New York in 1992.
Answer: John James Audubon.

46) Which green plant did Gregor Mendel use in his work on genetics?
Answer: Pea plants.

47) Give the phrase for "manners" that includes letters of the English alphabet.
Answer: P's and Q's.

48) Give the phrase for "the basic facts, elements, or principles" that includes letters of the English alphabet.
Answer: The ABC's of.

49) One economist notes that, in constant dollars, the average earnings of a 25- to 35-year-old male high school graduate in 1983 had dropped by about 20% from the average $24,300 earned in 1973. Calculate the decrease by finding 20% of $24,300.
Answer: $4,860.

50) Canada once granted asylum to a Saudi Arabian woman who was persecuted because of her views on the status of women in her country. Spell *asylum*, meaning "protection."
Answer: A-S-Y-L-U-M.

1) Which 250-foot-tall rotating apparatus with 36 coaches debuted at the 1893 World's Columbian Exposition at Chicago? It was named for its inventor, a civil engineer.
Answer: Ferris Wheel.

2) Kimba Wood was the second nominee to remove her name from consideration for attorney general in the Clinton administration. Spell *nominee*.
Answer: N-O-M-I-N-E-E.

3) Give the synonym for "gigantic" that identifies the Kentucky cave in a national park.
Answer: Mammoth (Mammoth Cave National Park).

4) What term designates any quadrilateral with both pairs of sides parallel?
Answer: Parallelogram.

5) More than 10,000 objects larger than a softball are orbiting the Earth from the debris of the 4,500 spacecraft put into orbit since the USSR launched which one in 1957?
Answer: *Sputnik*.

6) Which of the following names the point at which a lever pivots: *wedge, axle, fulcrum,* or *piston*?
Answer: Fulcrum.

7) Which of the following designates the crime of illegally taking company funds for personal use: *arson, kleptomania, embezzlement,* or *polygamy*?
Answer: Embezzlement.

8) Marian Anderson was the first black soloist to sing with New York's major opera company. What word meaning "characteristic of a major city" names this opera company?
Answer: Metropolitan.

9) What term designates a parallelogram with 4 sides of equal length but no right angles?
Answer: Rhombus.

10) In which country did F.W. de Klerk and Nelson Mandela endorse a new constitution that ended 3 centuries of white domination?
Answer: South Africa.

11) In the 1990s, a 600-ton lead counterweight was placed to stabilize the Tower of Pisa, which has a 13-foot lean. Name the boot-shaped country in which this tower is located.
Answer: Italy (the tower has a 13-foot lean).

12) President Franklin Roosevelt issued the executive order for the legal detention of which ethnic group of Americans on February 19, 1942?
Answer: Japanese-Americans.

13) What name is given to the low-lying Florida islands between the U.S. mainland and Cuba?
Answer: Keys.

14) If 1,500 people voted in a local election, and one woman received 80% of the vote, how many votes did she get?
Answer: 1,200.

15) Several Nobel Peace Prize laureates united in Thailand in 1993 to try to win the release of 1991 Nobel Prize winner Aung San Suu Kyi and others held in Myanmar. Spell *Thailand*.
Answer: T-H-A-I-L-A-N-D (Myanmar is still popularly known as Burma).

16) Name the 7th planet from the sun. It was discovered on March 13, 1781.
Answer: Uranus (discovered by English astronomer William Herschel).

17) For his book *Holes*, Louis Sachar won the medal presented annually to the best children's book of the year. Name this medal.
Answer: Newbery (medal; *Snowflake Bentley* won the Caldecott for best illustrated book).

18) "The Star-Spangled Banner" was officially adopted as the national anthem on March 3, 1931. Complete the question that ends this song: "Oh! say, does that star-spangled banner yet wave / O'er the ...?"
Answer: "land of the free and the home of the brave."

19) Saturn's satellite Titan with its 3,190 mile diameter is larger than the 2 smallest planets. Name them.
Answer: Mercury and Pluto.

20) Give the German word for "lightning warfare," a type of fast-moving warfare developed by the Germans in WWII.
Answer: *Blitzkrieg*.

21) Name the Georgia-born founder of the Girl Scouts of America. Her surname is a synonym for "to make a soft sound" or "to moo."
Answer: Juliette Gordon Low.

22) Name the President to whom the nation's 2nd largest federal building was dedicated in May 1998 shortly after Washington's National Airport was renamed for him.
Answer: Ronald Reagan (the building is on Pennsylvania Avenue in Washington, D.C.).

23) Name the capital of South Carolina, which surrendered to General William T. Sherman on February 17, 1865.
Answer: Columbia.

24) Find the largest prime factor of 20, 30, and 60.
Answer: 5.

25) Joseph Fernandez was ousted in 1993 as New York City's school superintendent because of his support for AIDS education and gay tolerance programs. Spell *superintendent*.
Answer: S-U-P-E-R-I-N-T-E-N-D-E-N-T.

26) According to a study, men under age 55 with a certain type of baldness are at greater risk for acute myocardial infarction. What does the Greek root *cardi-* mean, as in *myocardial* or *electrocardiogram*?
Answer: Heart (an acute myocardial infarction is a heart attack).

27) Identify the 2 verbs in the following sentence: "Former Interior Secretary Manuel Lujan authorized $170,000 in bonuses for 12 senior employees 5 minutes before Bill Clinton took the oath of office."
Answer: *Authorized* and *took*.

28) Renowned ballet and opera troupes were searching for interim quarters as the 168-year-old Bolshoi Theater in Russia underwent repairs that could cost $300 million. Spell *renowned*, meaning "famous."
Answer: R-E-N-O-W-N-E-D.

29) J.P. Morgan incorporated the first "billion dollar corporation," U.S. Steel, on February 25, 1901. How many zeroes are in the number for one billion?
Answer: 9.

30) Which capital city was founded by Francisco Pizarro after he conquered the Incas in Peru?
Answer: Lima.

31) Virginia-born soldier and politician Sam Houston served as governor in both Tennessee and Texas. Spell *Tennessee*.
Answer: T-E-N-N-E-S-S-E-E.

32) Identify the American Revolutionary hero whose maxim was "a warrior is always ready." He is known as the "Father of the American Navy."
Answer: John Paul Jones.

33) Identify the Arizona national park established on February 26, 1919.
Answer: Grand Canyon National Park.

34) The Clinton administration once cut the Office of Drug Control Policy to 25 employees. Does the group of 25 represent about 1/3, 1/4, 1/5, or 1/6 of the original 146?
Answer: 1/6.

35) Name the city northeast of Toledo that has been Spain's capital since 1561.
Answer: Madrid.

36) A fax machine transmits copies of original messages. For which word meaning "a copy" is *fax* a shortened form?
Answer: Facsimile.

37) The Salvation Army, which William Booth founded in England, was officially established in the U.S. in New York on March 10, 1880. Spell *officially*.
Answer: O-F-F-I-C-I-A-L-L-Y.

38) According to the Bible, after the exodus from Egypt, which river did the Israelites cross to reach the Promised Land?
Answer: Jordan River.

39) Which substance made of amino acids is used to build and repair cells in the body and is found in such foods as fish and meat?
Answer: Protein.

40) The Korean War left 8,200 MIAs, 4 times the number from Vietnam, a fact angering many who say the Senate Select Committee on POWs and MIAs neglects them. Give the full meaning of both *POW* and *MIA*.
Answer: Prisoner of War and Missing In Action.

41) To help pay the costs of the Civil War, the U.S. issued its first paper money in 1861. Name the President and the secretary of the treasury on today's $5 and $10 bills.
Answer: Lincoln on $5 and Hamilton on $10 (reversed in the bills issued 3/10/1861).

42) Which Virginian, known as the "Father of the Constitution," served as the 4th President of the U.S.? His surname also identifies the capital of Wisconsin.
Answer: James Madison.

43) Which U.S. state has been called the "Keystone of the Democratic Arch"? Its capital is Harrisburg.
Answer: Pennsylvania.

44) Find the quotient when .23 is divided into 10.81.
Answer: 47.

45) In a 1993 mock trial, defense lawyer F. Lee Bailey tried to clear the name of Dr. Samuel Mudd, who set the broken leg of the assassin who killed President Lincoln. Name him.
Answer: John Wilkes Booth.

46) Robert Koch announced his discovery of the germs of tuberculosis on March 24, 1882. Is tuberculosis a disease primarily of the nerves, lungs, liver, or heart?
Answer: Lungs.

47) The reference book *Final Curtain* tells how 4,000 movie, TV, and music personalities died. Which of the following designates "a public notice of a death": *epitaph, finale, invocation,* or *obituary*?
Answer: Obituary.

48) Both the TV miniseries *Roots* and the miniseries *Queen* are based on the lives of Alex Haley's ancestors. Which of the following designates "a study of one's family tree, or ancestors: *genealogy, graphology, psychology,* or *ophthalmology*?
Answer: Genealogy.

49) How many years are in 4 decades plus 1 score?
Answer: 60 (40 + 20).

50) Name the country of former dictator Manuel Noriega. His country provides sea passage between the Atlantic and Pacific oceans.
Answer: Panama.

1) Is a *maritime* disaster a volcanic eruption, an earthquake, a plane crash, or the sinking of a ship?
    Answer: Sinking of a ship.

2) In which state, known for groundhog Punsxutawney Phil, did Baron von Steuben begin drilling General Washington's infantry at Valley Forge?
    Answer: Pennsylvania (on February 23, 1778).

3) Into which body of water does the Jordan River empty?
    Answer: Dead Sea.

4) According to one estimate, a movie star gets about $650,000 after taxes for every $1 million paycheck. What percent of $1 million is the $350,000 paid in taxes?
    Answer: 35%.

5) In which state did Governor Folsom end a long debate when he said the Confederate battle flag won't be put back atop the Capitol in Montgomery?
    Answer: Alabama.

6) On March 26, 1953, Dr. Jonas Salk announced a new vaccine capable of immunizing humans against which crippling disease?
    Answer: Polio (poliomyelitis or infantile paralysis).

7) Name the legendary giant lumberjack of the U.S.
    Answer: Paul Bunyan.

8) The Roman Catholic feast of the Annunciation, celebrated on March 25, commemorates the day an angel told Mary that she was to be the Mother of Christ. Name this angel.
    Answer: Gabriel.

9) The area of a rectangular garden plot is 100 square feet. If the width of this garden is 5 feet, what is its length?
    Answer: 20 feet.

10) Which country donated a sculpture to Switzerland's Olympic museum in an attempt to secure a bid to host the 2000 Olympics in Beijing, its capital?
    Answer: China.

11) Identify the winner of the 1997 Sugar Bowl, the team voted No. 1 after defeating Florida State 52-20. This school's teams are nicknamed the "Gators."
    Answer: University of Florida.

12) How long is a term for a congressman in the U.S. House of Representatives?
Answer: 2 years.

13) Name the country whose longest river is the Loire (lwär), which flows through a valley known for its chateaux.
Answer: France.

14) What letter is the Roman numeral for 500?
Answer: D.

15) Which type of tax due each year on April 15 generates about $130 billion, the largest single tax item in the Clinton administration's budget?
Answer: Income tax.

16) Give the full name of the AMA, the U.S.'s largest organization for doctors, which was denied representation on President Clinton's health-care reform task force.
Answer: American Medical Association.

17) In which U.S. state did Paul Bunyan and his blue ox, Babe, allegedly create ten thousand lakes when their footprints filled with water?
Answer: Minnesota.

18) In which 2 states does major league baseball hold spring training? One is nicknamed the "Sunshine State," and the other is home to one of the Seven Natural Wonders of the World.
Answer: Florida and Arizona (Arizona's Grand Canyon is one of the Seven Natural Wonders of the World).

19) On January 24, 1978, some debris from the USSR's satellite *Cosmos 954* reached ground after the satellite fell into Earth's atmosphere and burned over Canada. Spell *debris*.
Answer: D-E-B-R-I-S.

20) Which month of the year is named for Julius Caesar, who was assassinated on the Ides of March in 44 B.C.
Answer: July.

21) Name the President whose daughter Amy in 1977 became the last presidential offspring, and only the 2nd this century, to attend a public school in Washington, D.C.
Answer: Jimmy Carter.

22) Name the state for which Hiram Revels began serving the unexpired Senate term of Jefferson Davis in 1870, thus becoming the first black in the U.S. Senate. Its capital is Jackson.
Answer: Mississippi (Revels began his term on February 25, 1870).

23) In which state did Congress establish Mount Rainier National Park on March 2, 1899?
Answer: Washington.

24) A rectangular floor has an area of 720 square feet. How many square yards of carpeting are needed to cover it?
Answer: 80 square yards.

25) Researchers once found 1,133 undersea volcanoes about 2,000 miles west of which continent, site of the world's largest rain forest?
Answer: South America.

26) Identify the bird of prey whose name has come to mean "an advocate of war" or "a person who favors aggressive policies."
Answer: Hawk.

27) Marilyn Tucker Quayle, returned to her profession as an attorney after her husband's term as Vice President ended. Spell *attorney*.
Answer: A-T-T-O-R-N-E-Y.

28) What does the word *love* mean in a tennis score, such as 40-love?
Answer: Zero (from French *l'oeuf* for "egg," which, of course, is shaped like a zero).

29) What is the product of the number of sides of a hexagon and the number of degrees in a right angle?
Answer: 540.

30) In which country that occupies an entire continent did a prime minister call for Britain's Queen Elizabeth to be replaced as head of state?
Answer: Australia (the Latin word *australis* means "southern").

31) Give the full name of the NAACP. It is the nation's oldest and largest civil rights group.
Answer: National Association for the Advancement of Colored People.

32) On March 4, 1893, which President was inaugurated for his second, nonconsecutive term of office? His surname also identifies Ohio's second largest city.
Answer: Grover Cleveland.

33) Which one of the following countries borders Somalia: Argentina, Ethiopia, Italy, or South Africa?
Answer: Ethiopia.

34) Saudi Arabia once agreed to donate $1.9 million annually for 4 years, or a total contribution of how much, to the Carter Center in Atlanta to support the international eradication of Guinea worm disease?
Answer: $7.6 million.

35) On April 12, 1955, American physician Dr. Jonas E. Salk announced a "safe and effective" vaccine for polio. Spell *vaccine*.
Answer: V-A-C-C-I-N-E.

36) The United Mine Workers once called off a strike it began when the miners' contract with the coal operators' association expired. Identify the soft coal for which this association is named.
Answer: Bituminous.

37) Identify the direct object in the following sentence: "The flooding Gila River has forced the evacuation of thousands who live near the Painted Rock Dam in Arizona."
Answer: Evacuation.

38) Six years after he was taken to Ireland by pirates, who escaped and became a monk in France, and later a missionary to Ireland? March 17 commemorates his feast day.
Answer: Saint Patrick.

39) On March 8, 1993, which celestial body was 17,326 miles closer to Earth than average in its elliptical orbit, teaming up with the Earth and sun in a rare alignment that created surging tides throughout the U.S.?
Answer: Moon.

40) Only one man was court-martialed and convicted for the My Lai massacre of unarmed civilians in Vietnam. In which decade did this massacre occur?
Answer: 1960s (on March 16, 1968).

41) In which state did the first atomic bomb explode on July 16, 1945, at the Alamogordo Air Base about 190 miles due south of the capital of Santa Fe?
Answer: New Mexico.

42) Name the Texas fort that was overrun by Mexican General Santa Anna on March 6, 1836. From this defeat came the slogan "Remember the _____," which inspired Texans to capture Santa Anna and win their independence on April 21.
Answer: The Alamo.

43) Name the New York City square where on New Year's Eve, lasers, strobes, and other lights are assembled to mark the dropping of a ball at the stroke of midnight.
Answer: Times Square.

44) The U.S. Senate confirmed Janet Reno as the first female U.S. attorney general. If all but 2 senators voted, and all who cast ballots voted for her, how many votes did she receive?
Answer: 98.

45) Name the world's third-tallest building, where a 1993 explosion caused by a bomb killed 5 people, and forced thousands to flee down dark, smoke-filled stairs. This building is in New York City.
Answer: World Trade Center.

46) Although he resigned in disgrace in 1973, former U.S. Vice President Spiro Agnew later got a marble bust on Capitol Hill. To which of the 3 classifications of rock does marble belong?
Answer: Metamorphic.

47) A redesign team gathered in 1993 at NASA headquarters in an effort to pare costs for *Freedom*, the $31 billion space station. Spell *pare*, meaning "to trim."
Answer: P-A-R-E.

48) Give the religious affiliation of Mohammed Salameh, the man arrested for bombing the World Trade Center when he tried to reclaim a deposit on a rented van.
Answer: Muslim or Moslem.

49) By what special name do we know a parallelogram with all sides congruent and all angles congruent?
Answer: Square.

50) Name the "Lady with the Lamp" who cared for the wounded during the Crimean War and is considered the founder of modern nursing. Her surname designates a song bird.
Answer: Florence Nightingale.

1) Answer the following question posed to the winner of the 1998 National Geography Bee: What is the European Union's most populous country?
   Answer: Germany (with a population of more than 80 million people).

2) Lee Harvey Oswald killed John F. Kennedy. Identify the gemstone that shares its name with the person who killed Oswald and was convicted of the murder on March 14, 1964?
   Answer: Ruby (Jack Ruby killed Oswald).

3) Name the U.S.'s tallest man-made monument, at 630 feet. It is located on the Mississippi River.
   Answer: Gateway Arch.

4) If each step is 12 inches high, how many steps are in a staircase 15 feet high?
   Answer: 15.

5) Name one of the 3 Baltic republics that became independent from the Soviet Union in 1991, two of whose names begin with the letter *L*.
   Answer: Estonia, Latvia, or Lithuania.

6) According to an EPA survey, nearly 20% of U.S. schools have unacceptably high levels of which gas that is the second leading cause of lung cancer?
   Answer: Radon.

7) Freedom-of-assembly rights are guaranteed under the First Amendment. Spell *guaranteed*.
   Answer: G-U-A-R-A-N-T-E-E-D.

8) The Soviet's Alexi Leonov took the first space walk on March 18, 1965. Which Greek root for "universe" completes the word for a Russian space traveler: _____*naut*?
   Answer: Cosmo- (cosmonaut).

9) What is the area of a rectangle with a length of 9 feet and a width of 7.2 feet?
   Answer: 64.8 square feet.

10) What name do the British and French share for their lawmaking bodies?
   Answer: Parliament (the French verb *parler* means "to talk").

11) For which U.S. President is the memorial that includes Gateway Arch named? He sent Lewis and Clark to explore the Louisiana Territory.
Answer: Thomas Jefferson (Jefferson National Expansion Memorial).

12) The Social Security Act was part of which U.S. President's New Deal program?
Answer: Franklin Roosevelt's.

13) Which of the following does not border Texas: Arizona, Arkansas, Louisiana, or New Mexico?
Answer: Arizona.

14) By what special name do we know a parallelogram with all angles congruent?
Answer: Rectangle (square).

15) Huge explosions once rocked India's largest stock exchange in Bombay. On which sea is Bombay located, a sea whose name is in the title of a collection of ancient tales including the story of "Ali Baba and the Forty Thieves"?
Answer: Arabian Sea (*The Arabian Nights' Entertainments*).

16) Name the electronic device surgically implanted into a body to control a worsening heart condition.
Answer: Pacemaker.

17) Which word that also identifies the number resulting from mathematical division completes the term *intelligence* _____ for which IQ stands?
Answer: Quotient.

18) Ross Perot initiated a project to highlight wasteful government spending. Identify the meat whose name is used to represent the "fat" or "unnecessary excess" in a budget.
Answer: Pork.

19) The world's biggest germ, a cigar-shaped bacterium visible to the naked eye, was discovered in Australian fish in 1993. What term is used to describe fish and any other animal whose body temperature varies with the external environment?
Answer: Cold-blooded (also, poikilothermous or ectothermic).

20) Conservatives won about 80% of the seats in France's National Assembly in 1993. In lowest terms, what fraction is equivalent to 80%?
Answer: 4/5.

21) The first women's collegiate basketball game was played at Smith College between the freshmen and sophomores on March 22, 1892. Spell *sophomores*.
Answer: S-O-P-H-O-M-O-R-E-S.

22) Which patriot in 1775 spoke these words in favor of arming the militia: "I know not what course others may take, but as for me, give me liberty or give me death"?
Answer: Patrick Henry.

23) On which major river of the Northwest is the U.S.'s largest concrete dam, the Grand Coulee Dam, located? This river shares its name with a U.S. state capital, and its name begins with the letter *C*.
Answer: Columbia River.

24) The prime number 19 contains the digit 1. What is the next prime number that contains the digit 1?
Answer: 31.

25) The Senate passed a bill making it a federal crime to harass a person by mail, phone, or across state lines. Which word that as a noun means "the main stem of a plant" and as a verb means "to track prey" completes the term _____*ing* used to designate this type of criminal activity?
Answer: Stalk (*stalking*).

26) Congress passed the Standard Time Act on March 18, 1918, authorizing the ICC to establish standard time zones. Name 3 of the 4 time zones in the continental U.S.
Answer: Eastern, Central, Mountain, and Pacific.

27) Captain William Bligh survived a 47-day voyage after being set adrift by crew members who took over his ship on April 28, 1789. What is such a rebellion at sea called?
Answer: Mutiny.

28) Which word designates both a high-ranking Roman Catholic official who with others of the same rank elects the Pope, and a bird with bright red feathers?
Answer: Cardinal.

29) Of the 435 members in the U.S. House, how many did not vote when President Clinton's deficit-reduction plan was passed by a vote of 243 to 183?
Answer: 9.

30) A U.S. Secretary of State once warned that "the price we pay could be frightening" if Russia falls into a state of lawlessness. Which of the following words designates a "state without any government": *anarchy, apartheid, monarchy,* or *republic*?
Answer: Anarchy.

31) Name the popular 1993 movie based on a 1960s TV series whose title designates a person on the run to escape capture by police.
Answer: *The Fugitive* (starring Harrison Ford).

32) In which of the original 13 colonies did Leonard Calvert establish a settlement west of the Chesapeake Bay on March 27, 1634?
Answer: Maryland.

33) In which mountain range is Mount Everest, the world's tallest mountain?
Answer: Himalayas.

34) A box contains 100 pennies, 60 nickels, and 40 dimes. If one coin is taken from the box at random, what is the probability that it will be a dime?
Answer: 1 out of 5 (40 out of 200 is also acceptable).

35) President Clinton has held summits with Boris Yeltsin in Vancouver, British Columbia. Which of the following U.S. cities is closest to Vancouver: Chicago, Detroit, Portland, or Seattle?
Answer: Seattle.

36) Through powerful binoculars, the brightest stellar explosion to appear in the Northern Hemisphere in decades was visible between the North Star and the Big Dipper, or Ursa Major in 1993. What is the Latin name for the North Star?
Answer: Polaris.

37) U.S. Secretary of State William H. Seward acquired Alaska from Russia on March 30, 1867. Spell *acquired*.
Answer: A-C-Q-U-I-R-E-D.

38) What name is given to the day that commemorates Christ's last entry into Jerusalem and begins Holy Week in Western Christian churches?
Answer: Palm Sunday.

39) Which scientist is credited with the first practical use of a telescope: Edison, Einstein, Franklin, or Galileo?
Answer: Galileo.

40) In 1993, Andorra voted to end its 7 centuries of being ruled by the French head of state and the bishop of a neighboring country. Name this neighboring country that is separated from France by the Pyrenees Mountains.
Answer: Spain.

41) Which warship was Horatio Nelson's first command in 1778? This ship shares its name with the animal associated with Wisconsin.
Answer: *Badger.*

42) In 1998, Democrat Charles Schumer of New York won a primary race for the senate by defeating a former female Democratic vice presidential nominee, namely which of the following: *Judy Bloom*, *Elizabeth Dole*, *Geraldine Ferraro*, or *Sally Ride*?
Answer: **Geraldine Ferraro.**

43) Which ocean did Vasco Núñez de Balboa call the "South Sea" when he became the first European explorer to see its eastern shore on September 25, 1513?
Answer: **Pacific Ocean (he was atop a peak in Panama).**

44) A pie is cut in half and each piece is then cut in half again. If each piece is cut in half one more time, how many pieces will there be?
Answer: **8 pieces.**

45) Of the following countries that have gained independence since 1990, which one was not formerly a part of Yugoslavia: *Macedonia*, *Croatia*, *Slovenia*, or *Ukraine*?
Answer: **Ukraine.**

46) What name is given to life, a being, or any influence that comes from outside the earth's limits? The film character E.T. is named with an abbreviation for this word.
Answer: **Extraterrestrial.**

47) Byron White was the only appointee of a Democratic president on the Supreme Court when he announced his retirement, effective the summer of 1993. Spell *appointee*.
Answer: **A-P-P-O-I-N-T-E-E (John F. Kennedy appointed White in 1962).**

48) Which religion calls its New Year's Day celebration Rosh Hashanah?
Answer: **Judaism (Jewish).**

49) By what name do we know a quadrilateral with diagonals that bisect each other?
Answer: **Parallelogram.**

50) Identify the Canadian province whose name is a compound of 3 words meaning "territory recently discovered."
Answer: **Newfoundland (it became the 10th Canadian province on March 31, 1949).**

1) Congress established the first plant for making coins on April 2, 1792, in Philadelphia. What term designates such a plant?
Answer: Mint.

2) Name the two states from which the U.S. acquired the land for the District of Columbia.
Answer: Virginia and Maryland.

3) Is Mount St. Helens in Washington located in the Black Hills, Cascades, Ozarks, or Smokies?
Answer: Cascades.

4) What is the reciprocal of the mixed number 4 3/4?
Answer: 4/19.

5) Name Martin Luther King Jr.'s assassin, who in May 1994 was denied his first bid for parole. His surname designates a straight line extending from a point.
Answer: James Earl Ray (he died, at age 70, on April 23, 1998).

6) Which of the following wind speeds designates the point at which a tropical storm becomes a hurricane: in **mph**, 74, 94, 124, or 154?
Answer: 74 mph.

7) A revolt took place on April 19, 1943, when Germans tried to deport residents of a ghetto in Warsaw, Poland. Spell *ghetto*, meaning "a section of a city occupied by a minority group."
Answer: G-H-E-T-T-O.

8) German golfer Bernhard Langer won his second Masters title in 1993. In which state is this tournament played in Augusta?
Answer: Georgia (he also won in 1985).

9) If two lines intersect in right angles, what are the two lines said to be?
Answer: Perpendicular.

10) Complete Great Britain's official name: the United Kingdom of Great Britain and Northern ____.
Answer: Ireland.

11) What is the banking term for the amount of money a person has in an account at a given time?
Answer: Balance.

12) On April 2, 1865, from which capital did President Jefferson Davis and most of his Confederate Cabinet flee after General Robert E. Lee abandoned it and Petersburg?
Answer: Richmond.

13) Which 2 U.S. capitals beginning with the letter *S* are located in states bordering the Pacific Ocean?
Answer: Sacramento (California) and Salem (Oregon).

14) How many more square yards of carpet are needed to cover a square room with a side of 12 feet than a room measuring 9 feet by 12 feet?
Answer: 4 square yards.

15) Two sailors broke a 140-year-old record when they sailed from San Francisco to Boston around which South American cape nearly a week ahead of the 76 days of the 1853 record-setting voyage?
Answer: Cape Horn (their trip in 1993 took 69 days, 19 3/4 hours).

16) Gen. Thomas "Stonewall" Jackson died of pneumonia following the amputation of his arm after being wounded by his own men. Spell *pneumonia*.
Answer: P-N-E-U-M-O-N-I-A.

17) Mildred Wirt Benson was publicly recognized at a conference as the original Carolyn Keene, the pen name used for books about which teen sleuth?
Answer: Nancy Drew (the first-ever Nancy Drew conference was held at University of Iowa).

18) Identify the Renaissance artist whose name completes the title of the Royal British Columbia Museum's 1998 exhibit _____: *Scientist, Inventor, Artist*.
Answer: Leonardo da Vinci.

19) The nickname of Maryland, the 7th state to ratify the Constitution, is the "Terrapin State." A terrapin is an aquatic turtle; what is the name for a land turtle?
Answer: Tortoise (Maryland ratified the Constitution on April 28, 1788.

20) In what century did Juan Ponce de León claim Florida for the King of Spain?
Answer: 16th century (on April 2, 1513).

21) What is a business owned by group of people known as shareholders called?
Answer: Corporation (accept company).

22) Which of the following was *not* among the 15 stamps the post office issued to commemorate the 1970s: jumbo jets; VCRs; *Sesame Street*; or walking on the moon?
Answer: Walking on the moon (which took place in 1969; the public chose it as the top subject of the 1960s).

23) James Earl Ray assassinated Dr. Martin Luther King Jr. on April 4, 1968, in Memphis, Tennessee. Spell *Memphis*.
Answer: M-E-M-P-H-I-S.

24) If 4 years at a college costs $92,000, how much would a student save by completing his degree in 3 years?
Answer: $23,000.

25) A counterfeiter makes copies of money with the intent of passing it off as the real thing with real value. Spell *counterfeiter*.
Answer: C-O-U-N-T-E-R-F-E-I-T-E-R.

26) In which country surrounded by the Pacific and Indian Oceans have scientists found fossils showing that life on Earth was surprisingly advanced more than 3.5 billion years ago? The Great Barrier Reef lies off its northern coast.
Answer: Australia.

27) Which 19th-century poet wrote the lines "Hang a lantern aloft in the belfry arch / Of the North Church tower as a signal light" in his poem "Paul Revere's Ride"?
Answer: Henry Wadsworth Longfellow.

28) What color, made from mixing blue and yellow, is used to name the card that gives approval for a foreigner to live in the U.S.?
Answer: Green (card).

29) Helena, Montana, residents were given the option of clearing fines by donating cans of food for the needy. With each can worth $5 toward a fine, what was the total amount of the cleared fines for the 12,013 cans collected?
Answer: $60,065.

30) On October 1, 1936, Francisco Franco was named leader of the nationalist government of which country located between Portugal and France?
Answer: Spain.

31) Is a person in his 80s referred to as an adolescent, centenarian, humanitarian, or octogenarian?
Answer: Octogenarian (*octo-* means "eight").

32) Senators sometimes use long speeches to delay action on bills. How many votes are required to break a filibuster in the Senate, a count that equals 3/5 of the membership?
Answer: 60 votes.

33) What is Vietnam's capital: Belgrade, Hanoi, Saigon, or Prague?
Answer: Hanoi.

34) The average Stone Age human lived 15 years. If the average life expectancy today for men in the U.S. is 4.8 times as long, how many years does that equal?
Answer: 72 years (life expectancy for women is 79 years).

35) In 1993, a U.N.-negotiated peace plan was signed for the first time by all 3 parties in the Bosnian conflict—Serbs, Muslims, and Croats. Spell the name of the country in which all three groups lived before its breakup.
Answer: Y-U-G-O-S-L-A-V-I-A.

36) What is the acronym for the U.S. space agency?
Answer: NASA (National Aeronautics and Space Administration).

37) In which Washington Irving story does Brom Bones rival Ichabod Crane for the hand of Katrina?
Answer: *The Legend of Sleepy Hollow.*

38) Spell *choreography*, which means "the art of planning the movements of a dance or ballet."
Answer: C-H-O-R-E-O-G-R-A-P-H-Y.

39) The parasite cryptosporidium, which sickened thousands in 1993, was washed into which lake that is the water supply for 800,000 Milwaukee residents and the largest body of fresh water in the contiguous U.S.?
Answer: Lake Michigan.

40) Which of the following wars began on April 21, 1898: Revolutionary War, Civil War, Spanish American War, or WWI?
Answer: Spanish American War.

41) Elizabeth Cady Stanton was elected the first president of the Woman Suffrage Association on May 15, 1869. Does *suffrage* mean "great pain," "right to own property," "liberation," or "right to vote"?
Answer: Right to vote.

42) Which amendment, ratified in 1913, provides for the direct election of senators: 1st, 10th, 17th, or 27th?
Answer: 17th Amendment.

43) August 21, 1993, was eliminated on Kwajalein [kwä′jə lən] in the Marshall Islands when it jumped from one side of the International Date Line to the other. In which ocean is Kwajalein located?
Answer: Pacific Ocean.

44) The area of a right triangle is 40 square inches. If the base of the triangle is 8 inches, what is its corresponding height?
Answer: 10 inches.

45) In 1993, NATO ships in the Adriatic Sea were authorized to shoot if necessary to stop ships carrying banned goods to Serbia. Which country is on the western shore of the Adriatic?
Answer: Italy.

46) In 1999, the vernal equinox, marking the first day of spring in the Northern Hemisphere, occurred on March 20. Spell *hemisphere*.
Answer: H-E-M-I-S-P-H-E-R-E (Earth Day is celebrated on this day).

47) Name the one-legged ship's cook and pirate leader who sets sail with Jim Hawkins to find hidden gold in Robert Louis Stevenson's novel *Treasure Island*.
Answer: Long John Silver.

48) Identify the insect whose name completes the title of composer Rimsky-Korsakov's "The Flight of the ____," a work that reproduces this insect's buzzing sound or drone.
Answer: Bumblebee.

49) A Frenchman and his crew on a sail-powered catamaran once met the challenge of Phileas Fogg in the Jules Verne book *Around the World in Eighty Days*. By how much did their 79 days and 6 hours beat the previous circumnavigation record of 109 days?
Answer: 29 days and 18 hours.

50) Who assumed the English throne on the death of King George VI on February 6, 1952?
Answer: Elizabeth II.

1) Promising higher achievement scores and more computers, a private, for-profit company once opened 4 public schools scattered throughout the U.S. Identify this company, which shares its name with the inventor of the phonograph.
Answer: Edison (Project; the 4 are in Texas, Kansas, Michigan, and Massachusetts).

2) Name the English playwright who died on April 23, 1616, the same day as Spanish writer Miguel de Cervantes, creator of Don Quixote. This playwright wrote *Romeo and Juliet*.
Answer: William Shakespeare.

3) In which city near Mount Rainier in the Cascade Mountains was the Space Needle opened on April 21 at the 1962 World's Fair?
Answer: Seattle (Washington).

4) What is 13 percent of 13?
Answer: 1.69.

5) In which ocean is Sri Lanka, the island off India's southern tip?
Answer: Indian Ocean.

6) A NASA spacecraft has revealed that which planet may have harbored life in oceans up to 75 feet deep that once covered its surface? This planet has been called Earth's twin.
Answer: Venus.

7) At a New York tribute to slain Prime Minister Yitzhak Rabin, Kathleen Turner read "O Captain, My Captain," Walt Whitman's poem about the death of which President?
Answer: Abraham Lincoln (widow Leah Rabin and Prime Minister Peres attended).

8) Which planet, named for the Roman god of the sea, was first seen on September 23, 1846? It is the eighth planet in the solar system.
Answer: Neptune.

9) Is Eritrea, a new nation with 45,405 square miles, about 1/2, 1/5, 1/10, or 1/20 the size of neighboring Sudan with its 966,757 square miles?
Answer: 1/20.

10) Which South American country did Portuguese explorer Pedro Alvares Cabral discover on April 22, 1500? It's larger than the mainland U.S.
Answer: Brazil.

11) Name either of the West Point graduates who completed 2 full terms as U.S. President.
Answer: Ulysses S. Grant or Dwight Eisenhower.

12) On April 25, 1898, who resigned his post as Assistant Secretary of the Navy to continue recruitment of the volunteers known as the "Rough Riders"?
Answer: Theodore Roosevelt.

13) The Portage Lake shoreline and 2 waterfalls in Alaska were once exposed when a large body of sliding ice made a dramatic retreat. What word designates such a field of ice?
Answer: Glacier.

14) What is the perimeter of a rectangle whose width is 4 cm and whose length is 9 cm?
Answer: 26 cm.

15) In which country did militants in 1997 kill 62 tourists at the ruins of a 3,400-year-old temple built by King Amenhotep III near the Nile River?
Answer: Egypt.

16) Which word using the same suffix as *pesticide* means "the act of killing oneself"?
Answer: Suicide.

17) Identify *combat* as a noun, verb, or adjective in the following: *Secretary of Defense Les Aspin ordered the armed services to let women fly combat aircraft.*
Answer: Adjective.

18) In Greek myth, which winged horse sprang from the beheaded body of Medusa and was later placed in the sky as a constellation?
Answer: Pegasus.

19) According to a science journal, which California geyser can forecast earthquakes up to 150 miles away? It has the same name as a famous Yellowstone National Park geyser.
Answer: Old Faithful.

20) Which city did the Germans take over on April 27, 1941, raising the Nazi swastika over the hill known as the Acropolis? It is the capital of Greece.
Answer: Athens.

21) Among the National Park Service's historical structures in need of repair is the 3-story, patched-up warden's house at which former prison in San Francisco Bay?
Answer: Alcatraz.

22) Which scientist, a refugee from Germany, wrote President Roosevelt the famous letter of August 2, 1939, that set in motion the development of the atomic bomb?
Answer: Albert Einstein.

23) Of which country did Benito Mussolini become premier on October 31, 1922? This country is shaped like a boot.
Answer: Italy.

24) Secretary of State William Seward purchased Alaska from Russia in 1867. With his payment of $7,200,000, about how much did he pay per square mile for the 591,000 square mile area: $120.00, $12.00, $1.20, or $.12?
Answer: $12.00.

25) Who first sailed around the world under the American flag? This adventurer, whose surname designates a color, also discovered the Columbia River, on May 12, 1792.
Answer: Robert Gray.

26) Name the positively charged particles in the atom.
Answer: Protons.

27) Senate Appropriations Committee head Robert Byrd ended his fight to have the Navy build an atomic clock in West Virginia. How many syllables does *appropriations* have?
Answer: 5.

28) Is a place where nuns lived called a *bureaucracy, convent, parsonage*, or *tabernacle*?
Answer: Convent.

29) What is the measure of the side of a square that has the same area as a rectangle whose width is 4 cm and whose length is 9 cm?
Answer: 6 cm.

30) Which English king succeeded to the throne on May 12, 1937, after the abdication of his brother Edward VIII? He and the Revolutionary War era king share the same name.
Answer: George (VI).

31) Belmont, Massachusetts, is now an attraction to Japanese tourists who want to see the former home of the young woman who married the Crown Prince of Japan. Which word from French designates "the woman whom a man has pledged to marry"?
Answer: Fiancée.

32) Which Louisiana city at the mouth of the Mississippi River fell to the Union in 1862?
Answer: New Orleans (on April 29, 1862).

33) Three colonies of rare giant tortoises are being threatened by volcanic eruptions on islands 600 miles west of Ecuador, namely, which of the following: Aleutians, Bahamas, Galapagos Islands, or Virgin Islands?
Answer: Galapagos Islands (the tortoises are Ecuador's major tourist attraction).

34) If you ate one ounce of a 3-pound cake, what fraction of that cake did you eat?
Answer: 1/48.

35) Name the continents Istanbul straddles. It is the world's only major city located on 2 continents.
Answer: Europe and Asia (Istanbul is in Turkey).

36) Identify the Egyptian town near which the ruins of King Amenhotep's temple are located. Its name begins with the same 3 letters as the English word completing the phrase "living in _____," meaning "surrounded by desirable riches."
Answer: Luxor (*luxury* is from Latin *luxuria*, meaning "excess").

37) Which word designates "a word with the same spelling as another but with a different meaning, and sometimes a different pronunciation"?
Answer: Homograph.

38) In medieval times villagers danced around a pole while holding ribbons attached to its top on May Day, or May 1. Spell *medieval*, which describes the Middle Ages, from about 500 to about 1500.
Answer: M-E-D-I-E-V-A-L.

39) Which sedimentary rock composed of calcium carbonate is formed from the skeletons of marine invertebrates?
Answer: Limestone.

40) Name the British citizen who at the age of 88 was granted honorary U.S. citizenship on April 9, 1963. His surname contains a word for "a place of worship."
Answer: Winston Churchill.

41) A 4-year-old boy pronounced dead when dug out after being buried by an avalanche in Austria in 1999 was successfully resuscitated. Spell *resuscitate*, meaning "to restore consciousness."
Answer: R-E-S-U-S-C-I-T-A-T-E.

42) Which President first declared Thanksgiving a national holiday, issuing a proclamation for its celebration on November 26, 1789?
Answer: George Washington (partly to give thanks for the new Constitution).

43) Which state, nicknamed the "North Star State," is the source of the Mississippi River? It is bordered on the west by the Red River of the North.
Answer: Minnesota.

44) What is the greatest common divisor of 65 and 26?
Answer: 13.

45) In which country did construction workers find a long-hidden statue of Ramses the Great, a famous pharaoh?
Answer: Egypt.

46) A Health and Human Services secretary once mistakenly said alcohol was a major cause of psoriasis, a skin disorder, before quickly correcting herself, saying she meant *cirrhosis*, a disease of the largest gland of the body. Name this gland.
Answer: Liver.

47) At a summit on human rights, former President Jimmy Carter recommended establishing a U.N. human rights commissioner. Spell *recommend*.
Answer: R-E-C-O-M-M-E-N-D.

48) According to scientists, murals in the Sistine Chapel in the palace of the Vatican in Rome are being damaged by perspiring visitors who exude 220 pounds of moisture a day. Are *murals* statues, wall paintings, altar cloths, or portraits of saints?
Answer: Wall paintings.

49) Russian president Boris Yeltsin once survived an impeachment vote in a battle with the Congress of People's Deputies. How many votes were needed for the 2/3 majority necessary for impeachment in the 1,033-member body?
Answer: 689.

50) Against which country did the U.S. declare war when it entered WWI on April 6, 1917?
Answer: Germany.

1) Robert E. Peary, along with black assistant Matthew Henson, allegedly reached the North Pole on April 6, 1909. Spell *assistant*.
   Answer: A-S-S-I-S-T-A-N-T.

2) In which state bordering Idaho and Arizona was a golden spike driven near Ogden on May 10, 1869, to mark the connecting point of the first transcontinental railroad?
   Answer: Utah.

3) A massive diesel fuel spill from a pipeline in Fairfax County, Virginia, reached 20 miles down which river to the Jefferson Memorial?
   Answer: Potomac River.

4) About what fraction of the total points in a 77 to 71 victory were scored by a player with his 25 points: 1/3, 1/4, 1/5 or 1/6?
   Answer: 1/6.

5) Name the world's largest country, with an area of over 6.5 million square miles.
   Answer: Russia.

6) What is the term for the unit of weight used to determine the value of a precious gem?
   Answer: Carat.

7) Spell *colonel*, the word for the military rank just below brigadier general.
   Answer: C-O-L-O-N-E-L.

8) According to a Henry Wadsworth Longfellow poem, Paul Revere made his famous ride "On the eighteenth of April" in which year, a year before independence was declared?
   Answer: 1775 ("On the eighteenth of April in Seventy-five" in "Paul Revere's Ride").

9) On which country did Congress officially declare war on May 13, 1846?
   Answer: Mexico.

10) Which President was the first to host a Russian leader—Nikita Krushchev—in the U.S., in 1959?
    Answer: Dwight Eisenhower.

11) The Union suffered about 13,000 casualties and the Confederacy about 11,000 at Shiloh in 1862. What color were the regulation uniforms worn by Union and Confederate soldiers, respectively?
Answer: Blue (Union) and Gray (Confederate).

12) Name the state where on May 10, 1775, Ethan Allen's Green Mountain Boys captured Fort Ticonderoga without firing a shot. It is bordered by Lake Erie and Lake Ontario.
Answer: New York.

13) About 225 miles south of Barrow, Alaska, archaeologists have found evidence of a camp dating back 11,700 years, making it possibly the oldest inhabited site in North America. On which ocean is Barrow located?
Answer: Arctic Ocean.

14) In the expression *y* to the *x*th power, what name is given to the number *x*?
Answer: Exponent.

15) According to a survey that examined such factors as infant and child mortality, immunizations, and teen suicide, the Midwestern state containing the geographic center of North America had the nation's healthiest kids. Identify this state, whose capital is Bismarck.
Answer: North Dakota.

16) In 1993, President Clinton reversed a Bush administration policy by agreeing to maintain 1990 CO_2 emissions levels into the year 2000. Which compound is named by the chemical formula CO_2?
Answer: Carbon dioxide.

17) Spell *capitol* as used in the following: After 130 years, the 7-ton statue *Armed Freedom* was lifted from the top of the nation's *capitol* for repairs and cleaning.
Answer: C-A-P-I-T-O-L.

18) Name the President whose body arrived for burial in Springfield, Illinois, May 3, 1865.
Answer: Abraham Lincoln.

19) Approximately how many meters tall is the 19-foot 6-inch statue *Armed Freedom*: 3, 6, 9, or 12 meters?
Answer: 6 meters.

20) Trade deficits with Japan and China have accounted for about 80% of the U.S.'s deficit. What is the dollar amount of the 20% of the $84.3 billion deficit that can be charged to other countries?
Answer: $16.9 billion.

21) Which prefix completes the word _____navigate for "to sail around the globe"?
Answer: *Circum-.*

22) In which city, the site of the Liberty Bell, did delegates from 12 states unanimously approve the U.S. Constitution on September 17, 1787?
Answer: Philadelphia.

23) President Clinton once took a boat ride on the Strait of Georgia between the city of Vancouver and Vancouver Island to view snow-capped mountains and the city's skyline. Spell *strait*, meaning "a narrow channel of water between 2 larger bodies of water."
Answer: S-T-R-A-I-T.

24) What adjective is used in mathematics to describe geometric figures that are identical in both size and shape?
Answer: Congruent.

25) Citing progress on human rights, the U.S. once released to Nicaragua $50 million in economic aid that had been suspended. Which of the following countries borders Nicaragua: Honduras, Iran, Mexico, or Nigeria?
Answer: Honduras.

26) Name the black and orange insect known for its annual migration from Canada to Mexico each winter.
Answer: Monarch butterfly.

27) Which character created by Beatrix Potter is named in the title of her book that is the U.S.'s best-selling children's book of all time?
Answer: Peter Rabbit (*The Tale of Peter Rabbit*).

28) Which consonant is silent in the correct pronunciation of the name *Des Moines*?
Answer: S.

29) Give both the mean and the median for the set 90, 77, 70, 63, and 50.
Answer: 70 (is both the mean and the median).

30) Name the wall Soviet leader Nikita Khrushchev built as a barrier to the West in 1961 two months after a summit with President Kennedy.
Answer: Berlin Wall.

31) From the steps of which Washington, D.C., memorial with a gigantic statue of a U.S. President did Marian Anderson sing on April 9, 1939, after being denied use of the DAR's Constitution Hall?
Answer: Lincoln Memorial.

32) In which state at which Court House did Robert E. Lee surrender to Ulysses S. Grant on April 9, 1865, to end the Civil War? Its earliest settlement was established in 1607.
Answer: Virginia at Appomattox Court House.

33) Queen Margrethe's birthday, April 16, is a national holiday in Denmark. On which of the following peninsulas is this country located: Balkan, Jutland, Iberian, or Korean?
Answer: Jutland.

34) An ace has been drawn from a 52-card deck and not replaced. If another card is drawn, what is the chance that it will also be an ace?
Answer: 1/17 (accept 3/51).

35) Amnesty International officials once investigated alleged human rights violations in which Asian country, the world's second most populated? Christopher Columbus's name for the New World's natives also identifies its natives.
Answer: India (China is most populated; Columbus's destination was the *Indies*).

36) In 1993, a ban on the hunting of which animal was reaffirmed by an international commission despite the urging of Japan and Norway for its lifting? Harpoons are used in its slaughter.
Answer: Whale.

37) Name the land to which fictional character Peter Pan takes his new friends, the Darling children, in J. M. Barrie's play subtitled *The Boy Who Wouldn't Grow Up*.
Answer: Never-Never-Land.

38) France is known for its style of preparing food. Spell the French word *cuisine*, meaning "the manner of preparing food."
Answer: C-U-I-S-I-N-E.

39) Identify the soft, black form of carbon used in pencils.
Answer: Graphite.

40) On April 14, 1986, the U.S. bombed the country of Libya in retaliation for the bombing of a West German discotheque. On which sea is Libya located?
Answer: Mediterranean Sea (military sites in Tripoli and Benghaze were bombed).

41) In which city did Jesse Jackson lead a protest at the 1993 season opener at Oriole Park at Camden Yards about baseball's minority hiring practices?
Answer: Baltimore.

42) In which decade did Congress pass a major civil rights act on April 11, one week after the assassination of Dr. Martin Luther King Jr.?
Answer: 1960s.

43) Name the 2 seas on which Egypt is located.
Answer: Mediterranean and Red seas.

44) Spain agreed to give monetary compensation to the more than 1,000 hemophiliacs that contacted the AIDS virus through blood transfusions in the 1980s. At the agreed upon rate of $86,000 per victim, what is the total cost for 1,000 people?
Answer: $86 million.

45) Name the colony that held its last democratic election under British rule in 1995 before being taken over by Communist China in 1997. The 2 words in its name rhyme.
Answer: Hong Kong.

46) Identify the lightning rod inventor who also is credited with the first newspaper cartoon.
Answer: Benjamin Franklin.

47) In an unprecedented move to allow foreign generals to supervise its troops, the U.S. exchanged command with Germany in 1993 as NATO combined forces into multinational groups. Spell *unprecedented*, meaning "without ever having happened before."
Answer: U-N-P-R-E-C-E-D-E-N-T-E-D.

48) In 1890, Utah Mormons renounced *polygamy*, or being married to more than one person at the same time. Change *poly-* to a prefix meaning "two" to create a word for "having 2 husbands or 2 wives."
Answer: Bigamy.

49) A jar contains 500 beads colored blue, red, green, and yellow. If 20% of the beads are blue, 20% are red, and 35% are green, how many are yellow?
Answer: 125 beads.

50) The IRA was blamed by the London police force for a bomb that shattered London's financial district in 1993, leaving 1 dead and 40 injured. What name including a word for "an area around a house" is used to mean "the London police"?
Answer: Scotland Yard.

1) Because of advanced technology, the Coast Guard has ended the use of which emergency transmission system employing dots and dashes?
Answer: The Morse code.

2) Mario Cuomo served as governor of which state where George Washington took the oath of office as the nation's first President?
Answer: New York.

3) Which state extends from Tennessee to the Gulf of Mexico?
Answer: Alabama.

4) With its approval of only $4 billion for unemployment benefits did the Senate approve about 20%, 30%, or 40% of President Clinton's $19.5 billion jobs package?
Answer: 20%.

5) In 1993, after 30 years of war, citizens of Eritrea voted to declare independence from which African country bordering Sudan, Somalia, and Kenya? It is one of 3 African countries whose names begin with *E*.
Answer: Ethiopia.

6) Which astronaut was the first American to travel into space, aboard *Freedom VII* on May 5, 1961? His surname by sound designates "a keeper of sheep."
Answer: Alan B. Shepard Jr.

7) In Algeria, the government canceled runoff elections after Islamic fundamentalists won a victory in initial balloting. Spell *initial*.
Answer: I-N-I-T-I-A-L.

8) Which major league pitcher on May 5, 1904, threw baseball's first perfect game? The annual award for outstanding major league pitchers is named for him.
Answer: Denton T. "Cy" Young.

9) What is the greatest common factor of the numbers 12 and 16?
Answer: 4.

10) The remains of a huge dinosaur classed as a new species of spinosaur were found in the Sahara in 1998. Spell the form of the verb *lie* that correctly completes the following concerning the discovery: *Its claw was _____ exposed in the desert in central Niger.*
Answer: L-Y-I-N-G (its scientific name is *Suchomimus tenerensis*).

11) Name the crop Alabama farmers were rushing to harvest in 1998 before the winds of Hurricane Georges blew the produce out of its seed pods called *bolls*.
Answer: Cotton.

12) Name the island, now incorporated as part of New York City, that Dutch colonizer Peter Minuit bought from the Indians after landing there on May 4, 1626.
Answer: Manhattan Island.

13) The British ship *Lusitania* was sunk by a German submarine in 1915 off the coast of the country nicknamed the "Emerald Isle." Name this country whose capital is Dublin.
Answer: Ireland.

14) What is the least common multiple of the numbers 12 and 16?
Answer: 48.

15) California farm labor organizer Cesar Chavez led a nationwide boycott of which fruit in the 1960s? Raisins were among the food products boycotted.
Answer: Grapes.

16) The national association for lawyers is known as the ABA. What does the "B" stand for? It is used to describe the exam a lawyer must pass, and is a homograph for a bank of sand.
Answer: Bar (American Bar Association).

17) Presidential commission hearings on military cutbacks were held in states that were to lose 15,000 civilian workers from proposed military base cuts. Spell *civilians*, meaning "those not in military service."
Answer: C-I-V-I-L-I-A-N-S.

18) Name the author of *Gulliver's Travels*. His surname is a synonym for *fast* and is often used to describe the current of a river.
Answer: Jonathan Swift.

19) Name the disease for which health pioneer Albert Sabin developed an oral vaccine.
Answer: Polio (poliomyelitis or infantile paralysis).

20) In which country did a Harvard- and Oxford-educated woman join the world's oldest surviving royal family when she wed the heir to the Chrysanthemum Throne in 1993?
Answer: Japan (Prince Naruhito wed Masako Owada).

21) Name the 2 countries that have larger populations than the U.S. Their capitals are Beijing and New Delhi.
Answer: China, 1st, and India, 2nd (Russia is 4th).

22) Name the Detroit-born aviator who made the first nonstop flight from the U.S. to Europe, on May 20-21, 1927.
Answer: Charles A. Lindbergh.

23) Many died when a ferry sank in the sea between Egypt and Saudi Arabia. Identify this body of water probably named for the color of algae on its surface.
Answer: Red Sea.

24) What did the Clinton's house number become when they moved to the White House on Pennsylvania Avenue? The house number is the same as 40 squared.
Answer: 1600.

25) According to a conservation group, which river that rises in Colorado and flows along the border between Texas and Mexico is the most endangered river in North America?
Answer: Rio Grande.

26) Meteors are visible in the U.S. and Europe in August from a meteor shower named for which constellation? It allegedly represents the son of Zeus who cut off the head of Medusa.
Answer: Perseus (known as the Perseid meteor shower).

27) A tentative agreement was reached to hold the first South African elections including the black majority on April 27, 1994. Spell *tentative*.
Answer: T-E-N-T-A-T-I-V-E.

28) Are the Lilliputians Gulliver meets in his travels gigantic people, miniature people, horses, or knights in armor?
Answer: Miniature people (the adjective *lilliputian* means "very small).

29) In which year, MCMLXIII in Roman numerals, did Martin Luther King Jr. make his famous "I Have a Dream" make the speech in Washington, D.C.?
Answer: 1963.

30) Name the monarch who celebrated the 45th anniversary of her coronation on June 2, 1998. She is the sixth longest-reigning English monarch.
Answer: Queen Elizabeth II.

31) After 8 months in office and following accusations of corruption, Morihiro Hosokawa resigned as prime minister of which country known as the "land of the rising sun"?
Answer: Japan.

32) The "Gulf of Tonkin Resolution" of August 7, 1964, gave President Lyndon Johnson the authority to do whatever was necessary in which country where the U.S. became involved in a war that lasted until 1975?
Answer: Vietnam.

33) In which country did the volcanic eruption of Mount Ruapehu [rü ə pā hü] in 1995 cause the evacuation of skiers around the area? It has a 2-word name and lies southeast of Australia.
Answer: New Zealand.

34) NASA once lost contact with a spacecraft on a $980 million mission three days before it was to photograph which planet, the 4th from the sun?
Answer: Mars.

35) Which Mideast country did the U.S. strike with Tomahawk missiles in retaliation for a plot to assassinate former President Bush while he was visiting Kuwait?
Answer: Iraq.

36) On which June date did summer begin in the Northern Hemisphere in 1993 at 5:00 a.m., Eastern Daylight Time? This number is 6 more than 1/2 the days in the month.
Answer: June 21.

37) A 14-year-old from Tennessee correctly spelled "kamikaze" to win the 66th National Spelling Bee. Spell *kamikaze*.
Answer: K-A-M-I-K-A-Z-E.

38) Name the country whose Little League baseball team was defeated 3-2 by a Long Beach, California, team in a world championship game. It is located on the isthmus joining Central and South America.
Answer: Panama.

39) Name the seasonal wind over the northern part of the Indian Ocean responsible for the summer floods in South Asia. The 2nd syllable of its name means "in the near future."
Answer: Monsoon.

40) Name the country that elected Kim Campbell its first female prime minister in 1993. Queen Elizabeth II is its head of state.
Answer: Canada.

41) The granddaughter of WWII dictator Benito Mussolini once ran for mayor of Naples. What term designates the relationship of a grandfather's sister to his grandchild?
Answer: Great aunt.

42) Supreme Court nominee Clarence Thomas received from the full Senate one more vote than necessary for confirmation. How many votes did he get?
Answer: 52.

43) What name is given to a narrow, natural channel of water joining 2 larger bodies of water, such as that discovered by Magellan near the tip of South America.
Answer: Strait (Strait of Magellan is north of Cape Horn).

44) Pope John Paul II joined 375,000 young people from 70 nations for a World Youth Day celebration in Denver. In feet, what is the altitude of this "Mile High City"?
Answer: 5,280 feet.

45) How many members are on the U.S. Supreme Court? Its 2 female members in 1999 represented less than 1/3 of its membership.
Answer: 9.

46) In which New York city was President William McKinley fatally shot on September 6, 1901? Its name also identifies the American bison that was almost extinct by 1889.
Answer: Buffalo (the city probably took its name from Buffalo Creek).

47) Give the first name of the ten-year-old girl who comes to live with her British uncle, Archibald Craven, in a house with "near a 100 rooms" in the book *The Secret Garden*. She shares this name with the nursery rhyme character known to be "quite contrary."
Answer: Mary (Lennox; Frances Hodgson Burnett's book was first published in 1911).

48) On September 8, 1974, President Ford pardoned former President Nixon for any offenses he might have committed against the U.S. Spell *committed*.
Answer: C-O-M-M-I-T-T-E-D.

49) Assuming the half year is a leap year, how many days are in 2½ years?
Answer: 913 days.

50) In which U.S. city named for Saint Francis of Assisi was the United Nations Charter signed by 50 nations on June 26, 1945?
Answer: San Francisco.

1) Name the female choreographer born in 1894 who pioneered in "modern dance." Her surname also designates a kind of sweet cracker.
   Answer: Martha Graham.

2) Which political party is often referred to as the GOP?
   Answer: Republican (GOP stands for the nickname "Grand Old Party").

3) In which South American country known for its rain forest did gold miners once massacre 30 Yanomami Indians?
   Answer: Brazil.

4) Which of the following numbers has 3 as a factor: 287, 689, 711, or 940?
   Answer: 711.

5) Name the city whose walls fell down when the Israelites led by Joshua marched around it and blew their trumpets, according to the Bible.
   Answer: Jericho.

6) Europeans knew nothing of which crop, also called maize, until Columbus landed in America in 1492?
   Answer: Corn.

7) Spell *negotiating*, meaning "to settle a dispute through discussion."
   Answer: N-E-G-O-T-I-A-T-I-N-G.

8) Is a special benefit attached to a position called a *lobby*, a *perk*, a *gratuity*, or a *crypt*?
   Answer: Perk (short for *perquisite*).

9) What is the surface area of a cube measuring 3 centimeters on each edge?
   Answer: 54 cm^2.

10) Who was inaugurated as Russia's first popularly elected president on July 10, 1991?
    Answer: Boris Yeltsin.

11) Name the first U.S. President after George Washington not to attend college, or name the capital of Mississippi.
    Answer: Andrew Jackson, or Jackson.

12) The ship known as "Old Ironsides," which was launched on September 20, 1797, is now permanently located in Boston. How many syllables does the word *permanently* have?
Answer: 4.

13) What word designates a place where grapes are grown and completes the name of the Massachusetts town where the Clinton family spent several summer vacations?
Answer: Vineyard (the town is Martha's Vineyard).

14) What is the total pay for an 8-hour day at the wage of $6.25?
Answer: $50.00.

15) Give the full name of the PLO, the organization Yasir Arafat heads.
Answer: Palestine Liberation Organization.

16) Pioneer John Chapman was nicknamed Johnny Appleseed because of his planting of apple trees along the frontier. What word designates a large grove of fruit trees?
Answer: Orchard.

17) What is the silent consonant in the word *debt*?
Answer: *B*.

18) What word designates total control of the production and selling of a commodity and also names a popular board game with play money?
Answer: Monopoly.

19) To promote the Administration's health-care plan, Hillary Rodham Clinton once held a town meeting at the Mayo Clinic in which state on Lake Superior known for its twin cities?
Answer: Minnesota (clinic is in Rochester; twin cities are St. Paul and Minneapolis).

20) Which country, whose name means "The Savior," gained its independence from Spain on September 15, 1821, along with Costa Rica, Guatemala, Honduras, and Nicaragua?
Answer: El Salvador.

21) The portrait of the first Republican President appeared over the mantel in the background of the Clinton's first Christmas card. Name this President who took office in 1861.
Answer: Abraham Lincoln.

22) HUD once seized control of an all-white housing project in Texas after the last black resident fled amid racial threats. Give the word represented by the *U* meaning "of the city" in the acronym HUD for Housing and _____ Development.
Answer: Urban.

23) The sand bars known as the Outer Banks were damaged by Hurricane Emily before she headed out to sea. Name the "Tar Heel" state off whose coast these sandbars are located.
Answer: North Carolina.

24) What is the correct time 3,000 seconds before 2:25 p.m.?
Answer: 1:35 p.m.

25) Identify the document whose signing on September 17, 1787, was reenacted at 96 national parks, 5 presidential libraries, and 3 regional archives in September 1993.
Answer: U.S. Constitution.

26) How many feet is the distance of 20,000 leagues named in the title of Jules Verne's *Twenty Thousand Leagues Under the Sea* if a league is 3 miles and a mile is 5,280 feet?
Answer: 316,800,000 feet (60,000 miles times 5,280 feet).

27) The body of former President Ferdinand Marcos was returned to the Philippines after being held in exile for 4 years in Hawaii. Spell *Philippines.*
Answer: P-H-I-L-I-P-P-I-N-E-S.

28) Name the contralto who was the first black singer to perform at the White House and to sing a leading role with the Metropolitan Opera in New York. Her surname is a variant spelling of the surname of a Danish author.
Answer: Marian Anderson (Hans Christian Andersen is the Danish author).

29) How much pocket money do you have with 3 quarters, 3 dimes, and a bill picturing Abraham Lincoln?
Answer: $6.05.

30) On September 14, 1812, which city was set on fire by its residents after Napoleon and his French troops invaded it? It is known for its Red Square.
Answer: Moscow (hunger and cold later defeated Napoleon's Grand Army).

31) Under orders from the League of Nations, Great Britain began to govern Palestine in 1923. Spell *league*, which designates both an alliance and a measure of distance.
Answer: L-E-A-G-U-E.

32) In which state did the "alleged former" Ku Klux Klansman David Duke lose to Democrat Edwin Edwards in the race for the governorship? Its capital is Baton Rouge.
Answer: Louisiana.

33) In which state was a monument honoring black soldiers in the Civil War erected at Petersburg National Battlefield Park just south of Richmond?
Answer: Virginia.

34) Answer the following question used on a test to assess problem-solving skills of U.S. students: Explain how Jose who ate half a pizza could have eaten more pizza than a friend who ate half of another pizza.
Answer: Jose ate half of a larger pizza.

35) Which state is the home of Yosemite National Park and a redwood forest known as Muir Woods?
Answer: California.

36) *Fusion* is an antonym of *fission*, which means "a process of splitting into parts." What does *fusion* mean?
Answer: A joining of parts (joining of nuclei).

37) Spell the word that is the subject of the following sentence: According to *The New York Times*, terrorists planned to kidnap former President Nixon along with his secretary of state to win release of Muslims being held in the World Trade Center bombing.
Answer: T-E-R-R-O-R-I-S-T-S.

38) On September 17, 1787, delegates from all 12 states represented at the Constitutional Convention approved the U.S. Constitution in Philadelphia. What word is used to describe a decision that is approved by all those casting ballots?
Answer: Unanimous.

39) Which natural force requires that objects that rise must eventually fall?
Answer: Gravity.

40) On October 12, 1960, Russian premier Nikita Khrushchev angrily pounded his shoe in the U.N. to protest the U.N.'s failure to vote on a Soviet proposal. What initials designated Russia, or the Soviet Union, at that time?
Answer: U.S.S.R. (Union of Soviet Socialist Republics).

41) Which country celebrates Thanksgiving Day on the 2nd Monday in October? Its flag features a red maple leaf.
Answer: Canada (on October 9 this year).

42) The House of Representatives formally charged President Andrew Johnson with wrongdoing in a proceeding that began on February 24, 1868. Identify the fruit whose name completes the verb *im____* that designates such action.
Answer: Peach (*impeach*).

43) Scientists once discovered in the Andes the remains of the ear-
liest dinosaur ever found, a dog-sized meat-eater of the species
Eoraptor, or "dawn stealer." On what continent are the Andes?
Answer: South America.

44) How much longer are women expected to live than men according to a report that life expectancy at birth was 78.9 years for
women and 72 years for men?
Answer: 6.9 years.

45) A British play based on the lunacy of the king who lost the
American colonies toured the U.S. in 1993. Name this king.
**Answer: King George (specifically, George III; play is
The Madness of George III).**

46) Which planet, known as "the evening star," can never be seen
for more than about 3 hours after sunset or 3 hours before sun-
rise because the greatest elongation of its orbit is at 47
degrees?
Answer: Venus.

47) What part of speech is *slick* in the following? "The Tampa Bay
harbor was temporarily closed after 2 barges and a freighter
collided, creating a 15-mile-long oil *slick* along Florida's west
coast."
Answer: Noun.

48) In which country, then a British dependency, was Mary
Lennox, the main character of *The Secret Garden*, born? She
tells of seeing there a young rajah adorned with jewels.
Answer: India.

49) If voters in a state decide to give every parent vouchers worth
$2,600 per child per year to use at any public or private school,
how much would a school with 500 students collect from these
vouchers in a year?
Answer: $1,300,000.

50) Identify the heir to the British throne who was born in London
on November 14, 1948.
Answer: Prince Charles.

1) A 7th grader won a National Spelling Bee by spelling *antediluvian*, meaning "before the flood." Spell the prefix *ante-*, meaning "before."
Answer: A-N-T-E-.

2) Name either one of the first two first ladies who spoke before Congress: one's husband was President during WWII, and the other's has built houses for Habitat for Humanity.
Answer: Eleanor Roosevelt or Rosalyn Carter.

3) Name the sea in which the U.S. Coast Guard mans U.S. helicopters, planes, and cutters along the Russian-U.S. maritime line to prevent foreign trawlers from fishing in Alaskan waters.
Answer: Bering Sea.

4) What is the charge for a 7-minute phone call that costs a total of 60 cents for the first 3 minutes and 15 cents for each additional minute?
Answer: $1.20.

5) The Smithsonian's Museum of Natural History has an exhibit with living subjects, all of which have 6 legs. Name the animals it features.
Answer: Insects.

6) Is Uranus's 32,300-mile diameter about 2, 3, 4, or 5 times that of Earth's 7,927-mile diameter?
Answer: 4 times.

7) Give the pen name for the children's book author who was awarded a special Pulitzer Prize in 1984. He wrote *The Cat in the Hat*.
Answer: Dr. Seuss (born Theodor Seuss Geisel).

8) The killing of Foreign tourists in Miami prompted European tabloids to rename the "Sunshine State" the "State of Terror." Spell *foreign*.
Answer: F-O-R-E-I-G-N.

9) When Florida spent $24,000 a day for officers from state agencies to guard its 76 highway rest stops in response to violence against tourists, in how many days did the expense top $1 million?
Answer: 42 days.

10) After President Yeltsin's forces overpowered anti-government protestors, Muscovites rushed home to beat the hour set for citizens to be off the streets. What is the name for a time at which people must leave the streets?
Answer: Curfew.

11) In 1999, the Phoenix Art Museum opened a show featuring the creations of 19th- and 20th-century milliners. Name the milliner's product, known by the French word *chapeau*.
Answer: Hat.

12) After 52 World Cup soccer games were hosted in 9 U.S. cities in 1994, which South American team won for a record 4th time by defeating Italy, 3-2, in a penalty-kick shootout?
Answer: Brazil.

13) The crater left by a rock on the Yucatan Peninsula is 186 miles across, nearly twice as big as earlier believed, strengthening the theory that the impact wiped out the dinosaurs. On which body of water is the Yucatan Peninsula?
Answer: Gulf of Mexico (it is called the Chicxulub crater).

14) A sidewalk frame is 16 feet long and 3 feet wide. If one bag of cement covers 8 square feet, how many bags will be needed to fill the frame?
Answer: 6 bags.

15) By a 45-43 vote over Beijing, which city in Australia was awarded the 2000 Summer Olympics?
Answer: Sydney.

16) The 2 lightest gases together with methane make up the atmosphere of the planet Uranus. Name these gases, whose chemical formulas are H and He.
Answer: Hydrogen and helium.

17) Complete the title of C.S. Lewis's book *The* _____, *the* _____, *and the Wardrobe*.
Answer: *Lion* and *Witch*.

18) A Department of Education report revealed that 47% of adult Americans read and write so poorly that they are unable to function effectively in the workplace. Spell *effectively*.
Answer: E-F-F-E-C-T-I-V-E-L-Y.

19) What name is given to the effect of the thick blanket of carbon dioxide surrounding Venus that results in surface temperatures near 460 degrees Centigrade?
Answer: Greenhouse effect.

20) President Sadat of Egypt was assassinated in October 1981. Which of the following is not within or on the border of Egypt: Red Sea, Nile River, Suez Canal, or Tiber River?
Answer: Tiber River.

21) Hillary Rodham Clinton was only the 3rd first lady to testify before Congress when in 1993 she spoke about the Administration's plan for reforming which system?
Answer: Health-care system.

22) After a 1,700-mile retreat, which Indian chief surrendered to U.S. troops in Montana in 1877, with these words: "From where the sun now stands, I will fight no more forever"? His name also designates the biblical figure with a coat of many colors.
Answer: (Chief) Joseph.

23) In which state did preservationists buy a 56-acre parcel of land adjacent to Harpers Ferry National Park to stop future development on the site?
Answer: West Virginia.

24) Using 3.14 as an approximation for *pi*, what is the area of a circle with a radius of 10 cm.?
Answer: 314 cm².

25) President Bush sent the CIA director to Egypt and Saudi Arabia in 1992 to discuss U.S. efforts to hasten the downfall of the Iraqi leader. Name this leader.
Answer: Saddam Hussein.

26) Which paralyzing disease crippled President Franklin Roosevelt?
Answer: Polio (poliomyelitis or infantile paralysis).

27) Complete the title of Maurice Sendak's book *In the Night _____* with a word for a room where culinary skills are practiced.
Answer: *Kitchen.*

28) What word designates both the written form of music for an orchestra and the record of points in a game?
Answer: Score.

29) Which of the following has the same number of sides as a parallelogram: *triangle*, *trapezoid*, *pentagon*, or *octagon*?
Answer: Trapezoid.

30) In seeking a permanent seat for his country on the U.N. Security Council, Japan's prime minister expressed remorse over its WWII aggression. Spell *council*, meaning "a group."
Answer: C-O-U-N-C-I-L (permanent members: China, France, Russia, U.K., and U.S.).

31) Harvard College held its first commencement, or graduation, exercises on September 23, 1642. Spell *commencement*, literally meaning "a beginning."
Answer: C-O-M-M-E-N-C-E-M-E-N-T.

32) Shawnee Indian chief Tecumseh was defeated and killed fighting for the British at the Battle of the Thames on October 5, 1813. During which war did this battle take place?
Answer: War of 1812.

33) Spell the name of the state, the third smallest, in which Yale University was founded. The school was moved to New Haven in 1716.
Answer: C-O-N-N-E-C-T-I-C-U-T.

34) Using 3.14 as an approximation for *pi*, what is the circumference of a circle with a radius of 10 cm.?
Answer: 62.8 cm.

35) In which Asian country is Hinduism the religion of about 83% of its population, the 2nd largest in the world?
Answer: India.

36) Benjamin Banneker, nicknamed the "First Black Man of Science," worked with Andrew Ellicott as a surveyor to lay out the boundaries of Washington, D.C. Spell *surveyor*.
Answer: S-U-R-V-E-Y-O-R.

37) The Versailles Peace Conference to end WWI formally opened on January 18, 1919. Name the silent double consonant in the spelling of *Versailles*.
Answer: L.

38) Identify the brass instrument named for the composer who conducted the U.S. Marine Corps Band and was nicknamed the "March King."
Answer: Sousaphone (named for John Philip Sousa).

39) Name the palm-sized Apple computer that has been satirized in *Doonesbury* because of its glitches. Its name identifies the British scientist known for his laws of gravity.
Answer: Newton.

40) William I earned his nickname "The Conqueror" on October 14, 1066, after he defeated King Harold and his English forces at the Battle of Hastings. Spell *conqueror*.
Answer: C-O-N-Q-U-E-R-O-R.

41) How much would the "7 swans a swimming" from the "Twelve Days of Christmas" song cost if each cost $750?
Answer: $5,250.

42) How many terms of office may a U.S. senator serve?
Answer: No limit on terms.

43) Name the African-American leader who negotiated the release
of the 3 U.S. soldiers held captive in Yugoslavia in 1999. His
surname is the same as that of the 19th-century President who
lived in a house called the Hermitage in Nashville, Tennessee.
**Answer: Jesse Jackson (Andrew Jackson lived in the
Hermitage).**

44) If on a map 1 inch equals 200 miles and the distance between
Augusta, Maine, and San Diego is 14.5 inches, what is the
mileage between the cities?
Answer: 2,900 miles.

45) Some 600 U.S. troops were once deployed to Haiti as part of a
6-month U.N. mission to help restore democracy. Spell *Haiti*.
Answer: H-A-I-T-I.

46) Facing a bad harvest, Japan once broke a political taboo and
allowed emergency imports of which crop that is a part of
almost every Japanese meal?
Answer: Rice.

47) Mrs. O'Leary's cow allegedly caused the October 8, 1871, fire
that destroyed a large part of Chicago. Spell *allegedly*, meaning "according to popular belief."
Answer: A-L-L-E-G-E-D-L-Y.

48) Does *indict* mean "to reprimand," "to formally charge with a
crime," "to find guilty of a crime," or "to imprison"?
Answer: To formally charge with a crime.

49) Find the perimeter of a regular octagon with sides of 0.8 centimeters.
Answer: 6.4 centimeters.

50) In which country did 85% of voters in 1997 support accepting
NATO's invitation of membership? Its capital is Budapest, and
its name is sometimes misspelled as a word meaning "needing
or wanting nourishment."
Answer: Hungary.

1) Spell the word for the ceremony that marks the beginning of a President's term of office.
Answer: I-N-A-U-G-U-R-A-T-I-O-N.

2) Which document contains the words "We hold these Truths to be self-evident, That all men are created equal"?
Answer: Declaration of Independence.

3) In which Canadian province was the annual meeting of the Group of 7 international leaders once held in Halifax? Its 2-word name means "New Scotland."
Answer: Nova Scotia.

4) Expressed as a Roman numeral, what is the square root of the Roman numeral CXXI?
Answer: XI.

5) A 1,200 acre *Gone With the Wind* theme park was once planned near which city that was burned during the Civil War? Margaret Mitchell was born there.
Answer: Atlanta (Georgia).

6) Identify the tube through which food passes from the back of the mouth to the stomach.
Answer: Esophagus (accept gullet).

7) Complete the word ____*space* used to designate the Internet world in which on-line communication takes place.
Answer: Cyberspace.

8) Agnes DeMille created the dance routines for the play *Oklahoma!* Is one who creates dance an *architect, cardiologist, choreographer*, or *stenographer*?
Answer: Choreographer.

9) If on a blueprint scale 1/4 inch represents 3 feet, how long is a pipe that measures 3 inches long on the blueprint?
Answer: 36 feet.

10) Which statue by French sculptor Frédéric Auguste Bartholdi was dedicated on October 28, 1886, on Bedloe's Island in New York?
Answer: *Statue of Liberty*, or *Liberty Enlightening the World*.

11) Name the "Mother of the Civil Rights Movement" who was inducted into the National Women's Hall of Fame for prompting the Montgomery, Alabama, bus boycott in 1955.
Answer: Rosa Parks (the Women's Hall of Fame is located in Seneca Falls, New York).

12) Based on a 1767 survey, the Mason-Dixon Line was set as the boundary between Maryland and which state settled by Quaker William Penn?
Answer: Pennsylvania.

13) Which U.S. state, once owned by Russia, has more inland water than any other state?
Answer: Alaska.

14) Approximately how much will it cost to feed one person for 30 days using the Pentagon's vegetarian meals at a cost of $3.95 for a day's worth of sustenance?
Answer: $120.

15) Stock shares of Nike once fell as much as 2½ points after its chief pitchman announced his retirement from the NBA's Chicago Bulls. Name him.
Answer: Michael Jordan.

16) The Pentagon's HDR, or Humanitarian Daily Ration, is a vegetarian meal suitable for sending to civilians in Muslim areas like Bosnia. What is the more common name for the legumes that contribute to the protein content of these meals?
Answer: Beans (or peas).

17) On October 17, 1945, Colonel Juan Peròn seized power to become dictator in Argentina. Spell either *seize*, meaning "to take," or *cease*, meaning "to stop."
Answer: S-E-I-Z-E or C-E-A-S-E.

18) In which novel is Injun Joe the real murderer of young Dr. Robinson?
Answer: *The Adventures of Tom Sawyer*.

19) Name the tiny blood vessels connecting arteries and veins that permit the passage of oxygen and other nutrients from the blood to the cells of the body.
Answer: Capillaries.

20) In 1992, Israeli troops prevented Palestinians from leaving an area on the Mediterranean coast. Which name designates this strip of land: *Gaza, Amazon, Klondike,* or *Siberia*?
Answer: Gaza Strip (the ban was lifted after 2 days).

21) Prague, Oklahoma, wanted the Olympic torch re-routed to pass through it instead of Yale, the city erroneously called the birthplace of Jim Thorpe, the Olympic athlete who was the first to win the 5-event and 10-event competitions. Name the 5-event competition.
Answer: Pentathlon (Thorpe was born near Prague in 1887).

22) A film based on the novel *The Killer Angels* and featuring CNN owner Ted Turner in a bit part tells of which 1863 Pennsylvania Civil War battle with 51,000 casualties?
Answer: Gettysburg.

23) Name the saltiest body of water in the world, a lake shared by Jordan and Israel. Its shore is the lowest place on the surface of the earth.
Answer: Dead Sea.

24) What is the correct time 3,000 seconds before 2:25 p.m.?
Answer: 1:35 p.m.

25) Name the country of F.W. de Klerk and Nelson Mandela, the 2 leaders who were jointly awarded the 1993 Nobel Peace Prize for negotiating the end of apartheid in their nation.
Answer: South Africa.

26) What word designates a facility for displaying living fish and other creatures that thrive in water?
Answer: Aquarium.

27) St. Paul's Cathedral in London honors architect Christopher Wren with the epitaph: "If you would see his monument, look about you." Spell *epitaph*.
Answer: E-P-I-T-A-P-H.

28) Of the following musicians, which one is primarily known as a composer of music for the piano: Franz Liszt, John Philip Sousa, Marian Anderson, or Peter Tchaikovsky?
Answer: Franz Liszt.

29) If a salesperson receives a weekly salary of $150 with a 10% commission on all sales, what is his weekly income when he sells $6,500?
Answer: $800.

30) In fulfillment of a 1991 parliamentary vote, Germany agreed to complete the move of its capital to which once divided city by the end of the year 2000?
Answer: Berlin.

31) All employees have an FICA deduction from their salary. Name the federal program providing retirement income that this FICA contribution supports.
Answer: Social Security (FICA stands for Federal Insurance Contributions Act).

32) What name is given to the period of economic hardship that began on October 24, 1929, when investors began panic selling of stocks, dumping more than 13 million shares?
Answer: (Great) Depression.

33) A Michigan 8th grader won a National Geography Bee by knowing that Pashtu and Dari are the languages of which mountainous landlocked central Asian country? Its capital is Kabul, and its name begins with *A*.
Answer: Afghanistan (Chris Galeczka won a $25,000 college scholarship).

34) If a person buys a horse for $50, sells it for $60, buys it back for $70, and then resells the horse for $80, how much money has this person made?
Answer: $20.

35) The Energy Department has acknowledged that the U.S. government concealed more than 200 nuclear weapons tests between 1940 and 1990. In which state, nicknamed the "Silver State," was the last secret test in the U.S. conducted?
Answer: Nevada (in 1990).

36) How many days were in the ancient Egyptian calendar based on the stars with its 12 months of 30 twenty-four hour days with an additional 5 holy days yearly?
Answer: 365.

37) Which of the following correctly completes the sentence "Anne gave the book to John and _____": *she, I, me,* or *we?*
Answer: Me.

38) The U.S. flag was formally raised over Alaska on October 18, 1867, following its purchase from Russia by William H. Seward. Spell *formally*.
Answer: F-O-R-M-A-L-L-Y.

39) According to health officials, polio, sometimes called infantile paralysis, could be eradicated within 2 to 4 years in the Western Hemisphere. Spell *paralysis*.
Answer: P-A-R-A-L-Y-S-I-S.

40) In 1993, thousands gathered at the Paris site where Marie Antoinette was executed 200 years ago during the French Revolution. Name the instrument used in her beheading.
Answer: Guillotine.

41) Which month of the year is said to come in like a lion and go out like a lamb?
Answer: March.

42) On October 24, 1861, to which U.S. President did Californian Stephen Field send the first transcontinental telegram? The message declared California's loyalty to the Union.
Answer: Abraham Lincoln.

43) Identify the river spanned by the George Washington Bridge connecting New York City and New Jersey. It was named for the English captain who explored the river in 1609.
Answer: Hudson River.

44) How many total days did *Columbia*'s mission last when it surpassed by 5 hours the shuttle record of 331.5 hours in space in 1993?
Answer: 14 days.

45) Of the following, which is Puerto Rico's nearest neighbor: Cuba, Mexico, Panama, or Florida?
Answer: Cuba.

46) The Endangered Species Act of 1973 is credited with helping bring back the Arctic peregrine falcon from near extinction. Spell *extinction*.
Answer: E-X-T-I-N-C-T-I-O-N.

47) Which of the following correctly completes the sentence "He had _____ 3 glasses of orange juice": *drank, drunk, drunken,* or *drinked*?
Answer: Drunk.

48) A 1995 CD includes "Free As A Bird," a song built around a vocal track recorded in 1974 by John Lennon, who was shot to death in 1980. Name his music group.
Answer: The Beatles (the surviving Beatles completed the song in February 1994).

49) Is the product of the digits in the number 1865 more, less, or the same as the product of the digits in 1955?
Answer: More (product of 1865 is 240; product of 1955 is 225).

50) Ukrainian lawmakers have voted to keep open the Chernobyl power plant, site of the world's worst nuclear power accident. Does Ukraine border Colombia, Iraq, Italy, or Poland?
Answer: Poland (Ukraine was a part of the former Soviet Union).

1) Which of the following words designates "a written order to appear for testimony in a court": *supposition, subpoena, obituary*, or *libel*?
Answer: Subpoena.

2) When House Minority Leader Robert Michel retired from Congress at the end of his 19th term in 1995, how many years had he served?
Answer: 38 years (House term is 2 years).

3) The Dan Quayle Center and Museum is located in his hometown of Huntington, Indiana. Name 2 of the 4 states bordering Indiana.
Answer: Illinois, Kentucky, Michigan, and Ohio.

4) What term names an integer greater than 1 whose only positive factors are 1 and itself?
Answer: Prime number.

5) President Clinton signed weapons accords with Russia in 1995, including a mutual agreement that the 2 countries will stop aiming their long-range nuclear missiles at each other. Spell *mutual*.
Answer: M-U-T-U-A-L.

6) Using alliteration as a guide, choose from the following the word for a group of geese: *bevy, covey, gaggle*, or *litter*.
Answer: Gaggle.

7) What word means "with the support of members from both parties, without regard for political allegiance": *bicuspid, biannual, bilingual*, or *bipartisan*?
Answer: Bipartisan.

8) The Tour de France, a 3-week cycling race, passes through the tunnel under which body of water in going from France to England?
Answer: English Channel.

9) What time is it in Denver, Colorado, when it is 4:00 p.m. in New York City?
Answer: 2:00 p.m.

10) The residents of a British island in the Caribbean were allowed to return home in 1998 after the collapse of the core of a volcano that had been erupting for 2 years. Name this island, or give the French word for "mountain" that begins its name.
Answer: Montserrat or *mont* (the island is in the British West Indies).

11) Which 2 words were merged to make the word *smog*?
Answer: *Smoke* and *fog*.

12) Spell the name of the state in which Abraham Lincoln dedicated the national cemetery at Gettysburg on November 19, 1863. It is sometimes called the "Quaker State."
Answer: P-E-N-N-S-Y-L-V-A-N-I-A.

13) Choreographer Jacques d'Amboise once brought together children from the extreme places on the globe for a New York dance performance. Did the 2 children representing the globe's highest place come from Egypt, Italy, Nepal, or the U.S.?
Answer: Nepal (it has 8 of the world's 10 highest mountains).

14) Give the result of rounding 1,645 to the nearest hundred.
Answer: 1,600.

15) China once broke an informal world ban on nuclear testing. Which of the following does *not* mean "stopping of an activity": *cessation, moratorium, debut,* or *suspension*?
Answer: Debut.

16) Halley's comet last appeared in 1985 and is expected to reappear in which year, as it completes its 76-year cycle?
Answer: 64 years.

17) Spell *personnel*, meaning "a group of people employed by an organization of business."
Answer: P-E-R-S-O-N-N-E-L.

18) Which of the following means "to take apart": *deport, dismantle, eradicate,* or *exhale*?
Answer: Dismantle.

19) Moose hunting is now permitted in Vermont to keep the growing moose population in balance with its habitat. What is the plural of *moose*?
Answer: Moose.

20) In which year did the Russian Revolution take place? The U.S. established diplomatic relations with the Soviet Union in 1933, sixteen years after the end of that revolution.
Answer: 1917.

21) Is a crime more serious than a misdemeanor called a *felony*, *heresy*, *odyssey*, or *parody*?
Answer: Felony.

22) In 1906, which President, known as the "Bull Moose," named Oscar Straus as the first Jew to hold a Cabinet post?
Answer: Theodore Roosevelt (Straus became secretary of commerce and labor.)

23) Which Texas hero, for whom the largest city in the state is named, served as governor in both Tennessee and Texas?
Answer: Sam Houston.

24) What number comes next in the sequence 9, 16, 25, 36, . . . ?
Answer: 49 (square 3, 4, 5, 6, then 7).

25) Under a new measure, which word in the Girl Scout pledge may now be replaced by one that meets the individual's beliefs?
Answer: God (Muslims, for instance, could substitute their name for God).

26) Doctors have developed a technique to produce identical twins from an organism in its earliest stage of development. Is such an organism called a *cerebrum*, *embryo*, or *fetus*?
Answer: Embryo.

27) Singer Carly Simon's fourth children's book is entitled *The Nighttime Chauffeur*. Spell *chauffeur*, meaning "a person hired to drive one's auto."
Answer: C-H-A-U-F-F-E-U-R.

28) Name the Laura Ingalls Wilder 1935 autobiographical book about a frontier family that has been featured on a U.S. postage stamp.
Answer: *Little House on the Prairie.*

29) The 30th edition of the Ford Mustang was introduced with the unveiling of a red convertible with a price tag of almost $22,000, about 9 times that of the original 1964 model. Did the original model cost about $1,400; $2,400; $3,400, or $4,400?
Answer: $2,400.

30) Name the king of England, crowned on October 26, 1760, who was in power at the time of the American Revolution.
Answer: George III.

31) Name the unofficial "national anthem" of the Confederate States of America allegedly written by Daniel Decatur Emmett.
Answer: "Dixie."

32) Which U.S. President, born in New York City, was the first President to win a Nobel Peace Prize? He believed in the African proverb "Speak softly and carry a big stick."
Answer: Theodore Roosevelt.

33) Of the five world oceans: Antarctic, Arctic, Atlantic, Indian or Pacific, which is the largest ocean on earth?
Answer: Pacific Ocean.

34) How much more would one pay for $10 of handgun ammunition with the tax increase from 11% to 50% proposed by Senator Moynihan of New York?
Answer: $3.90 more.

35) On which of the following squares is the U.N. Headquarters located: Red Square, Dag Hammarskjöld Plaza, St. Peter's Square, or Tiananmen Square?
Answer: Dag Hammarskjöld Plaza (Dag Hammarskjöld was a U.N. secretary general).

36) A group of islands, such as those that make up the country of Indonesia, is known as an *archipelago*. What is a large group of stars like the Milky Way called?
Answer: Galaxy.

37) Winston Churchill, who was the British prime minister during WWII, was re-elected to succeed Clement Attlee on October 26, 1951. Spell *succeed*, meaning "to replace another in a position."
Answer: S-U-C-C-E-E-D.

38) What word beginning with the letter *K* names the Jewish diet regulating both food choices and ways of preparation?
Answer: Kosher (diet).

39) Name the French scientist who was the first person to win a Nobel in two fields: physics and chemistry. She and her husband discovered radium.
Answer: Marie Curie.

40) In which century did the British Parliament pass the Stamp Act requiring publications and legal documents in the American colonies to bear a tax stamp?
Answer: 18th century (Stamp Act took effect on November 1, 1765).

41) In 1869, Rutgers played Princeton in the U.S.'s first college football game. How many more players does a starting team in football have than a starting team in basketball?
Answer: 6 (football team, 11; basketball, 5).

42) Which day of the week in which month is general election day in the U.S.?
Answer: Tuesday in November (first Tuesday after the first Monday).

43) Spell the name of the mountain range through which Daniel Boone blazed the Wilderness Road.
Answer: A-P-P-A-L-A-C-H-I-A-N.

44) What is the sum of 2 consecutive numbers whose product is 42?
Answer: 13.

45) What 3 letters follow the final period in an e-mail address for a business, such as the on-line bookseller Amazon.____?
Answer: com (as in *Amazon.com*).

46) Which planet completes a full rotation of the sun in 59 days, faster than any other planet in the solar system?
Answer: Mercury.

47) Judge Thomas was the first justice to be confirmed without a positive recommendation from the Judiciary Committee. Spell *recommendation*.
Answer: R-E-C-O-M-M-E-N-D-A-T-I-O-N.

48) Which song was Katherine Lee Bates inspired to write when she viewed the land below from the summit of Pikes Peak in 1893? It begins with these lines: "O beautiful for spacious skies / For amber waves of grain."
Answer: "America the Beautiful."

49) If you increase an investment of $50 by 20%, then decrease the new amount by 10%, by how many dollars have you increased your original investment?
Answer: $4 (you now have $54).

50) In 1996, which European country set off its 6th—and, according to President Chirac, the last—in a series of nuclear tests in the South Pacific? *Oui* means "yes" in its language.
Answer: France.

1) During which war did Julia Ward Howe write "The Battle Hymn of the Republic" the day after she heard the song "John Brown's Body Lies A-Mouldering in the Grave"?
    Answer: Civil War.

2) Which of the following was NOT one of the original 13 colonies: Connecticut, Florida, Georgia, or Virginia?
    Answer: Florida.

3) Which state known for its Black Hills became the 40th state on November 2, 1889?
    Answer: South Dakota.

4) What is the tens' digit in the product of 649 and 231?
    Answer: 1.

5) Of the U.S.'s 40 million school-age children, about how many children make up the group of 5% considered gifted?
    Answer: About 2 million.

6) What is removed from water in the process known as desalination?
    Answer: Salt.

7) Who is wrongly accused of murdering Dr. Robinson in *The Adventures of Tom Sawyer*?
    Answer: Muff Potter.

8) Are *diary* and *dairy*, which can be made from the same letters, called synonyms, homophones, anagrams, or homographs?
    Answer: Anagrams.

9) What is the cost of 2 tacos and 4 sodas if each taco costs 80¢ and each soda costs 60¢?
    Answer: $4.00.

10) Which of the following words means "dry" and is used to describe an area like Australia's Outback: *arid, barren, lunar,* or *toxic*?
    Answer: Arid.

11) Imelda Marcos, who was charged with graft and tax evasion in 1991, had to put up a sum of money for her release from jail until her trial. What is such a payment called?
    Answer: Bail.

12) In 1998, after a House hearing on military readiness, several members suggested that the U.S. may need to return to its practice of requiring youth to serve in the military. What word beginning with the letter *D* names this process of assigning people to military service?
Answer: Draft.

13) On November 3, 1903, Panama declared itself independent from which South American country named for the explorer who landed in the New World in 1492?
Answer: Colombia.

14) About how many times more plentiful is Iceland's supply of fresh water with its 666,667 cubic meters per person, than that of the African country of Djibouti [ji bü´ tē] with its 23 cubic meters per person: 5,000; 15,000; 25,000; or 35,000?
Answer: 35,000.

15) After a fight was interrupted by a parachutist dropping into the ring, Evander Holyfield regained the heavyweight title by defeating Riddick Bowe. Spell *parachutist*.
Answer: P-A-R-A-C-H-U-T-I-S-T.

16) A woman in Carlisle, Iowa, gave birth to 7 babies in 6 minutes in 1997. What word designates 7 babies born to one mother at the same time?
Answer: Septuplets.

17) Which of the following, like *plotting*, is spelled with a double letter: shining, bidding, hiding, or daring?
Answer: Bidding.

18) The Supreme Court once heard a suit against a rap group for recording a humorous imitation of "Oh, Pretty Woman." Spell the term for "a person's right to reproduce a literary or artistic work."
Answer: C-O-P-Y-R-I-G-H-T.

19) German-born American physicist Albert Einstein was awarded the Nobel Prize in 1921. Which letter of the alphabet completes his famous equation ____ = mc^2, important in the development of atomic energy?
Answer: E.

20) Scotland's National Party copied the IRA in conducting a fundraising drive in the U.S. to help with its plan to secede from England, or what is sometimes referred to as U.K. What do the initials U.K. stand for?
Answer: United Kingdom (of Great Britain and Northern Ireland).

21) The Vietnam Women's Memorial in Washington, D.C., was officially unveiled 300 feet from the Vietnam Veterans Memorial on which holiday observed on November 11?
Answer: Veterans Day.

22) In 1993, Maryland's governor pushed for legislation to eliminate the gas chamber as a means of execution. What is the 2-word legal term for a death sentence?
Answer: Capital punishment.

23) Identify the small South American country named for the equator.
Answer: Ecuador.

24) Randy's best high jump was 4 3/4 feet. Expressed as a mixed number in simplified form, how many feet below the meet record of 6 7/12 feet was Randy's jump?
Answer: 1 5/6 feet.

25) A satellite that once went out of control and fell into the Pacific Ocean was launched by China from which desert, the world's coldest and most northern: the Gobi, Mojave, or Sahara?
Answer: Gobi Desert.

26) Identify the hot, dry winds that sometimes fan major firestorms, destroying homes in California. They share their name with the Mexican general whose forces overran the Alamo.
Answer: Santa Ana winds.

27) Rachel Carson's book *Silent Spring*, which warned of the danger of pesticides, was released in 1962. Which word using the same suffix as *pesticide* means "the act of killing another person"?
Answer: Homicide.

28) Golden Books have introduced children's books in Spanish. What is the English title for the children's story entitled *Los Tres Osos* in the Spanish book?
Answer: *The Three Bears*.

29) What is the largest of 5 consecutive whole numbers whose average is 28?
Answer: 30.

30) Venezuela lies on the northern coast of South America. Spell the name of the sea the country borders.
Answer: C-A-R-I-B-B-E-A-N (Sea).

31) In sports, what is the word for a manager or player in his first season on the job?
Answer: Rookie.

32) Name the U.S. Capitol hall in Washington, D.C., with marble statues of the nation's heroes.
Answer: Statuary Hall (House of Representatives met there from 1817 until 1857).

33) Which U.S. state, whose name comes from Indian words meaning "sky-tinted waters," is bordered by Wisconsin, the Dakotas and Iowa?
Answer: Minnesota.

34) How many gallons of gas will it take for the approximate 3,000-mile trip from New York to San Francisco in a super car averaging the over 80 miles per gallon that is the 2003 goal of a joint effort of the government and the Big Three automakers?
Answer: 37½ (or 38) gallons; the 2003 target is 82 miles per gallon).

35) In which decade of the 1800s was the Civil War fought?
Answer: 1860s.

36) In 1993, eight people emerged after spending 2 years studying the relationships of organisms and their physical environment in Biosphere 2. Name the science in which such relationships are studied.
Answer: Ecology.

37) Former first lady Rosalyn Carter said the Clinton health plan discriminates against the mentally ill. Spell *discriminate*.
Answer: D-I-S-C-R-I-M-I-N-A-T-E.

38) Identify 2 of the words that contain double consonants in the following sentence: After a 10-day mission, the space shuttle *Discovery* made the first nighttime landing at Kennedy Space Center in Florida.
Answer: *Mission, shuttle, nighttime*, and *Kennedy*.

39) Sue made a 15-minute long distance phone call which cost $.35 for the first 3 minutes and $.10 for each additional minute up to 20. There is also a $1.25 surcharge. What was the total cost of the phone call?
Answer: $2.80.

40) The U.N. once placed an order prohibiting trade of arms and oil to rebels in Angola. Is a ban on trading called a *filibuster*, *embargo*, *accord*, or *indictment*?
Answer: Embargo.

41) James Madison moved into a house named for its 8 sides after the British burned the White House in 1814. Name the polygon that has 8 sides.
Answer: Octagon (Octagon House).

42) President Clinton signed the National Service Act with the same two pens used to create the Civilian Conservation Corps and the Peace Corps. Which 2 U.S. Presidents, known by the initials FDR and JFK, signed papers enacting these earlier programs?
Answer: **Franklin D. Roosevelt and John F. Kennedy (respectively).**

43) An F-5 tornado was among those that struck in Oklahoma and Kansas in 1999. What 2-word nickname is given to the area from north-central Texas through Oklahoma, Kansas, and Nebraska, and into the Dakotas because of the number of tornadoes that occur there?
Answer: **Tornado Alley.**

44) According to the Census Bureau, 1 in 5 fathers with working wives was the primary caretaker for their preschool children. On this basis, how many of every 100 fathers with working wives were primary caretakers of their children?
Answer: **20 (the average in 1988 was 1 in 7).**

45) Which Caribbean island, whose name means "rich port," voted 48% to 46% to remain a U.S. commonwealth rather than to apply for admission as the 51st U.S. state?
Answer: **Puerto Rico (4% voted for independence).**

46) According to the CDC, measles has virtually disappeared in the U.S. because of increased immunizations. Spell *inoculation*, the method used for preventing measles.
Answer: **I-N-O-C-U-L-A-T-I-0-N.**

47) Are rebels who engage in surprise attacks called *cobras, guerrillas, tigers,* or *sharks*?
Answer: **Guerrillas (as distinguished from the homophone *gorillas*, for the animals).**

48) The Supreme Court's Sandra Day O'Connor wrote the Supreme Court decision declaring that women need not prove they have been psychologically damaged to win sexual harassment damage charges. Spell *harassment*.
Answer: **H-A-R-A-S-S-M-E-N-T.**

49) What is the median age of the Supreme Court justices if their ages are 45, 53, 57, 57, 61, 63, 68, 73, and 85?
Answer: **61.**

50) On which continent is Zaire, which celebrates its national holiday on November 24?
Answer: **Africa.**

1) Name the American frontiersman who became a U.S. representative from Tennessee and died defending the Alamo.
   Answer: Davy (David) Crockett.

2) Zachary Taylor, the 12th President, was born in Virginia. Name any 3 of the other 7 Presidents born in this state known as the "Mother of Presidents."
   Answer: Washington, Jefferson, Madison, Monroe, W.H. Harrison, Tyler, and Wilson.

3) To which of the following U.S. cities is Canada's capital, Ottawa, closest: Seattle, Minneapolis, Chicago, or Boston?
   Answer: Boston.

4) What is the area of the smallest square that can surround a circle with an area of 16π?
   Answer: 64 square units.

5) The bubonic plague killed a fourth of Europe's population in the 1300s. By what other colorful name is this plague known?
   Answer: Black Death.

6) In humans, 55% of the blood is a straw-colored liquid which transports the red and white blood cells. What is the scientific name for this liquid?
   Answer: Plasma.

7) Identify the abandoned pirate ship in Robert Louis Stevenson's *Treasure Island* that shares its name with the island on which Haiti and the Dominican Republic are located.
   Answer: *Hispaniola*.

8) The estate of a composer made his papers available to the public via computer. Is a person who has died described as *exhumed, extinct, defunct,* or *deceased*?
   Answer: Deceased.

9) What is the quotient when 1 is divided by 1/3?
   Answer: 3.

10) Name the Spanish explorer who first saw the Mississippi River in 1541.
    Answer: Hernando De Soto.

11) With its stars arranged in alternating rows of 6 stars and 5 stars, how many rows of stars does the current U.S. flag have?
    Answer: 9 (4 rows of 5 and 5 rows of 6 for a total of 50 stars).

12) Which group was granted the right to vote in U.S. elections by the 26th Amendment, proposed by Congress on March 23, 1971?
Answer: 18-year-olds.

13) Spell the name of the Caribbean island that celebrated its 500th birthday with street festivals, art shows, and the Central American Games in San Juan in 1993.
Answer: P-U-E-R-T-O R-I-C-O.

14) What is the cube root of the square root of 64?
Answer: 2.

15) President Clinton turned 53 on his birthday, August 19, 1999. In which year was he born?
Answer: 1946.

16) Guidelines issued by the American Academy for the Advancement of Science Literacy stated that 8th graders should know that the moon circles the Earth in about how many days?
Answer: 28 (accept 27, for *World Book* states that it is 27 1/3 days).

17) Spell *passed* in the following: Although the House *passed* the Brady bill, a Senate filibuster prevented it from going to President Bush, who opposed it.
Answer: P-A-S-S-E-D.

18) The Louvre, which was opened to the public in Paris on November 8, 1793, was originally a royal residence. Spell *originally*.
Answer: O-R-I-G-I-N-A-L-L-Y.

19) The son of the man who invented the Heimlich technique for ejecting an object from the windpipe of a choking person was once a mayoral candidate. What is the scientific name for the windpipe: *aorta, esophagus, larynx,* or *trachea*?
Answer: Trachea.

20) Mount Vesuvius erupted on August 24, A.D. 79, destroying the cities of Pompeii, Stabiae, and Herculaneum in the southern part of which country on the Mediterranean?
Answer: Italy.

21) For which American frontiersman was the capital of Nevada named?
Answer: Kit Carson (his given name was Christopher).

22) In which decade did Shirley Chisholm become the first black woman to serve in the U.S. Congress: 1920s, '40s, '60s, or '80s?
Answer: 1960s.

23) Three Atlanta men once set out on what they called the "Grits to Gators Bike Ride," a 400-mile trek from Georgia's Okefenokee Swamp to which swamp in South Florida?
Answer: The Everglades.

24) What percent of a half dollar is a dime?
Answer: 20%.

25) What is the acronym for the free trade agreement passed by the U.S. House and Senate and by our North American neighbor Mexico?
Answer: NAFTA (North American Free Trade Agreement).

26) Work by the 1995 winners of the Nobel Prize in chemistry led industrial countries to agree to phase out by 1996 the ozone-depleting chemicals known as CFCs. Name the chemical element represented by either of the 2 *C*'s in CFC.
Answer: Chlorine or carbon (CFCs are chlorofluorocarbons; winners were U.S.'s Mario Molina and Sherwood Rowland and Dutch citizen Paul Crutzen).

27) When politicians engage in a gubernatorial race, for which position are they running?
Answer: Governor.

28) Sojourner Truth was the first black woman to make speeches against slavery. Is one who makes formal speeches called an *apprentice, aviatrix, choreographer,* or *orator*?
Answer: Orator.

29) If Walter hiked 21 miles in 3 hours and 30 minutes, how long would it take him to hike 28 miles at the same pace?
Answer: 4 hours, 40 minutes (accept 4 2/3 hours).

30) Give the full name of WHO, the U.N. agency that declared December 1 as World AIDS Day, in 1988.
Answer: World Health Organization.

31) If Puerto Rico became the 51st state and the stars were arranged in rows of 9 stars and rows of 8 stars, how many rows of stars would the flag have?
Answer: 6 (3 rows of 8 and 3 rows of 9 for a total of 51 stars).

32) In which state did Father Edward Flanagan found Boys Town on December 1, 1917, at a site located about 11 miles west of Omaha? Its nickname is the "Cornhusker State."
Answer: Nebraska.

33) In 1961, President Kennedy decided to increase the U.S. advisers in Vietnam to 16,000 within 2 years. Of Cambodia, India, Laos, and China, which does not border Vietnam?
Answer: India.

34) How many representatives did not vote when the 435-member House rejected a bill to let D.C. become a state by a vote of 277-153?
Answer: 5.

35) In which state bordering Georgia did black mayors once meet in Tuskegee, site of the college for blacks founded by Booker T. Washington?
Answer: Alabama.

36) A rare earthquake warning was once issued for Parkfield, California, the town called the "earthquake capital." Name the notorious fault on which it lies.
Answer: San Andreas Fault.

37) Name Jack London's book about a wild wolf-dog that is gradually tamed and taken from the Yukon to California, where the dog protects his new master's family from assault.
Answer: *White Fang.*

38) Name the title character in the Broadway musical based on the biblical story about a boy with a coat of many colors who was sold into slavery by his brothers.
Answer: Joseph (the play is *Joseph and the Amazing Technicolor Dreamcoat*).

39) Nutritionists told the FDA that olestra, a synthetic chemical that doesn't clog arteries, is safe to eat as a replacement for fat, one of the 3 main classes of nutrients that provide energy to the body. Name the other 2 major classes of nutrients providing energy.
Answer: Carbohydrates and proteins.

40) Which country celebrates its founding as a British colony on January 26, the 1788 date when a shipload of convicts arrived at Botany Bay? It's located below the equator.
Answer: Australia.

41) Identify the colors whose names complete the labels "Tickle Me ____" and "Robin's Egg ____" for 2 of the 16 colors Crayola added to its product line-up in the 1990s.
Answer: "Pink" and "Blue."

42) Based on full membership, how many votes were needed in the 435-member House of Representatives for approval of the North American Free Trade Agreement?
Answer: 218.

43)   The Appalachian Trail, one of 150 areas to benefit from a park improvements bill, runs from Maine to which state bordering the Carolinas?
       Answer: Georgia.

44)   If a kilometer is approximately equivalent to .62 miles what is the approximate measure in kilometers of a 26-mile course: 16, 32, 42, or 52?
       Answer: 42 (kilometers).

45)   In which year did Christopher Columbus found the first European colony in the Americas? A tiny crucifix has been uncovered near this site on the island of Hispaniola.
       Answer: 1492.

46)   An eclipse of the moon occurred on November 28-29, 1993. Which of the following words describes such an eclipse: *astral*, *briny*, *lunar*, or *solar*?
       Answer: Lunar.

47)   Name author Washington Irving's native state, where he died at Tarrytown in 1859. His character Rip Van Winkle lived in its Catskill Mountains.
       Answer: New York.

48)   Which country, home of composers Handel, Mozart, and Schubert, celebrates October 26 as its national holiday? It is the setting for the show *The Sound of Music*.
       Answer: Austria.

49)   Of 4,288 total Democratic delegate votes, how many are needed for the simple majority to nominate a candidate?
       Answer: 2,145.

50)   Prince Carl was elected King Haakon VII by the people of Norway on November 18, 1905. Give either of the adjectives meaning "from Norway."
       Answer: Norse or Norwegian.

1) What is the full name for the shortened form *pro-am* used to name a kind of golf tournament or other sporting contest?
Answer: Professional-amateur.

2) What word designates "a President's refusal to sign a bill"?
Answer: Veto.

3) Which body of water does South America's Colombia border on its western shore?
Answer: Pacific Ocean.

4) If a right triangle has an angle of 35%, what are the measures of the other 2 angles?
Answer: 55% and 90%.

5) Which Communist country handed over 33 coffins to the U.S. with what it said were the remains of U.N. servicemen killed in a war in the 1950s?
Answer: North Korea.

6) What word meaning "the science of flying" is represented by the first *A* in NASA?
Answer: Aeronautics (NASA: National Aeronautics and Space Administration).

7) A court ruled that salvagers who spent millions to find a sunken ship were entitled to its treasure. Name the Jules Verne sea captain for whom the 2-ton robot used in the search was named.
Answer: Captain Nemo (in *Twenty Thousand Leagues Under the Sea*).

8) What does the word *purple* describe in the first stanza of the song "America the Beautiful," which was sung at the ceremony celebrating the Capitol's 200th anniversary?
Answer: Mountains ("for purple mountain majesties / Above the fruited plain").

9) How many yards does a person run in a half-mile race, or 2,640 feet?
Answer: 880 yards.

10) Is a meeting of leaders of countries referred to as a *caucus, summit, cartel,* or *referendum*?
Answer: Summit.

11) Congress may pass more legislation to stop noisy air tours over national parks since activists say a law passed years ago did not restore quiet to which Arizona park?
Answer: Grand Canyon National Park.

12) General Ambrose Burnside, defeated by General Lee in Virginia on December 13, 1862, is known for his whiskers. What word for "side whiskers" comes from his name?
Answer: Sideburns (Burnside was defeated at Fredericksburg, Virginia).

13) Many people have been killed in accidental falls at the Grand Canyon. Which of the following is NOT a synonym for "canyon": *chasm, gorge, mesa,* or *ravine*?
Answer: Mesa.

14) What is the sum of the number of positive factors for 19 and 12?
Answer: 8 (19 has 2 positive factors; 12 has 6 positive factors).

15) Name the London home of Queen Elizabeth II that was opened to tourists for the first time in the summer of 1993.
Answer: Buckingham Palace.

16) Smallpox has been eliminated by a vaccination program. Spell *vaccination.*
Answer: V-A-C-C-I-N-A-T-I-O-N (smallpox is the first disease conquered by humans).

17) Which children's Christmas song was the biggest recording hit of "Singing Cowboy" Gene Autry, who died at age 91 in 1998? It contains the phrase "had a very shiny nose."
Answer: "Rudolph, the Red-Nosed Reindeer" (it's the 2nd best-selling single ever).

18) Gilbert Stuart is famous for his 3 paintings of George Washington. What term designates a painting of a person?
Answer: Portrait.

19) Who was granted a patent for the cotton gin on March 14, 1794?
Answer: Eli Whitney.

20) In which Parisian cathedral did Napoleon crown himself emperor on December 2, 1804? A famous Catholic university in the U.S. bears the same name, meaning "our lady."
Answer: Cathedral of Notre Dame.

21) U.S. and European trade negotiators met to try to settle differences for completing the agreement known as GATT. Which word completes its full name: General Agreement on _____ and Trade?
Answer: Tariffs.

22) What name is given to the first Ten Amendments to the U.S. Constitution, which became effective following ratification by Virginia in 1791?
Answer: Bill of Rights.

23) A stone pathway was built in Israel for tourists to retrace Jesus' footsteps from the Last Supper to the Garden of Gethsemane on which mount? It bears the name of the fruit of the tree whose branch has long been a symbol of peace.
Answer: Mount of Olives.

24) What is the difference between 0.2 percent of 20,000 and 0.02 percent of 20,000?
Answer: 36 (0.2 percent is 40; 0.02 percent is 4).

25) What color is the ribbon on the 29-cent stamp issued to encourage awareness of AIDS? This color is often associated with anger.
Answer: Red (stamps were first issued on December 1, 1993).

26) Identify the 2 continents on which the leopard lives in the wild.
Answer: Africa and Asia.

27) Since the administration of President Theodore Roosevelt, most U.S. Presidents have been scheduling visits to foreign countries. Spell *scheduling*.
Answer: S-C-H-E-D-U-L-I-N-G.

28) Antonín Dvořák's *New World Symphony* premiered at Carnegie Hall on December 16, 1893. Name 3 of the 4 sections that make up a symphony orchestra.
Answer: String, wind, percussion, and brass sections.

29) How much more is the $1,424,778 in taxes a $15 million business would pay in Philadelphia than the $1,118,239 the same company would pay in Atlanta?
Answer: $306,539.

30) Are North Korea and South Korea separated by the *International Date Line*, the *equator*, the *38th parallel*, or the *102nd meridian*?
Answer: 38th parallel (the line of latitude at 38% N.).

31) France and England failed to qualify for the final lineup of the 1994 World Cup in the U.S. In which sport is this World Cup awarded every 4 years?
Answer: Soccer.

32) Which of the following states does not include any part of the territory acquired by the Louisiana Purchase of December 20, 1803: Iowa, Kentucky, Missouri, or Montana?
Answer: Kentucky (originally part of Virginia).

33) Which body of water lies on Algeria's northern shore?
Answer: Mediterranean Sea.

34) At midnight, the temperature was 27 degrees and by 5:00 a.m., it had dropped 8 degrees. From that point, it began to warm, reaching a high at 3:30 p.m. that was 14 degrees warmer than at 5:00 a.m. What were the day's low and high temperatures?
Answer: 19 and 33 degrees.

35) The NFL franchise team awarded to Jacksonville, Florida, is nicknamed for a large feline animal. Is a *feline* a bird, cat, dog, or horse?
Answer: Cat (the team is called the Jaguars).

36) Enrico Fermi helped achieve the first controlled nuclear chain reaction at a laboratory at the University of Chicago on December 2, 1942. Spell *laboratory*.
Answer: L-A-B-O-R-A-T-O-R-Y.

37) Complete this literary threesome: Wynken, Blynken, and
_____.
Answer: Nod.

38) At a state dinner in 1999, actor Robert Duvall performed an Argentine dance for the Argentine president. Identify this dance, whose name completes the saying "it takes two to _____."
Answer: Tango.

39) Complete this scientific threesome: protons, neutrons, and
_____.
Answer: Electrons.

40) Which country has restored the double-headed eagle as its official emblem in place of the famed hammer and sickle used to represent peasants and workers?
Answer: Russia.

41) Rhodes scholarships are awarded annually for study at Oxford University. Spell *scholarship*.
Answer: S-C-H-O-L-A-R-S-H-I-P.

42) What was the primary crop cultivated by Jamestown colonist John Rolfe, who on April 5, 1614, married the Indian princess Pocahontas?
Answer: Tobacco.

43) Which Texas city on the Rio Grande near the Mexican border has a Spanish name meaning "the pass" or "the crossing"?
Answer: El Paso.

44) A U.S. $1 coin lasts about 30 years while a $1 bill lasts about a year and 4 months. How many dollar bills would have to be printed to last the lifetime of a dollar coin?
Answer: 23.

45) The 1995 television special *My First 85 Years* celebrated the life of which famous French oceanographer?
Answer: Jacques Cousteau.

46) Complete this scientific threesome: igneous, sedimentary, and _____.
Answer: Metamorphic.

47) On November 26, 1864, Lewis Carroll sent a handwritten manuscript of his new work to 12-year-old Alice Liddell as an early Christmas present. Name it.
Answer: *Alice's Adventures in Wonderland.*

48) According to a director at the Washington's National Gallery of Art, 5 of its works are inaccurately attributed to 17th-century Dutch artist Rembrandt. Spell *inaccurately*.
Answer: I-N-A-C-C-U-R-A-T-E-L-Y.

49) By what percent was the adult entry fee once cut at Euro-Disney near Paris with its reduction from 250 francs to 175 francs?
Answer: 30%.

50) Emperor Akihito and Empress Michiko were the first Japanese rulers to visit France. Which of the following words is *not* a synonym for ruler: *sovereign, tributary, monarch,* or *emir*?
Answer: Tributary.

1) The Department of Agriculture has issued a children's version of the food pyramid using graphics to illustrate food groups. Which food group is at the base of this pyramid indicating that it is the one from which the most servings per day should come?
   Answer: Grains (bread, cereal, rice, and pasta; the pyramid calls for 6-11 servings a day).

2) The Continental Army camped for the winter on December 19, 1777, at Valley Forge, Pennsylvania. Name 3 of the 6 states bordering Pennsylvania.
   Answer: Delaware, Maryland, New Jersey, New York, Ohio, and West Virginia.

3) Dutch navigator Abel Tasman discovered and named New Zealand in 1642. Identify the country off whose southeast coast New Zealand is located.
   Answer: Australia.

4) What is the length of a rectangle with a 48-square-inch area and a 4-inch width?
   Answer: 12 inches.

5) After its government executed 9 human rights activists in 1995, Nigeria was suspended from an association comprised of Britain and its former colonies. What word meaning "riches" is added to the word *common* to form the compound word naming this organization?
   Answer: Wealth (Commonwealth, or Commonwealth of Nations).

6) The EPA reported that drinking water in some cities contained unhealthy levels of which soft, metallic element represented by the symbol Pb?
   Answer: Lead.

7) Spell the only adverb in the following: The Clinton Administration tentatively approved hiring 1,600 energy experts to oversee cleanup of the U.S.'s old atom-bomb factories.
   Answer: T-E-N-T-A-T-I-V-E-L-Y.

8) Is the director of a museum called an *artisan, curator, novice,* or *liaison*?
   Answer: Curator.

9) Find the exact surface area of a cube with 4-inch edges.
    Answer: 96 square inches.

10) In March 1999, an average of stock prices on the U.S. market
    broke 10,000 for the very first time ever. Complete its name:
    Dow _____ Industrial Average.
    Answer: Jones (it reached 10,001.78).

11) Give the Greek prefix for "over" or "excessive" that completes
    the word _____*tension*, the medical name for high blood
    pressure.
    Answer: Hyper- (hypertension).

12) According to Governor William Bradford's *History of Plymouth
    Plantation*, in which year did the Pilgrims land at Plymouth,
    Massachusetts, on December 20: 1585, 1607, 1620, or 1692?
    **Answer: 1620 (1585: Roanoke Island; 1607: Jamestown;
    1692: witch trials).**

13) Name the state where President Bush's vacation compound at
    Kennebunkport was left in rubble by 20-foot waves in 1991.
    Answer: Maine.

14) As many as 1,000 of the U.S.'s poorest communities applied for
    a share of $3.5 billion in federal money for urban revitaliza-
    tion. If the shares were meted out equally, how much of the
    $3.5 billion would each of the 1,000 applicants receive?
    Answer: $3.5 million.

15) Surgeon General Elders set off a controversy when she said
    violent crime would probably be reduced if drugs were legal-
    ized. Spell *surgeon*.
    Answer: S-U-R-G-E-O-N.

16) The fossil remains of a relative of a present-day seabound mam-
    mal show that it once walked on land. Name this mammal, the
    largest animal that has ever lived.
    Answer: Whale (blue whale is the largest animal).

17) Former British Prime Minister Margaret Thatcher testified
    that she didn't know her administration had loosened
    restraints on arms sales to Iraq in the 1980s. Spell *loosened*.
    Answer: L-O-O-S-E-N-E-D.

18) On which date, 12 days after Christmas, is the Christian festi-
    val of Epiphany celebrated to mark the adoration of the infant
    Jesus by the Magi?
    **Answer: January 6 (also called Twelfth Day and Feast
    of Lights/or Three Kings).**

19) A headline once called composting "Nature's alchemy." What did the ancients hope to produce with alchemy?
Answer: Gold (to change base metals into gold).

20) Despite opposition by many POW/MIA families and some veterans groups, President Clinton in 1994 lifted a 19-year-old ban on trade with which Southeast Asia country?
Answer: Vietnam.

21) The American Expeditionary Forces' official newspaper was published for the first time on February 8, 1918. With what nickname for the flag, or "Old Glory," was it entitled?
Answer: "Stars and Stripes" (the newspaper was called _The Stars and Stripes_).

22) More than 200 American Indians were massacred by the U.S. cavalry on December 29, 1890, at Wounded Knee. Spell _massacred_.
Answer: M-A-S-S-A-C-R-E-D.

23) Which of the following does NOT border Wyoming: Colorado, Montana, Nevada, or Utah?
Answer: Nevada.

24) With the number of Americans with high blood pressure having dropped from about 64 million a decade ago to about 50 million today, what percent of today's population of 260 million have high blood pressure: 10%, 20%, 30%, or 40%?
Answer: 20%.

25) Name the country that U.S. planes began bombing in 1999 as part of a NATO effort to bring peace to the region after President Milosevic refused to let troops oversee a peace deal in the province of Kosovo.
Answer: Yugoslavia.

26) Which word designates both "an animal's home" and "a group of 5 to 10 Cub Scouts"?
Answer: Den.

27) Which of the following means "a pardon": _amnesty_, _apathy_, _gratuity_, or _truce_?
Answer: Amnesty.

28) In which European city has the second phase of a $1 billion renovation doubled the exhibition space of the Louvre Museum? It is the site of the Eiffel Tower.
Answer: Paris.

29) How much greater was the nation's largest retailer's $67.38 billion of sales in 1994 than its $55.48 billion in the previous year?
Answer: $11.9 billion.

30) After urging the citizens of Belarus to reject communism, President Clinton visited the Belarus burial site of 50,000 victims of which Communist dictator? His adopted name means "man of steel" and begins with an *S*.
Answer: Joseph Stalin.

31) Which word for "a large city" names both Superman's base of operation and an Illinois town that is now the site of a museum with 40,000-items of Superman memorabilia?
Answer: Metropolis (the museum is called the Super Museum).

32) Name the Massachusetts town known for its witch trials in 1692.
Answer: Salem.

33) Name the second longest U.S. river, one that rises in the Rocky Mountains and empties into the Mississippi. The state whose postal abbreviation is MO shares its name.
Answer: Missouri River.

34) If 2½ cups of apples are needed to make one pie, how many cups of apples are needed to make 10 pies?
Answer: 25 cups.

35) The world's longest escalator, a half-mile-long stairway, is located in which former British dependency released in 1997? It shares part of its name with the monstrous gorilla of film fame called King ____.
Answer: Hong Kong.

36) What is the 2-part scientific name for man indicating genus and species?
Answer: *Homo sapiens*.

37) "Compassion" and "Perseverance" are among the chapter titles in former Secretary of Education Bennett's book *The Book of Virtues: A Treasury of Great Moral Stories*. Spell *perseverance*, meaning "sticking to a course of action."
Answer: P-E-R-S-E-V-E-R-A-N-C-E.

38) Complete this biblical threesome: gold, frankincense, and _____.
Answer: Myrrh.

39) A gasoline gauge registers 1/8 full. After 12 gallons are added to the tank, the gauge registers 7/8 full. What is the capacity of the tank?
Answer: 16 gallons.

40) On November 14, 1935, President Franklin Roosevelt proclaimed a group of islands between Japan and Indonesia to be a free commonwealth. Name this island nation, whose capital is Manila.
Answer: Philippine Islands.

41) What word is used specifically to describe animals that eat meat: *carnivorous, herbivorous, invertebrate*, or *cold-blooded*?
    Answer: Carnivorous.

42) According to the book *Lost Star*, which pilot who disappeared at sea while on an around-the-world flight in 1937 was really engaged in a spy mission undertaken in return for funding for the flight?
    Answer: Amelia Earhart.

43) In 1999, President Edward Shevardnadze endorsed the NATO bombing of Yugoslavia. Name his country, the former Soviet republic that bears the name of a U.S. state.
    Answer: Georgia.

44) What is the time at 1.6 hours past 2:30 p.m.?
    Answer: 4:06 p.m. (1.6 hours is 1 hour and 36 minutes).

45) In which African nation have Islamic militants damaged the tourist-dependent economy despite the attraction of such sites as the Great Sphinx, a huge statue with the head of a man and the body of a lion?
    Answer: Egypt.

46) What is the boiling point for water on the Fahrenheit temperature scale?
    Answer: 212% (named for Gabriel D. Fahrenheit; most countries use Celsius scale).

47) Which author describes the end of the Mississippi River's steamboat era in his 1883 *Life on the Mississippi*?
    Answer: Mark Twain (Samuel Langhorne Clemens).

48) Calling it the biggest thing since fire, scientists at Princeton University raised hopes of commercially producing energy by fusion by the year 2035. Which Greek mythological figure allegedly stole fire from the gods and gave it to man?
    Answer: Prometheus.

49) Physicist Robert Boyle formulated the law that says the volume of a gas at constant temperature varies inversely to the pressure applied to the gas. Spell *varying*, the present participle of *vary*, meaning "to change."
    Answer: V-A-R-Y-I-N-G.

50) Give the current name for the Russian city freed on January 27, 1944, after an 880-day German siege, or name the fictitious city in which Mark Twain's Tom Sawyer lived.
    Answer: St. Petersburg (called Leningrad at the time of the siege).

1) What day of the week is named in the French phrase *Mardi Gras*?
Answer: Tuesday (literally for "Fat Tuesday").

2) What was Newt Gingrich's title as head of the House of Representatives: *House Secretary*, *Speaker of the House*, *President of the House*, or *Attorney General*?
Answer: Speaker of the House (elected by the majority party in the House).

3) In which Canadian province is the city of Montreal?
Answer: Quebec.

4) If a drug costs $1.50 in Britain, how much would it cost at a 60% increase in the U.S.?
Answer: $2.40.

5) Following the Security Council's unanimous vote to condemn a Hebron massacre, Syria, Jordan, and Lebanon agreed to resume talks with Israel. Spell the word *unanimous*, meaning "in total agreement."
Answer: U-N-A-N-I-M-O-U-S.

6) Which of the following, like man, belongs to the class called Mammalia: *cobra*, *whale*, *frog*, or *robin*?
Answer: Whale.

7) Which word meaning "to talk unintelligibly" makes up part of the one-word title of a Lewis Carroll poem?
Answer: Jabber (poem is "Jabberwocky").

8) Name the Christian period of 40 days that begins on Ash Wednesday, or give the past tense of the verb *lend*.
Answer: Lent.

9) How many zeros does the number one trillion have?
Answer: 12.

10) A Christian martyr named Valentine is said to have been beheaded on the Flamian Way in the Roman Empire on February 14, A.D. 269. Spell *martyr*.
Answer: M-A-R-T-Y-R.

11) According to an old legend, animals of the class Aves choose their mates on Valentine's Day, February 14. Which animals make up this class?
Answer: Birds.

12) Name the President who followed Richard Nixon and granted him a "full, free and absolute pardon" on September 8, 1974. His surname also designates a large U.S. automaker.
Answer: Gerald Ford.

13) Name 2 of the states in which the following 3 academies are located: the U.S. Military Academy, the Naval Academy, and the Air Force Academy.
Answer: New York (West Point); Maryland (Annapolis); and Colorado (Colorado Springs).

14) A ribbon 24 inches long is cut into two pieces. If one piece is twice the length of the other, what is the length of the shorter piece?
Answer: 8 inches.

15) According to a Census Bureau report, 9 of the 10 fastest-growing states in the 1990s were west of the Mississippi. Which Southern state, the largest east of the Mississippi, is in the top 10?
Answer: Georgia (ranks 8th; it unseated Florida as the South's top growth area).

16) Fifth-grade boys in an Oceanside, California, class shaved their heads so a friend who underwent cancer treatment wouldn't feel out of place. Name the cancer treatment that can cause hair to fall out.
Answer: Chemotherapy.

17) Which of the following words does not end in *-ee*: *absentee*, *employee*, *nominee*, or *warranty*?
Answer: Warranty.

18) In which city was Chelsea Clinton once invited to dance with the famous Bolshoi Ballet?
Answer: Moscow (during a European tour).

19) Which planet, named for the Greek god of the underworld, was discovered by an Arizona astronomer on February 18, 1930? It is usually the farthest from the sun.
Answer: Pluto (found by Clyde Tombaugh).

20) February 15 marks the anniversary of the Soviet Union's withdrawal of troops from Afghanistan in 1990. Which nation, whose name begins with *I*, borders Afghanistan on the west?
Answer: Iran.

21) Lewis Grizzard, a Southern humorist known for his newspaper columns and 20 books, including *Elvis Is Dead And I Don't Feel So Good Myself*, died in 1994 after heart surgery. Spell *deceased*, a synonym for "dead."
Answer: D-E-C-E-A-S-E-D.

22) On February 18, 1861, who said in his inaugural address, "All we ask is to be left alone"?
Answer: **Jefferson Davis (as president of the Confederacy).**

23) Which of the following seas neither borders Asia nor lies within it: *Black, Caspian, Dead, Red,* or *Tasman?*
Answer: **Tasman.**

24) If the scale on a blueprint is 1/2 inch to 1 foot, then how long is a wall 3 inches long on the blueprint?
Answer: **6 feet (accept 72 inches).**

25) A billionaire president of Mexico's largest banking group became one of 2,000 businessmen kidnapped for money in Mexico in the 1990s. What word designates a "sum of money requested by kidnappers in exchange for their prisoner"?
Answer: **Ransom.**

26) What is the source of all light that comes from a comet?
Answer: **Sun.**

27) Name the language spoken by European Jews that combines German dialects with Hebrew and other languages with such words as *chutzpah,* meaning "gall" or "nerve."
Answer: **Yiddish.**

28) The Democratic National Committee picked up the $8,365 tab for the custom-made costumes Vice President Al Gore and his wife Tipper wore to an annual Halloween party. Which 2 Disney characters whose names begin with *B*, in a story featuring Gaston, did the Gores portray?
Answer: **Beauty and the Beast.**

29) What is the next highest cube after 27?
Answer: **64.**

30) Which structure, first completed in 214 B.C. and rebuilt in the late 1400s, did President Clinton visit in China in late June 1998, following in the footsteps of all U.S. Presidents since President Nixon, who went there in 1972? It is some 4,000 miles in length.
Answer: **Great Wall (of China).**

31) The U.S. Forest Service marked the golden anniversary in the 1990s of which bear who warns of the dangers of forest fires?
Answer: **Smokey (the) Bear.**

32) Name the state where Molly Pitcher distinguished herself by replacing her husband in loading and firing cannon at the Battle of Monmouth in 1778. Its capital is Trenton.
Answer: **New Jersey.**

33) From which Midwest state did a rider set out on April 3, 1860, to begin the Pony Express service to deliver mail to California? Its capital is Jefferson City.
Answer: Missouri (the rider departed from St. Joseph, Missouri).

34) The Hubble Space Telescope was launched in 1990 with an expected life of 15 years. In which year is it expected to cease operation?
Answer: 2005.

35) Which 1964 conservative Republican presidential nominee urged both Republicans and Democrats "to get off [President Clinton's] back" about Whitewater? His surname is made of 2 words identifying the metal sought in the Klondike and the compound known as H_2O, respectively.
Answer: Barry Goldwater.

36) Is the path that most comets follow when they travel around the sun described as *bovine, circular, elliptical*, or *spherical*?
Answer: Elliptical.

37) Spell the past tense of *flee* to complete the following: On April 2, 1865, Confederate President Jefferson Davis _____ from the capital of Richmond.
Answer: F-L-E-D (along with most of his Cabinet).

38) Which color is used to name the kind of jazz with African-American roots for which Columbus, Georgia, native Ma Rainey was famous?
Answer: Blue (Rainey is known as "Mother of the Blues").

39) Is a light year a measure of *speed, distance, volume*, or *time*?
Answer: Distance (distance that light travels in one year, about 9.5 trillion km).

40) Which stringed instrument did Italian virtuoso Niccolò Paganini play with such skill and speed that he was thought to be in league with the devil?
Answer: Violin.

41) A mathematician helped develop the calculations for orbital navigation and space rendezvous in several space programs. Does the word *rendezvous* designate "an exploration," "a meeting," "a walk," or "a breathing apparatus"?
Answer: A meeting.

42) Spell the word for a kind of government that completes Woodrow Wilson's famous line from a 1917 speech to Congress: "The world must be made safe for _____."
Answer: D-E-M-O-C-R-A-C-Y.

43) What is the postal abbreviation for the state in which Camp David, the presidential retreat, is located?
Answer: MD (Maryland).

44) To reduce costs, Volkswagen, began a 4-day, 29-hour work week. About how much less would a worker earn at the same hourly wage in 29-hours than in the usual 40-hour week: 5%, 15%, 25%, or 35% less?
Answer: 25%.

45) On which of the following rivers were cruises downriver from Hungary canceled in 1999 because of the war in Yugoslavia, through which it flows: *Danube, Nile, Seine,* or *Tiber*? In song, it's known as "the beautiful blue _____."
Answer: Danube.

46) What is the name for the tremors following an earthquake?
Answer: Aftershocks.

47) Name the Polish-born American who is the only Yiddish writer to have won the Nobel Prize for literature. He is known for his book *The Fools of Chelm and Their History*, and his last name designates the occupation of Elvis Presley and Bruce Springsteen.
Answer: Isaac Bashevis Singer (he won the Nobel in 1978).

48) Which popular Christmas season plant was named after an American diplomat, Dr. Joel Roberts Poinsett?
Answer: Poinsettia.

49) If Paula had 54 rabbits and she sold 4/9 of them, how many rabbits did she have left?
Answer: 30.

50) From which country did William Seward, the U.S. secretary of state, acquire Alaska on March 30, 1867?
Answer: Russia.

1) DST, or daylight-saving time, first went into effect on March 31, 1918. To make the change to DST at 2:00 a.m. in the spring, a person should reset his clock to what time?
Answer: 3:00 a.m.

2) Harry Blackmun, age 85, announced in 1994 that he was resigning from which of the following: CIA, FBI, State Department, or Supreme Court?
Answer: Supreme Court.

3) An American diplomat was kidnapped in the nation of Yemen, which is bordered on the north by Saudi Arabia. On which continent is Yemen located?
Answer: Asia.

4) What is the geometric term for the oval space between the White House and the Washington Monument where the National Christmas Tree is placed?
Answer: Ellipse.

5) A strike of flight attendants against American Airlines ended when President Clinton persuaded both sides to agree to submit their dispute to an impartial person for settlement. Is such a process called *arbitration, connotation, interrogation,* or *respiration*?
Answer: Arbitration.

6) If a grain of sand becomes embedded in the mantle of a mollusk such as an oyster, the animal secretes layers of nacre to enclose the grain. What is the resulting object called?
Answer: A pearl.

7) Over 200 needlepoint Christmas stockings were hung at the White House in 1995 in keeping with a holiday theme based on which poem by Clement Moore that tells of "stockings hung by the chimney with care"?
Answer: 'Twas the Night Before Christmas (accept A Visit from St. Nicholas).

8) According to tradition, who founded Rome on April 21, 753 B.C.?
Answer: Romulus.

9) With a starting wage of $17 an hour for a full-time driver, how much does a new driver make in a 40-hour week?
Answer: $680 a week.

10) Which event took place in Boston on December 16, 1773, when patriots boarded British vessels and threw 342 chests into the harbor?
Answer: Boston Tea Party.

11) Of CEO, NATO, PLO, and FDA, which is a true acronym?
Answer: NATO (true acronyms are pronounced as words rather than as initials).

12) The 13th Amendment to the Constitution prohibited slavery in the U.S. Were those opposed to slavery called *Bolsheviks*, *abolitionists, chauvinists*, or *capitalists*?
Answer: Abolitionists.

13) Name Chicago Cubs player Sammy Sosa's home country, whose city of Santo Domingo, founded in 1496, is the Western Hemisphere's oldest European settlement. Its initials are D.R.
Answer: Dominican Republic.

14) To total 100%, what percentage of their allowances do American children spend on food according to an article reporting that they spend 29% on toys, 16% on movies and video games, 13% on clothing, and 6% on gifts and other items?
Answer: 36%.

15) On which continent are Rwanda and Burundi, the countries whose presidents were killed in 1994?
Answer: Africa (they were killed in a plane crash).

16) On March 30, 1842, Dr. Crawford Long of Georgia became the first medical person to use a drug to put someone to sleep during surgery. Is a drug that brings unconsciousness or insensitivity to pain called an *antiseptic, antibiotic, antitoxin,* or *anesthetic*?
Answer: Anesthetic.

17) A new series of Dover Thrift Editions of classic literature cost only a dollar each because no one has to pay for the right to reprint them. Is a payment made for the right to print a piece of writing called an *excise tax, royalty, stipend*, or *tariff*?
Answer: Royalty (works not requiring royalties are said to be in the public domain).

18) In 1999, Oklahoma City faced the very difficult task of disposing of tornado debris in a 19-mile-long strip. Identify the mythical hero whose name is the basis for an adjective meaning "very difficult" because of the 12 difficult labors he completed.
Answer: Hercules (a headline about this tornado read "Disposal of debris a *herculean* task").

19) Which of the following is the main artery that carries blood from the left ventricle of the heart to the body: *atrium*, *aorta*, *solar plexus*, or *femoral*?
Answer: Aorta.

20) A 1989 rebel attack on the government in the Philippines was stopped with U.S. help. Is a violent rebel attack on government called a *debut*, *cul de sac*, *coup*, or *coronary*?
Answer: Coup.

21) Muir Woods National Monument in California, named for American conservationist John Muir, is known for which kind of giant trees?
Answer: Redwoods (or giant sequoias).

22) Which state on the Delmarva Peninsula became the first to ratify the proposed U.S. Constitution on December 7, 1787? It borders Maryland, Pennsylvania, and New Jersey.
Answer: Delaware (known as the "First State of the Union").

23) Seattle's Space Needle from the 1962 World's Fair marks its 32nd anniversary on April 21. Is Seattle on the Chesapeake Bay, Puget Sound, Yukon River, or Columbia River?
Answer: Puget Sound.

24) If a rectangular piece of property measures 200 by 300 feet, what is the area of the property in square feet?
Answer: 60,000 square feet.

25) Philip Calvert and his wife were identified in 1994 as the mystery occupants of lead coffins buried in which state in the 1680s? Calvert was the fourth Colonial governor of this state bordering Delaware, Pennsylvania, and West Virginia.
Answer: Maryland.

26) Of the following gems, which are considered organic, or formed by living substances: garnet, jade, pearl, and coral?
Answer: Pearl and coral (the other 2 are classified as mineral substances).

27) Name the fictional Knight of La Mancha, created by Spanish author Cervantes. On his horse Rocinante, this character attacked windmills he perceived as monstrous giants.
Answer: Don Quixote.

28) Apple Computer co-creator Steve Job became an instant billionaire when prices for stock in his Pixar Animation Studios soared. Name Pixar's 1995 computer-generated hit movie featuring Buzz Light-Year.
Answer: *Toy Story*.

29) How much simple interest would you pay on a credit card balance of $2,400 at the end of one month with an annual rate of interest of 20%?
Answer: $40.00.

30) Which Middle Eastern city, considered the birthplace of 3 major religions—Judaism, Islam, and Christianity—did Great Britain capture on December 9, 1917?
Answer: Jerusalem.

31) A new $20 bill with high-tech features to thwart counterfeiters began circulating in the fall of 1998. Which President, nicknamed "Old Hickory," is pictured on this bill?
Answer: Andrew Jackson (his portrait is enlarged and off-center on the new bill).

32) Which city's business section was destroyed by an earthquake on April 18, 1906?
Answer: San Francisco's.

33) Despite a malfunction of one radar device on *Endeavour*, the other took its first images of the Upper Peninsula of which state in 1994?
Answer: Michigan (the only state with Upper and Lower peninsulas).

34) Give the equivalent for the following: liters in a kiloliter and centimeters in a meter.
Answer: 1,000 (liters) and 100 (centimeters).

35) Spell both of the following words which are homophones for the surnames of 2 of Gonzaga's basketball players in 1999: *calvary*, naming the hill where Christ was crucified, and *leisure*, meaning "free time."
Answer: C-A-L-V-A-R-Y and L-E-I-S-U-R-E.

36) Where in the human body are the sebaceous glands located?
Answer: In the skin (dermis).

37) In the Dewey Decimal system of filing books, is fiction shelved according to title, author, subject, or date of issue?
Answer: Author (alphabetically, by author's last name).

38) *Bibliothèque* and *biblioteca* are the French and Spanish words for "library." What does the Greek root *biblio-* used in these and in the English word *bibliography* mean?
Answer: Books.

39) Name the band of tissue that connects bones at the joints.
Answer: Ligament.

40) Which Caribbean country celebrates on January 1 the end of Spanish rule on this date in 1899? This island is known as the "Pearl of the Antilles."
Answer: Cuba.

41) Which library now located just east of the U.S. Capitol was established on April 24, 1800, and destroyed when the British burned the Capitol in 1814?
Answer: Library of Congress (it was reopened in the Capitol in 1815).

42) In which century was the Revolutionary War fought? Congress announced its end on April 19, 1783.
Answer: 18th century.

43) Mount Pinatubo in the Philippines erupted on June 11, 1991. Are the Philippines closer to Brazil, China, Saudi Arabia, or the U.S.?
Answer: China.

44) What would a single person with an income of $5,000 have paid in income tax when the first nation-wide income tax went into effect in 1914 with a 1% rate and a $3,000 exemption for single taxpayers?
Answer: $20.00 ($3,000 dollars is about $35,000 in today's dollars).

45) In 1994, President John F. Kennedy's wife was buried next to him at Arlington National Cemetery. Name this former first lady.
Answer: Jacqueline Kennedy (Onassis; she married Aristotle Onassis after her first husband's death).

46) During a 1993 total lunar eclipse, the moon entered the inner part of Earth's shadow about 11:40 EST. Is this shadow called the *aurora, orbit, solstice,* or *umbra*?
Answer: Umbra (the penumbra is the outer part of Earth's shadow).

47) *Don't Look Back* is a book about which baseball player who pitched in the Negro leagues for more than 20 years before being allowed to become the first black pitcher in the American League? His surname is a homophone for a leaf of a book.
Answer: Satchel Paige.

48) Name the golf tournament won in 1999 by Spain's Jose Maria Olazabal in Augusta, Georgia.
Answer: Masters.

49) What is the cost of 20 first class postage stamps at the current rate of 33¢ a stamp?
Answer: $6.60.

50) Cicero, a Roman orator, was ordered killed on December 7, 43 B.C., by members of the Second Triumvirate who would not tolerate his opposition. Spell *opposition*.
Answer: O-P-P-O-S-I-T-I-O-N.

1) Which Spanish phrase, meaning "the little girl," names the "cold water event" that occurs as the reversal of the conditions caused by El Niño, or the warming of waters?
Answer: La Niña.

2) Give President Clinton's middle name, which is also the surname of the President who made his home in Virginia at Monticello.
Answer: Jefferson (William Jefferson Clinton).

3) Which U.S. state is the second smallest state in area?
Answer: Delaware.

4) What is 500% of 30?
Answer: 150.

5) As requested in the will of Menachem Begin, the former Israeli prime minister who died in 1992, there were no funeral speeches praising him. Which term designates a formal speech of praise: *sermon*, *eulogy*, *benediction*, or *parable*?
Answer: Eulogy.

6) Doctors feel lymph nodes in the neck to check for the enlargement that indicates production of blood cells to fight infection. Which kind of blood cells fight infection?
Answer: White blood cells (called lymphocytes).

7) Identify the word *property* as a subject, direct object, indirect object, or appositive in the following: Many South Koreans once sold *property* in the belief that the world would end.
Answer: Direct object.

8) Which section of the band includes trumpets, trombones, and tubas?
Answer: Brass.

9) As of 1998, Nigeria, Africa's most populous country, had 110.5 million people. How many more people did the U.S. have with its population of 270.3 million?
Answer: 159.8 million.

10) In Stage 2 of the Middle East peace talks in the 1990s, Israel and its Arab neighbors held one-on-one meetings. Which prefix joined with *lateral* makes a word meaning "involving 2 sides or parties"?
Answer: *Bi-* (*bilateral* meetings were held).

11) Name the form of radar that has increased the time of warning for a tornado from negative 10-to-15 minutes, or after it has touched ground, to an average 12 minutes in advance since being introduced in the '90s. Its name begins with the letter *D*.
Answer: Doppler radar.

12) Movie star Charlton Heston, known for his role as Moses in *The Ten Commandments*, was inducted as president of the influential NRA in June 1999. What is the full name of the NRA?
Answer: National Rifle Association.

13) The great salt lake between Russia and Iran famous for its caviar is now threatened by pollution, overfishing, and poaching. Identify this lake, whose name begins with the letter *C* and ends with the word *sea*.
Answer: Caspian Sea (known for caviar from its beluga, osetra and sevruga sturgeons).

14) How many dimes can a person have if he has at least 1 nickel, 1 quarter, and 1 penny, and the total amount in coins is exactly $1?
Answer: 6 dimes ($1.00 minus 31¢ = 69¢).

15) In which South American nation, whose name begins with *V*, did President Carlos Perez survive a coup attempt in 1992?
Answer: Venezuela.

16) The over 100 joints in the human body are classified as *hinge joints*, *swivel joints*, *ball and socket joints*, and *suture joints*. Into which category do shoulder and hip joints fit?
Answer: Ball and socket joints.

17) Jefferson Davis officially became president of the Confederacy on February 18, 1861. Which word designates the ceremony to install a president?
Answer: Inauguration.

18) A political party formed by Soviet Jews in Israel bears the name *Da*, meaning "yes" in Russian. What is the Spanish word for "yes"?
Answer: *Sí*.

19) Steel is an alloy that results from combining carbon with what elemental metal?
Answer: Iron.

20) In which year was the Berlin Wall constructed? It was opened November 9, 1989, after 28 years.
Answer: 1961.

21) Which of the following designates a floating bridge: *monsoon, pontoon, latrine,* or *convoy*?
Answer: Pontoon.

22) Which state, nicknamed the "Land of Enchantment," was admitted to the Union on January 6, 1912? Albuquerque is its largest city.
Answer: New Mexico.

23) Name the present-day state where abolitionist John Brown was hanged at Charles Town in 1859. It was carved out of another by residents opposed to separation from the Union.
Answer: West Virginia.

24) What is the least common multiple of the numbers 12 and 16?
Answer: 48.

25) President Clinton once voiced support for Boris Yeltsin in his efforts to restore law and order after the Russian parliament building was stormed. What name identifies both this building and the Washington, D.C., building at 1600 Pennsylvania Avenue?
Answer: White House.

26) In which of the three states of matter—liquid, gas and solid—are the atoms the farthest apart?
Answer: Gas.

27) Name the author of such fairy tales as "The Ugly Duckling" and "The Red Shoes."
Answer: Hans Christian Andersen.

28) By presidential proclamation, January 13 is a memorial day for which songwriter, composer of "Camptown Races" and "My Old Kentucky Home." His surname also designates parents who care for children on a temporary basis without legal adoption.
Answer: Stephen Collins Foster.

29) What was the average ticket price for Steven Spielberg's film *Jurassic Park,* which broke the record for the highest-grossing premiere weekend when 10 million tickets were sold for $50.2 million?
Answer: $5.20.

30) Name the U.S. leader and the British leader who met in Casablanca, Morocco, on January 14, 1943, to decide the course of WWII.
Answer: Franklin Roosevelt and Winston Churchill.

31) Pete Sampras, who defeated Andre Agassi for his 3rd U.S. Open title in 1995, had 60 winning serves, including 24 that his opponent could not return. What is such a serve called?
Answer: Ace.

32) What is the official title of the Cabinet member who heads the U.S. Department of Justice?
Answer: Attorney general.

33) Name the U.S.'s tallest building, a 1,454-foot tower in Chicago.
Answer: Sears Tower.

34) What is the product of 3, 4, 5, and 6?
Answer: 360.

35) Which word designating a color and the substance of an elephant's tusks completes the name of the African country, _____ Coast?
Answer: Ivory.

36) Hundreds of thousands of people once fled from the city of Surat in India after an outbreak of an airborne form of bubonic plague claimed 51 lives and hospitalized hundreds. Spell *plague.*
Answer: P-L-A-G-U-E.

37) Which of the following verbs means "to get even for earlier actions": *renovate, revere, recuperate,* or *retaliate*?
Answer: Retaliate.

38) Procedures and forms in government and business that slow down progress are labeled as which color tape?
Answer: Red (tape).

39) By how many degrees Celsius do the boiling point and freezing point of H_2O differ?
Answer: 100 degrees.

40) Denmark granted Iceland self-government on December 1, 1918, though it remained under the Danish king until 1941. Is Iceland north, east, south, or west of Greenland?
Answer: East (Greenland is still a part of Denmark).

41) What word beginning with *N* designates addictive drugs that create a dreamlike state?
Answer: Narcotics.

42) U.S. Presidents give an annual address to the public about the U.S.'s condition. Complete its title: State of the _____.
Answer: (State of the) Union.

43) Environmentalists once filed a warning with the Forest Service protesting the logging of old-growth trees in California's national forests in which mountains named from the Spanish for "a saw"? The word *serrated* used to describe a knife with jagged points on its edge comes from the same Latin root.
Answer: Sierra Nevada (*sierra* means "a range of mountains with a notched profile").

44) If 600 sheets of paper make a stack 2 inches high, how many sheets are there in a pile 1/2 a foot high?
Answer: 1,800.

45) In 1993, the Associated Press became the first U.S. news organization to return to Vietnam full-time since the end of the war 18 years earlier. In which year did that war end?
Answer: 1975.

46) By how many degrees Fahrenheit do the boiling point and freezing point of H_2O differ?
Answer: 180 degrees (from 32 degrees to 212 degrees).

47) Richard Nixon held what he called at the time his "last" press conference on November 7, 1962, after losing a gubernatorial race, or a race to become governor, in California. Spell *gubernatorial*.
Answer: G-U-B-E-R-N-A-T-O-R-I-A-L.

48) Which holiday was observed on January 7, 1996, by the Russian Orthodox Church, with President Yeltsin and other dignitaries attending services at a newly rebuilt cathedral?
Answer: Christmas (the cathedral had been destroyed by Soviet dictator Josef Stalin).

49) What is the maximum number of quarters that can be given as change for a $5 bill used to pay for a $3.70 lunch?
Answer: 5.

50) Hostages John McCarthy and Edward Tracy were freed in August 1991 after almost 5 years in captivity in which country, whose capital is Beirut?
Answer: Lebanon.

1) What word meaning "business or trade" is represented by the first *C* in *ICC*, the initials of the federal agency that was abolished on New Year's Day 1996?
Answer: Commerce (the Interstate Commerce Commission was established in 1887).

2) "I am the last President of the United States," said President James Buchanan in December 1860, following which state's secession from the Union?
Answer: South Carolina's.

3) Spell the name of the state where a movie cameraman was rescued in 1992 from Kilauea, a volcano on the slope of Mauna Loa.
Answer: H-A-W-A-I-I.

4) If a rectangular solid block of stone 7 feet long and 5 feet wide has a volume of 140 cubic feet, what is its height?
Answer: 4 feet.

5) Name the national park along the border between North Carolina and Tennessee where hikers were ordered out in the wake of a devastating storm that hit the eastern U.S. in 1993.
Answer: Great Smoky Mountains (or Smoky Mountains).

6) With the Earth making one full rotation on its axis every 24 hours, how many degrees does it rotate in 4 hours?
Answer: 60 degrees.

7) Which work by which author includes the line: "I'm really a very good man; but I am a very bad Wizard"?
Answer: *The Wonderful Wizard of Oz* by L. Frank Baum.

8) Keiko, the killer whale star of the movie *Free Willie*, is being moved from a cramped pool in Mexico City to a new $7 million outdoor pool in Oregon. Which of the following does NOT describe Keiko: *invertebrate*, *mammal*, *amphibious*, or *aquatic*?
Answer: Amphibious.

9) How many years elapsed between the closing of the border between East and West Berlin on August 13, 1961, and the dismantling of the Berlin Wall, November 9, 1989?
Answer: 28 years.

10) Which world leader said in 1991, "The main work of my life is done. I did all I could. If others were in my place, they would have already gone. But I have managed . . . to push through the main ideas of perestroika"?
Answer: Mikhail Gorbachev.

11) In 1994, the Interior Department proposed removing from the endangered species list which majestic bird on the verge of extinction in the 1970s? It's the U.S.'s symbol.
Answer: Bald eagle.

12) In which year was the 19th Amendment extending the right to vote to women ratified: 1880, 1900, 1920, or 1940?
Answer: 1920.

13) Which landlocked Canadian province celebrates a festival of winter sports called "Jasper in January"? Its name completes the term _____ *clipper* used to designate a winter storm traveling from it southeast into the Great Plains, followed by cold polar air.
Answer: Alberta.

14) What is the greatest common factor of the numbers 48 and 16?
Answer: 16.

15) Fragments of a giant comet named for its co-discoverers slammed into Jupiter with great force in July 1994. Give the synonym for *cobbler* that completes its name: _____-Levy 9.
Answer: Shoemaker (also known as Comet 9).

16) In astronomy, what word beginning with R designates the circular motion of a planet or other body around another, for example, the Earth's travel around the Sun?
Answer: Revolution.

17) A genetically engineered tomato called Flavr Savr went on the market in the West and Midwest in 1994 after FDA approval. Spell *genetically*.
Answer: G-E-N-E-T-I-C-A-L-L-Y.

18) Vice President Gore was on crutches 5 months following surgery on a tendon linking the heel bone to the calf muscle. For which Greek hero is this tendon named?
Answer: Achilles (according to Greek myth, only his heel was vulnerable to injury).

19) A crested dinosaur from the Jurassic period representing a new genus and species was discovered in 1994 on which once-warm continent that was part of Gondwanaland?
Answer: Antarctica.

20) What word meaning "countries working together for a common goal" names the group of nations including the U.S. to whom Japan surrendered on September 2, 1945?
Answer: Allies (the Japanese informally surrendered on August 14).

21) By what name is a hurricane's center, a calm area about 20 miles in diameter, known?
Answer: Eye.

22) Name 2 of the 5 baseball players honored by monuments in Yankee Stadium, one of which was dedicated there in 1999 in memory of the recently deceased player known as the "Yankee Clipper."
Answer: Joe DiMaggio (as of 1999), Lou Gehrig, Mickey Mantle, Miller Huggins, Babe Ruth.

23) Name the largest freshwater lake wholly within the U.S. It separates a state into 2 parts.
Answer: Lake Michigan (Michigan has an upper and a lower peninsula).

24) If a person is paid 10% commission and sells $6,000 worth of merchandise, how much money does she earn in commissions?
Answer: $600.

25) An element used to make atomic bombs was seized in Germany in 1994 after allegedly being smuggled out of Russia. Identify this element whose name includes that of the planet farthest from the sun.
Answer: Plutonium.

26) According to scientists, the Earth is 4.5 billion years old. Which of the following is the equivalent of 4.5 billion: 45 million; 450 million; 4,500 million; or 45,000 million?
Answer: 4,500 million.

27) Spell *oppressors*, meaning "those who control by force."
Answer: O-P-P-R-E-S-S-O-R-S.

28) Some questioned why the FBI did not take more seriously David Koresh's talk of images of "fire mixed with blood" in the last book of the Bible. Name this book.
Answer: Revelation (also known as The Apocalypse).

29) Baseball's 1994 strike halted several players' shots at records, including San Diego's Tony Gwynn. What is the batting average for a player who has been at bat 20 times and has 7 hits?
Answer: .350 (7 divided by 20).

30) Name the Icelandic explorer credited with discovering North America in A.D. 1000.
Answer: Leif Eriksson (Ericson).

31) What is the name for a crab that lives in the shell of a mollusk? Its name also designates a person who lives alone without contact with other people.
Answer: Hermit crab.

32) The U.S.'s first fully automated privately-built road requiring a fee for travel on it opened in California in 1996. Spell the word that designates "a fee paid for highway travel."
Answer: T-O-L-L (the road was built to ease traffic congestion in Orange County).

33) Texas had its driest summer ever in 1934, when the southern Great Plains entered a period of excessive dryness. Complete the term _____ *Bowl* used to name the vast dry area of that time.
Answer: Dust Bowl.

34) The U.S. won the gold medal in the 12th World Championship of Basketball. How many points did they score with their 107 3-point baskets in the tournament?
Answer: 321 (U.S., represented by Dream Team II, defeated all 8 opponents).

35) Director Stephen Spielberg, talk-show host Oprah Winfrey, and the dinosaur Barney were 1993-94's 3 best-paid entertainers. What is their total take, with earnings of $335 million, $105 million, and $84 million respectively?
Answer: $524 million.

36) Which vitamin found in citrus fruits did the late Linus Pauling, a Nobel Prize winner in chemistry, recommend in large doses as a preventive for colds, cancer, and other ills?
Answer: Vitamin C (he also won the Nobel Peace Prize, in 1962).

37) What word beginning with *E* means "to remove all the people from an area"?
Answer: Evacuate.

38) Give a synonym for Quakers that completes the name of the school Chelsea Clinton attended: Sidwell _____ School.
Answer: Friends.

39) O.J. Simpson's blood matched that found at the murder scene according to genetic analysis. Is such testing known as AARP, RNA, DNA, or RAM analysis?
Answer: DNA (stands for *d*eoxyribo*n*ucleic *a*cid).

40) Name the English town that is the headquarters for global timekeeping. Its name contains the name of a color.
Answer: Greenwich.

41) Identify the Crustacean that in its attempt to find a mate waves the larger of its 2 front claws around, giving the appearance of a violinist using a bow. It can tunnel a foot or more into the sand.
Answer: Fiddler crab.

42) The Battle of Saratoga (or Freeman's Farm) in New York on September 19, 1777, was one of the first of 2 battles of the same name that marked a turning point of which war?
Answer: American Revolution (Revolutionary War).

43) Based on evidence that the Ucayali River is its true source, a research team now says the Amazon is longer than the Nile River. On which continent is the Amazon River?
Answer: South America.

44) If the zones of a target are worth 10, 25, and 50 points each, what is the maximum number of times a person who scores 425 points could have hit the bull's eye?
Answer: 8 times.

45) Haiti's military leaders agreed in 1994 to give up power after meeting with Sen. Sam Nunn, Gen. Colin Powell, and which former U.S. President sent by President Clinton?
Answer: Jimmy Carter.

46) Because of the light it provides for gathering crops, the full moon nearest the autumnal equinox is often named with which word beginning with *H* for "ingathering or reaping"?
Answer: Harvest.

47) The musical show *Parade* is based on the 1915 *lynching* of Leo Frank, a Jewish businessman, in what some say was the U.S.'s worst act of *prejudice* against Jews. Spell both *lynching* and *prejudice*.
Answer: L-Y-N-C-H-I-N-G and P-R-E-J-U-D-I-C-E.

48) According to the National Society of Film Critics, the best 1995 movie was about a porcine animal who herds sheep. What kind of animal is described as *porcine*?
Answer: Pig (*Babe* is the film).

49) In which year did the Lewis and Clark expedition depart from St. Louis? They returned on September 23, 1806, after an absence of 2 years, 4 months, and 10 days.
Answer: 1804 (on May 14, 1804).

50) Former President Carter has been nominated for the Nobel
     Peace Prize several times since he helped negotiate peace
     between Israel and Egypt in 1978. Spell the verb *negotiate*.
     Answer: **N-E-G-O-T-I-A-T-E.**

1) The U.S.S. *Constitution* was launched on September 20, 1797, in Boston, where it is now permanently docked. Which metal, represented by Fe, is named in its nickname?
Answer: Iron ("Old Ironsides").

2) Which word completes the title "I Have a _____" for the speech Dr. Martin Luther King Jr. delivered during a march on Washington on August 28, 1963?
Answer: Dream.

3) The U.S. Military Academy was founded on March 16, 1802, at West Point, New York, on which river?
Answer: Hudson River.

4) What mixed number in reduced form results from adding 5/6 to 2/3?
Answer: $1\frac{1}{2}$.

5) What word beginning with *C* designates "an alliance between various groups" and completes the name of the group made up of conservative Christians called Christian _____?
Answer: (Christian) Coalition.

6) Name the central shaft that turns in a wheel to make it rotate. It resembles the word for the central shaft on which the Earth turns.
Answer: Axle.

7) What is the silent consonant in *coup*, meaning "a small group's sudden overthrow of a government"?
Answer: *P* (*coup*, short for *coup d'état*).

8) Is the sousaphone a *woodwind*, *brass*, *stringed*, or *percussion* instrument?
Answer: Brass.

9) A map's key shows that 1 inch represents 70 miles. If 2 cities are 350 miles apart, how many inches apart will they be on the map?
Answer: 5 inches.

10) Of *suffrage*, *aggression*, or *emancipation*, which completes the following: Japan plans to spend about $1 billion from 1994 to 2004 to make amends for its _____ in WWII?
Answer: Aggression.

11) Actress Jessica Tandy won a 1948 Tony, a 1988 Emmy, and a 1989 Oscar. Of the Tony, Emmy, and Oscar, which is awarded for a TV performance?
Answer: Emmy (the Tony is for stage; the Oscar for film).

12) Name the African American appointed as a Supreme Court justice in 1991, making him the 2nd African American to serve on the Court. His surname also names Jesus' apostle known as "Doubting ____."
Answer: Clarence Thomas.

13) Boutros Boutros-Ghali, a former secretary-general of the U.N., is from Egypt. Give the capital of his country.
Answer: Cairo (Ghali is the first African in this position).

14) What improper fraction results from adding 3/4 to 1/2?
Answer: 5/4.

15) The 38,000 pairs of empty shoes placed around the Capitol Reflecting Pool in 1994 represented those who died each year from what cause that the Brady Bill was passed to combat?
Answer: Guns (Brady Bill is a gun control measure).

16) What word designates the force that slows action when 2 surfaces come in contact with each other? Changing one of its vowels results in a math term for "part of a whole."
Answer: Friction.

17) French public schools once banned head scarves, worn mostly by Arab and Turkish immigrant girls who practice the Muslim religion. Spell the plural of *scarf*.
Answer: S-C-A-R-V-E-S.

18) A *Frank and Ernest* cartoon showed the Earth complaining that it didn't mind those walking on top but really objected to the *spelunkers*. What are *spelunkers*?
Answer: Cave explorers.

19) The $7 million jet pack used by astronauts making the 7th and 8th free spacewalks weighed 83 pounds less in space than it did on Earth. How much did it weigh on Earth?
Answer: 83 pounds (it, like everything else, weighed nothing in space).

20) Which number completes French leader Georges Clemenceau's alleged statement about Woodrow Wilson's Fourteen Points for a peace settlement after WWI, "Even God Almighty has only ___ points"?
Answer: 10 (referring to the Ten Commandments).

21) Identify the thinking machine that became operational on January 12, 1992, in the movie *2001: A Space Odyssey*. This machine's 3-letter name can be found by identifying the letters that precede those in the name IBM.
Answer: HAL.

22) Shawnee Indian chief Tecumseh was killed in the Battle of the Thames on October 5, 1813, in Canada about 60 miles east of which Michigan city known as "Motor City"?
Answer: Detroit (Michigan).

23) In which state, known for its cliff dwellings built by the ancestors of the Pueblo Indians between A.D. 1000 and 1300, was Super Bowl XXX played at Sun Devil Stadium in Tempe?
Answer: Arizona.

24) When the baseball strike could not be settled in 1994, the World Series was cancelled for the first time since the year MCMIV in Roman numerals. How many years earlier was that?
Answer: 90 years.

25) In 1991, in which country did the emir push a lever to stop the flow of the country's last oil fire?
Answer: Kuwait.

26) In 1992, Candidate Bill Clinton followed doctor's orders to rest his vocal cords for five days. Are the vocal cords located in the *cerebellum, larynx, spleen*, or *esophagus*?
Answer: Larynx.

27) Robin Williams' film *What Dreams May Come* echoes a Greek myth of a husband pursuing his wife, Eurydice, in the afterlife. Which of the following names this husband who charms Hades with his music: *Cerberus, Daedalus, Orpheus*, or *Prometheus*?
Answer: Orpheus.

28) Which colors complete the following common metaphors used in a *Frank and Ernest* cartoon describing a "colorful" couple: _____ *with envy* and _____ *with rage*?
Answer: Green (with envy) and purple (with rage).

29) What is the decimal equivalent of 3/5?
     Answer: 0.6.

30) What name beginning with *P* designates the area also known
     as the Holy Land? The League of Nations put this area under
     Great Britain's control on September 29, 1923.
     **Answer: Palestine (parts of modern Israel, Jordan,
     and Egypt).**

31) Which of the following do Japanese do to greet each other:
     press fists together, kiss 3 times on the cheeks, bow from the
     waist, or nod the head while bending the knees?
     Answer: Bow from the waist.

32) In which state was America's bloodiest one-day battle fought at
     Antietam on September 17, 1862, when Lee met McClellan?
     This state is the home of Fort McHenry.
     **Answer: Maryland (Antietam is also called Sharps-
     burg).**

33) Which Northwestern state along with Idaho was hit with fires
     in 1991, with the largest occurring near Spokane?
     Answer: Washington.

34) If a train traveling at a constant speed of 30 mph takes 25
     hours to travel from Chicago to New York, how fast must the
     train travel to make the trip in 15 hours?
     Answer: 50 mph.

35) Which country, bordered by Guatemala and Nicaragua, was
     pounded by Hurricane Mitch in late 1998, leaving several
     thousand people dead and some 200 villages without power?
     Its name begins with the letter *H*.
     **Answer: Honduras (up to 1,500 died when flooding
     caused a mudslide in Nicaragua).**

36) Give the name for the building blocks that make up all living
     matter.
     Answer: Cells.

37) The doll Barbie is the subject of a new book tracing her roles
     from her birth in postwar Germany. What is the word for "the
     life story of someone other than the author"?
     **Answer: Biography (the book is entitled *The
     Unauthorized Biography of a Real Doll*).**

38) Name the architect of St. Peter's in Rome, who also sculpted
     David and *The Pietà*. His name contains the word for a spiri-
     tual being pictured in art with wings and a halo.
     Answer: Michelangelo (Buonarroti).

39) What is the chemical name for the compound whose solid form, commonly called dry ice, is often used to create the impression of fog or steam in stage plays?
Answer: Carbon dioxide (CO_2).

40) From which U.S. city to which European one did Charles Lindbergh make the first solo trans-Atlantic flight on May 20-21, 1927?
Answer: From New York to Paris.

41) What word completes the term _____ *egg* meaning "money set aside for future use"? The term completes the title of an investment guide by a group of older women.
Answer: Nest (*Beardstown Ladies' Stitch-in-Time Guide to Growing Your Nest Egg*).

42) Name the January 22, 1973, Supreme Court case that struck down laws restricting abortions during the first 3 months of pregnancy.
Answer: *Roe v. Wade*.

43) Which tunnel under the Hudson River between New York City and Jersey City, New Jersey, was completed in November 1927? It bears the name of a province of the Netherlands.
Answer: Holland Tunnel (there are 7 of these tunnels today).

44) Find the arithmetic mean of the following data set: 4, 5, 9, 4, 1, 10, 5, 1, 6.
Answer: 5.

45) In which European capital built on 7 hills did President Bush and 15 other NATO leaders attend a summit in 1991?
Answer: Rome.

46) In 1994, researchers identified a hereditary unit believed to cause breast cancer. What is the term for the inherited unit in a chromosome that determines a trait in an organism?
Answer: Gene (the newly found gene is called BRCA1, for Breast Cancer 1 gene).

47) In 1999, an earthquake in northern India near the Chinese border left the main road into the area blocked by boulders, earth, and other debris. Spell both *boulders* and *debris*.
Answer: B-O-U-L-D-E-R-S and D-E-B-R-I-S.

48) Minnesota Fats was made famous by a 1961 movie about his life as a pool player. A person skilled in pool who pretends he's inexperienced in order to win money is known as what kind of carnivorous fish?
Answer: Shark.

49) With an exchange rate of 7 kroner per dollar, what was the approximate dollar cost of a McDonald's hamburger, fries, and drink costing 50 kroner in Lillehammer, Norway, the site of the 1994 Winter Olympics?
Answer: $7.

50) Hungary declared independence on October 23, 1989, thirty-three years after Russian troops crushed a revolt against Soviet rule. In which year did that revolt occur?
Answer: 1956.

1) Is an Alpine home with a sloping roof known as an *adobe*, a *chalet*, a *citadel*, or a *monastery*?
   Answer: Chalet.

2) How many years elapsed between the 1919 ratification of the 18th Amendment prohibiting the manufacture and sale of liquor and the 21st Amendment of 1933 that repealed it?
   Answer: 14 years.

3) Which of the following is the capital of Hungary: Budapest, Prague, Bonn, or Copenhagen?
   Answer: Budapest.

4) Find the modes of the following data set: 4, 5, 9, 4, 1, 10, 5, 1, 3.
   Answer: 1, 4, 5 (must have all three).

5) In 1994, after a visit to assess diplomatic relations, 5 U.S. senators urged the President to lift the 20-year-old trade embargo against Vietnam. Spell *assess*, meaning "to evaluate."
   Answer: A-S-S-E-S-S.

6) The park Congress created in Montana in 1910 is named for the more than 50 sliding fields of ice within it. Complete its name: _____ National Park.
   Answer: Glacier (National Park).

7) On January 3, 1876, the first free kindergarten in the U.S. opened in Massachusetts. Spell *kindergarten*.
   Answer: K-I-N-D-E-R-G-A-R-T-E-N.

8) Frank Yankoric, who in 1986 won the first Grammy awarded for the polka, just died at age 83. Name the keyboard instrument with bellows that is linked with the polka.
   Answer: Accordion.

9) What is the value of the expression 2 to the 3rd power?
   Answer: 8.

10) Identify the Irish estate manager from whose name came the word for "refusing to do business with as a means of protest." His name contains a word for "a young male."
    Answer: Charles C. Boycott (his tenants carried out a boycott).

11) In which year—1841, '51, '61, or '71—did Mrs. O'Leary's cow allegedly cause the October 8 fire that destroyed a large part of Chicago about 6 years after the Civil War?
Answer: 1871 (with the loss of about 300 lives).

12) Which U.S. President did Vice President Al Gore once quote on a trip to Russia when he told Russian citizens that "the only thing that is necessary for evil to triumph is for good men to do nothing"? He held the presidency from 1861 to 1865.
Answer: Abraham Lincoln.

13) In which state are the Badger State Winter Games held? It borders Lakes Superior and Michigan.
Answer: Wisconsin.

14) If the base of a cube has an area of 36 inches, what is the volume of the cube?
Answer: 216 cubic inches.

15) A Bosnian girl whose diary about the war in Sarajevo became a best-seller in France says she hoped many times she would not suffer the same fate of which girl who kept a diary during WWII and died in a Nazi death camp? Her surname means "open and honest."
Answer: Anne Frank (the French evacuated Zlata Filipovic and her parents).

16) Niels Bohr of Denmark won a 1922 Nobel for research on atoms and their radiations. In which field, the science of matter, energy, and motion, did he win the award?
Answer: Physics.

17) Madeleine L'Engle's young adult novel *Troubling A Star* is a story of intrigue set in the Antarctic. Name her earlier novel in which Mrs. Whatsit is a character.
Answer: *A Wrinkle in Time*.

18) Brass instruments make up one of the 3 sections of a marching band. Name either of the other 2 instrumental sections.
Answer: Percussion or Woodwinds.

19) Former tennis star Vitas Gerulaitis was killed by the fumes emitted from a faulty propane heater. Name the toxic agent in these fumes.
Answer: Carbon monoxide.

20) In which country did a poisonous gas leak at a Union Carbide plant in Bhopal in December 1984 kill more than 2,000? Its capital is New Delhi.
Answer: India.

21) Name either the rock singer on the 1993 stamp that holds the record for sales with 124 million or the blonde movie star on 1995's top-selling stamp, with 46.3 million.
Answer: Elvis Presley or Marilyn Monroe, respectively.

22) On which day is Memorial Day, or Decoration Day, now celebrated as a legal holiday?
Answer: Last Monday in May (it dates from the Civil War).

23) The U.N. once administered Cambodia for 18 months following the signing of a peace agreement among its 4 warring factions. On which continent is Cambodia?
Answer: Asia.

24) According to the Census Bureau, U.S. population rose by 2.7 million in 1993, bringing the total population to about how many million, or in Roman numerals CCLX million?
Answer: 260 million people.

25) Gary, Indiana, was once named "murder capital" of the U.S. with 85.6 homicides per 100,000 residents. On which Great Lake is it located?
Answer: Lake Michigan.

26) According to a University of Montreal study, even a small amount of which stimulant found in coffee, tea, and sodas can cause a miscarriage or retard a baby's growth?
Answer: Caffeine.

27) Name the area of New York City around 125th Avenue where African-American poet Langston Hughes established himself as a writer in the 1920s. Its name begins with *H*.
Answer: Harlem.

28) Is a piano a *woodwind*, *brass*, *percussion*, or *stringed* instrument?
Answer: Stringed instrument.

29) A herd of 50 elephants once moved toward Calcutta, a city of 10 million. If the elephants had continued to move at the same rate of about 180 miles a week, within how many days would they have reached Calcutta, a distance of 60 miles?
Answer: 3 days (at a rate of 26 miles a day, in 2.3 days).

30) Which country invaded which country on August 2, 1990?
Answer: Iraq invaded Kuwait.

31) Name the non-aquatic mammals that scientists have determined are 2 to 3 times more efficient at locating objects by reflected sound than are the Navy's sonar systems. They are often found living in belfries.
Answer: Bats.

32) Name the first U.S. President to visit Moscow, doing so in 1972. He graduated from Whittier College, a Quaker school in California.
Answer: Richard Nixon.

33) In which state, admitted to the Union in 1959, is the annual Iditarod Trail Sled Dog Race held?
Answer: Alaska (from Anchorage to Nome, 1,159 miles away).

34) At the end of 1993, what was the cost of a Dell computer that cost 18% less than the $2,500 it had cost at the end of 1992?
Answer: $2,050.

35) Name the leader who took control of the Kremlin's nuclear weapons following Mikhail Gorbachev's resignation speech in 1991.
Answer: Boris Yeltsin.

36) To which of the 3 classes of rock does clay belong?
Answer: Sedimentary.

37) What name from the Bible completes the title of the whimsical Dr. Seuss book _____ *Katz and His Coat of Many Colors*?
Answer: Joseph (who is known for his coat of many colors).

38) Complete the title of the Aesop fable "The Ant and the _____," which concerns preparation for the future and is the basis for Disney and Pixar's new animated film *A Bug's Life*.
Answer: "(The Ant and the) Grasshopper."

39) Foods rich in which vitamin—A, B, C, or D—are important for preventing and curing scurvy?
Answer: Vitamin C (ascorbic acid).

40) In the 1990s, which country refused to permit a remake of the film *Anna and the King of Siam* because of what it says are historical inaccuracies about its king in the film? Its capital is Bangkok.
Answer: Thailand (formerly known as Siam).

41) A University of North Carolina women's soccer team set a U.S. record with its 89 consecutive wins. How many players does a soccer team put on the field to start a game?
Answer: 11.

42) On January 10, 1776, Thomas Paine published his pamphlet *Common Sense* advocating freedom from Britain. Spell *pamphlet*.
Answer: P-A-M-P-H-L-E-T.

43) On which continent is Libya, whose intelligence agents have been charged with planting the bomb that destroyed Pan Am Flight 103 in 1988?
Answer: Africa.

44) What is the total number of years represented by a golden anniversary, a bicentennial, and a quincentennial?
Answer: 750 years (50 plus 200 plus 500).

45) Name the creatures aboard *Endeavour* that were the first, other than insects, to be fertilized and born in space. These amphibious creatures change in form as they mature.
Answer: Tadpoles (or frogs).

46) A satellite was deployed from *Discovery* in 1991 to study the layer of the upper atmosphere that protects the earth from ultraviolet rays. Name this layer.
Answer: Ozone layer.

47) Spell the word beginning with the letter *C* that names the coloring and shape an insect or other animal has, or takes on, as a means of blending into the environment.
Answer: C-A-M-O-U-F-L-A-G-E.

48) Financier Andrew Carnegie provided funds for about 2,800 libraries. Is one who uses his own money for the public good a *miser*, an *egotist*, an *optimist*, or a *philanthropist*?
Answer: Philanthropist.

49) Janet got 32 questions right on a test and received a grade of 80%. If the questions were of equal value, how many questions were on the test?
Answer: 40.

50) Which country invaded Poland on September 1, 1939, to start World War II?
Answer: Germany.

1) In 1994, facing its worst ever water shortage, Puerto Rico had the National Guard set up desalination equipment. What does desalination equipment remove from water?
Answer: Salt.

2) Alabama withdrew from the Union on January 11, 1861. Spell the word beginning with *S* that means "to withdraw from a political union."
Answer: S-E-C-E-D-E.

3) In which sea did more than 900 people drown in 1994 when a ferry en route from Estonia to Sweden sank: the Baltic, Caribbean, Mediterranean, or Red?
Answer: Baltic Sea.

4) Are geometric figures that have the same shape but not the same size said to be *congruent, isosceles, parallel*, or *similar*?
Answer: Similar.

5) Yasir Arafat, Palestine's first elected president, is called *rais*, the word for "president" in the language spoken by Palestinians, namely which of the following: Arabic, Hebrew, French, or Greek?
Answer: Arabic.

6) Which sedimentary rock, formed by weathering and the decomposition of rock, is used to manufacture brick, glass, cement, and concrete?
Answer: Sand.

7) To combat water shortage, Puerto Rico opened a pipeline to bring water from the rainy western part of the island to the rest of the country. What Latin prefix for "water" is added to *duct* to name such a pipeline?
Answer: *Aqua- (aqueduct).*

8) Complete the following lines from the verses of a well-known folk song: "Oh, give me a home where the buffalo roam, / Where the deer and the _____ play."
Answer: Antelope (from the song "Home on the Range").

9) Approximately how many kilometers are there in one mile?
Answer: 1.6 kilometers.

10) Germany was called before the U.N. Human Rights Commission in the 1990s for the first time to answer complaints about its failure to halt Nazi violence against foreigners. What prefix is attached to Nazi to mean "new": *ante-*, *neo*, *pre-*, or *ortho-*?
Answer: *Neo-* (neo-Nazi).

11) In 1993, the Atlanta Braves' Greg Maddux became the first National League player to win back-to-back Cy Young awards since the 1960s. What position does a Cy Young honor?
Answer: Pitcher.

12) Democrats wanted to make Georgia the first Southern state to vote on 1992 presidential candidates. What term names an election to select the candidates who will run for office?
Answer: Primary (election).

13) Which of the following names do the Japanese use for their nation: Nippon, Canaan, Fuji, or Siam?
Answer: Nippon (it means "land of the rising sun").

14) Approximately what fraction of the $300 million of federal emergency home-heating aid given to 23 states in one winter did Michigan receive with its allotment of $48.8 million?
Answer: 1/6.

15) Name the Walt Disney movie that premiered on 4 giant movie screens before 100,000 people at New York's Central Park in 1995. Its main character is Powhatan's daughter.
Answer: *Pocahontas*.

16) Identify the rock formed by the metamorphism of limestone.
Answer: Marble.

17) On October 8, 1918, Corporal Alvin York won the Medal of Honor for capturing a hill and 132 enemy soldiers in France in World War I. Spell both *medal*, meaning "award," and *meddle*, meaning "to interfere."
Answer: M-E-D-A-L and M-E-D-D-L-E.

18) Give the surname of the architect featured on a PBS special offering a tour of his designs, such as "Falling Water," a home outside Pittsburgh built on a rock over a waterfall. The Ohio brothers credited with the first plane flight share this surname.
Answer: (Frank Lloyd) Wright.

19) What name is given to the temporary set of teeth sometimes called milk teeth or baby teeth?
Answer: Deciduous teeth (accept primary or temporary teeth).

20) Complete the name of the country, the People's Republic of
_____, which President Nixon visited in 1972, even though it
was not diplomatically recognized by the U.S.
Answer: China (Nixon arrived there on February 21).

21) Many companies misspelled *millennium* in their rush to get
the word on their products in 1999. Spell *millennium*.
Answer: M-I-L-L-E-N-N-I-U-M.

22) The Treaty of Paris ending the American Revolutionary War
was approved by the Continental Congress on January 14,
1784. What word means "to give formal approval to, usually by
means of a vote": *acquiesce, corroborate, nullify*, or *ratify*?
Answer: Ratify.

23) Which city is called "Music City, U.S.A." because of its role as
a recording center for country music and the 70-year-old Grand
Ole Opry radio show?
Answer: Nashville (Tennessee).

24) In reduced terms, what is the probability of drawing a red marble
out of a bag with 3 green, 2 red, 5 yellow, and 6 blue marbles?
Answer: 1/8 (2/16 reduced to 1/8).

25) Indian rebels once held talks with the Mexican government in
one of the 4 oldest temples in the Americas. What word beginning with *C* designates such a large church?
**Answer: Cathedral (this cathedral was San Cristobal
de las Casas).**

26) Name the coarse-grained, hard igneous rock of which Georgia's
Stone Mountain with its carving of Civil War figures is made.
Answer: Granite.

27) Name the heroine of a sequel whose first line is, "This will be
over soon, and then I can go home to Tara."
**Answer: Scarlett O'Hara (in sequel to *Gone With the
Wind*).**

28) Which baseball great, nicknamed "the Great Bambino," was
born in Baltimore, Maryland, on February 6, 1895? He hit 714
homeruns in 22 major league seasons.
Answer: George Herman "Babe" Ruth.

29) What is the remainder when 120 is divided by 13?
Answer: 3.

30) Czechoslovakia was created in a bloodless revolution in Prague
on October 28, 1918, and was divided into 2 parts in 1993.
Name the people of either of the 2 new countries.
Answer: Czechs or Slovaks.

31) Which college football team, nicknamed the "Seminoles," was voted national champion after defeating Nebraska 18-16 in the Federal Express Orange Bowl in 1994?
    Answer: Florida State.

32) In which state did President Franklin Roosevelt die at the Little White House in Warm Springs on April 12, 1945? Its capital city hosted the Summer Olympics in 1996.
    Answer: Georgia.

33) Ecuador once suspended new licenses for tourist operations in an effort to protect the Galapagos Islands. Do these Pacific Ocean islands lie east, west, north, or south of Ecuador?
    Answer: West.

34) Find the area of a rhombus whose base is 12 inches and whose corresponding altitude is 8 inches.
    Answer: 96 square inches.

35) San Franciscans were once dismayed by a thus far unexplained green rainfall described as iridescent. Spell *iridescent*, meaning "with colors like a rainbow."
    Answer: I-R-I-D-E-S-C-E-N-T (health inspector suspects it came from a plane).

36) Which of the following words is used to describe slightly salty water such as that found in marshes near the sea: *brackish*, *carbonated*, *placid*, or *variegated*?
    Answer: Brackish.

37) South African President Nelson Mandela once publicly feuded with Nobel Peace Prize winner Desmond Tutu over salary increases for the new parliament. What prefix, meaning "highest," is used with *bishop* to designate Tutu's title as head of the Anglican Church in South Africa?
    Answer: *Arch-* (archbishop).

38) For the first time since the Palestinian uprising began 6 years ago, thousands of tourists in 1994 celebrated Christmas in which city believed to be the site of Jesus' birth?
    Answer: Bethlehem.

39) Which explosive brought great wealth to Swedish-born chemist Alfred Nobel, the founder of the Nobel prizes?
    Answer: Dynamite.

40) By presidential proclamation the 2nd Monday in October is celebrated as Christopher Columbus Day. On which day in which year did Columbus land in the New World?
    Answer: October 12, 1492.

41) Canadian James Naismith, organized the first official basketball game on January 20, 1892, in Massachusetts. How many players are in a basketball team's starting lineup?
Answer: 5.

42) Name the captain of the *Bonhomme Richard,* who in a battle with the *Serapis* on September 23, 1779, said, "I have not yet begun to fight." His initials are J.P.J.
Answer: John Paul Jones.

43) Giuseppe Palunelli followed an annual New Year's Day tradition of leaping from Rome's Cavour Bridge into which river: the Nile, Rhine, Thames, or Tiber?
Answer: Tiber River.

44) If the base of a cube has an area of 36 square inches, what is the volume of the cube?
Answer: 216 cubic inches.

45) Ford Motor Co. once recalled its new Contour and Mercury Mystique sedans because of the danger of having fuel vapors burst into flames. What word beginning with *I* means "to burst into flames"?
Answer: Ignite.

46) What percentage of the water on earth is found in the salty oceans: 67, 77, 87, or 97%?
Answer: 97%.

47) Give the verb in the following sentence: European scientists recently harnessed nuclear fusion for the first time.
Answer: *Harnessed.*

48) Who led the Mormons in their migration west from Illinois to a new "promised land" in Utah in 1846: Billy Graham, Brigham Young, Warren Christopher, or Richard Byrd?
Answer: Brigham Young (they departed from Nauvoo, Illinois, on February 10, 1846).

49) If a wheel rotates 12 times per minute, how many degrees does it rotate in 5 seconds?
Answer: 360 degrees.

50) Name the document on which King John placed his seal on June 15, 1215, at Runnymede, England, granting many rights to English nobles. Its initials are M.C.
Answer: Magna Carta.

1) The captain of one of the more than 35 crews left stranded at sea by ship owners who went bankrupt in the global financial crisis of the 90s said he was inspired to seek help in the U.S. after looking at its motto on a dollar bill. What is this motto?
Answer: In God we trust.

2) The cornerstone of the White House, the oldest public building in Washington, D.C., was laid in which year, 16 years after the signing of the Declaration of Independence?
Answer: 1792 (on October 12).

3) Albert Schweitzer established a hospital in Lambaréné, Gabon, in Africa in 1913. Name any of the other 4 African countries whose names begin with G.
Answer: The Gambia, Ghana, Guinea, and Guinea-Bissau.

4) About how many times his $69,843 CIA salary is the $540,000 price CIA agent and alleged traitor Aldrich Ames paid for his home?
Answer: About 8 times more (7.7 times).

5) Which royal titles were held by Kristin and Hakon, who lived about 800 years ago in Norway and became in 1994 the first human mascots in Olympic history when the Winter Olympics were held in Lillehammer, Norway?
Answer: Prince and princess.

6) In 1994, Chicago closed its schools because of cold weather for the first time ever when –21°F was recorded. Convert –21°F to Celsius, using the equation °C = 5/9 (°F – 32).
Answer: –29.4°C (the temperature broke a 1930 record of –16°F).

7) On October 2, 1872, how many days did Jules Verne's character Phileas Fogg bet it would take him to go around the world? The number equals 4 score.
Answer: 80 days (*Around the World in Eighty Days*).

8) The largest traveling exhibit in U.S. history, which visited 11 cities, was a celebration of the 150th anniversary of which Washington, D.C., museum?
Answer: Smithsonian Institution.

9) What fraction with a denominator of 21 is equivalent to 3/7?
Answer: 9/21.

10) In which city later renamed Leningrad did riots and strikes on March 9, 1917, mark the beginning of the Russian Revolution?
Answer: St. Petersburg.

11) In February 1926, historian Dr. Carter G. Woodson helped launch African-American History Month. Is the top academic degree in history a D.D.S., J.D., M.D., or Ph. D.?
Answer: Ph. D. (Doctor of Philosophy).

12) Name the President whose library is located in Independence, Missouri. His surname completes the name of the popular 1998 film *The* _____ *Show*, about a life scripted for TV.
Answer: Harry S Truman.

13) Which state whose name begins with *A* was the 48th state admitted to the Union, on February 14, 1912?
Answer: Arizona.

14) How old was Chelsea Clinton on her February 27 birthday in 1999? Her father was 52 at the time, and she was born when he was 33.
Answer: 19 years old.

15) Which federal agency that manages emergencies is quickly on hand to coordinate disaster relief: CIA, FEMA, HUD, or NASA?
Answer: FEMA (Federal Emergency Management Agency).

16) For every increase of 1 on the Richter scale, there is a tenfold increase in ground motion. How much more powerful is a 7.0 earthquake than a 5.0 one?
Answer: 100 times (a 6.0 earthquake is 10 times stronger than a 5.0 one).

17) On March 8, 1481, which English printer completed the translation of the first illustrated book printed in England: William Caxton, Robert Fulton, Johannes Gutenberg, or Cyrus McCormick?
Answer: William Caxton.

18) Dmitri Shostakovich dedicated his 1941 *Symphony No.7* to the city of Leningrad, now St. Petersburg, which was then under siege by the German army. Spell *symphony*.
Answer: S-Y-M-P-H-O-N-Y.

19) Name the two types of light sensitive receptor cells located in the retina of the eye.
Answer: Rods and cones.

20) Which war began with an invasion on June 25, 1950?
Answer: Korean War (armistice was signed on July 27, 1953).

21) On October 16, 1859, John Brown seized the U.S. arsenal at Harper's Ferry, Virginia, as part of a plan to free the nation's slaves. By definition, what is stored in an arsenal?
Answer: Weapons (Harpers Ferry is in present-day West Virginia).

22) Who became the youngest recipient of the Nobel Peace Prize on October 14, 1964? He donated his $54,000 prize to further the cause of the civil rights movement.
Answer: Martin Luther King Jr.

23) Which of the following designates a valley in the ocean: *reef*, *trench*, *atoll*, or *nadir*?
Answer: Trench (the Marianas Trench in the Pacific is the world's deepest trench).

24) In which decade was *Explorer I,*, the first successful U.S. satellite, launched on January 31? The exact year is represented by MCMLVIII in Roman numerals.
Answer: 1950s (1958; the U.S.S.R.'s *Sputnik* was launched in 1957).

25) The Supreme Court in 1996 let stand a $1.5 million damage award against 4 people who because of their religion let a boy die from diabetes rather than permit medical treatment for him. Are followers of this religion that opposes treatment by physicians known as Mormons, Christian Scientists, Muslims, or Unitarians?
Answer: Christian Scientists.

26) Which of the following accounts for the formation of most mountains: shifting of the plates beneath the Earth's surface, erosion produced by flowing water, impact from meteorites crashing into the Earth, or glacial movement across the land?
Answer: Shifting of the plates beneath the Earth's surface.

27) Complete the title of Margaret Wise Brown's best known work, *Goodnight* _____.
Answer: *Moon* (Leonard Marcus's 1992 biography features Brown).

28) American Express was once fined for illegally using Olympic insignia in advertising. How many rings appear in this official design?
Answer: 5.

29) If a person runs a mile in 4 minutes, how many miles will he run in 4 hours at the same pace?
Answer: 60.

30) Which country lost a disastrous battle to the British in Quebec, Canada, and surrendered on September 18, 1759?
Answer: France (battle was on the Plains of Abraham).

31) How many days are in a leap year on the Gregorian calendar first issued by the Pope in 1582 and now in current use?
Answer: 366 days (issued by Pope Gregory XIII on 2/24/1582).

32) To help raise money for the Victorian house in Canton, Ohio, that opened in 1998 as the First Ladies Library, the founding group commissioned a series of dessert plates signed on the back by the 6 living first ladies. Name 3 of the 6.
Answer: Lady Bird Johnson, Betty Ford, Rosalyn Carter, Nancy Reagan, Barbara Bush, and Hillary Rodham Clinton.

33) Prime Minister Shamir said in 1992 he was no longer bound to follow the 1978 peace accords signed by Israel and Egypt at the U.S. presidential retreat in Maryland. Name this retreat.
Answer: Camp David.

34) Give the result of dividing the number of *S*'s in *Mississippi* by the square root of 4.
Answer: 2.

35) Name 2 of the 3 countries that once cut short a round of peace talks with Israel because of the Hebron massacre. Their capitals are Damascus, Beirut, and Amman.
Answer: Syria, Lebanon, and Jordan, respectively.

36) Name the solid cylinders that go up and down in larger cylinders in an internal combustion engine used in an automobile.
Answer: Pistons.

37) Name the author of the works contained in the a 9-volume boxed set of authentic Sherlock Holmes stories.
Answer: Arthur Conan Doyle.

38) What word beginning with *E* names a picture or impression printed from a metal plate?
Answer: Etching.

39) Name the part of an auto's internal combustion engine where fuel and air are mixed.
Answer: Carburetor (accept fuel injection system).

40) Which country between Germany and Hungary did Hitler's Nazi troops invade on March 12, 1938? It is drained by the Danube River, and its capital is Vienna.
Answer: Austria.

41) Give the Spanish word for "saint," which appears in the U.S. name for Saint Nicholas, whose feast day is still celebrated by many European countries on December 6.
Answer: Santa (Claus; a variant of Dutch *Sinterklaas*).

42) In which state did the first atomic bomb explosion occur on July 16, 1945? It is bordered by Oklahoma and Texas.
Answer: New Mexico.

43) Name the Egyptian canal that opened in November 1869.
Answer: Suez Canal.

44) Give the result of dividing 3 times the *L*'s in *Philippines* by the square root of 9.
Answer: 1.

45) Which country, consisting of 4 main islands, hosted the 1998 Winter Olympic Games in Nagano?
Answer: Japan.

46) What prefix is used before the word *technology* to create a word meaning "technology that uses living things to process or change other materials"? This prefix means "life."
Answer: *Bio-* (biotechnology).

47) Identify the grammatical function of the noun *woman* in the following sentence: Shirley Chisholm was the first black *woman* to serve in the U.S. Congress.
Answer: Predicate nominative (subject complement).

48) Identify the Roman god of fire, for whom Charles Goodyear's process of making rubber stronger and more resistant to heat and cold was named.
Answer: Vulcan (the process is called vulcanization).

49) What is the surface area of a cube measuring 5 centimeters on each edge?
Answer: 150 square centimeters.

50) In which country did the names of thousands of people disappear from the country's history during the purges conducted by its leader Joseph Stalin?
Answer: Soviet Union.

1) Name the annual 7-day post-Christmas festival initiated in the U.S. in 1966 to celebrate the hopes, talents, and accomplishments of black Americans.
   Answer: Kwanzaa (Swahili for "first fruits"; about 18 million worldwide celebrate it).

2) Identify the biblical character whose name sounds like the acronym naming the National Oceanic and Atmospheric Administration, which dreamed up Doppler radar.
   Answer: Noah (the acronym is NOAA).

3) In which of the following did the euro actually first appear on December 31, 1998, since it lies farther east than the other 10 Euro-zone nations and is therefore an hour ahead of them: Finland, France, Germany, or Austria?
   Answer: Finland.

4) A piece of cheese weighed 1 pound and 8 ounces. How much did it cost at $1.20 a pound?
   Answer: $1.80.

5) Name the British monarch who marked the 47th anniversary of her coronation in 1999.
   Answer: Queen Elizabeth II.

6) Which planet, the 7th from the sun, became the first to be discovered with a telescope? It is known to have 5 large moons and 15 small ones, and was discovered by Sir William Herschel on March 13, 1781.
   Answer: Uranus.

7) The iron-ore rich Mesabi Range in Minnesota was discovered by surveyors on September 19, 1844. Spell *Minnesota*.
   Answer: M-I-N-N-E-S-O-T-A.

8) Which religion celebrates an 8-day feast called Chanukah, or the Feast of Lights in December?
   Answer: Judaism (Jewish).

9) What is the greatest common divisor of 12, 16, 36?
   Answer: 4.

10) In which year did the 2 Germanys become one on October 3?
    Answer: 1990.

11)   Which country did Jawaharlal Nehru serve as prime minister from 1947, when it became independent, until his death in 1964?
      Answer: India.

12)   In which state did the nation's first Vietnam War museum open in 1998, funded primarily by a donation from Atlantic City's casinos? It's known as the "Garden State."
      Answer: New Jersey.

13)   Which of the following names Japan's main island, where its capital, Tokyo, is located: Guam, Honshu, Mali, or Oahu?
      Answer: Honshu.

14)   Which of the following is nearest in value to 234 (567: 1,200; 12,000; or 120,000?
      Answer: 120,000.

15)   The U.N. once set a deadline for total withdrawal of its 6,200 peacekeepers from Mozambique in southeastern Africa. On which ocean does Mozambique lie?
      Answer: Indian Ocean.

16)   An architect who designs a concert hall or theater must be an expert in the study of sound and how it travels. What is this study called?
      Answer: Acoustics.

17)   Identify the legendary son of Launcelot (or Lancelot) whose name is used today to identify any young man with a pure heart.
      Answer: Sir Galahad.

18)   Which musical instrument was presented to President Clinton by the mayor of Dinant, Belgium, the hometown of its inventor?
      Answer: Saxophone (Adolphe Sax is the inventor).

19)   Who invented the incandescent light bulb on October 21, 1879?
      Answer: Thomas Edison.

20)   In which country bordered by Guatemala on the south did archaeologists just find a huge throne built about A.D. 760 by the Maya Indians?
      Answer: Mexico (the throne was found in the ruins of a temple at Palenque).

21)   What name is given to the 3rd Monday in February, the day of celebration for Lincoln's and Washington's birthdays?
      Answer: Presidents' Day.

22) Which black separatist leader was assassinated on February 21, 1965, in New York City? He became a Muslim while in prison and later became a Muslim minister.
Answer: Malcolm X.

23) Scientists have reported a fossil find of a 9-foot-long oviraptor, or dinosaur, that died while squatting on a nest of eggs, suggesting the dinosaurs' influence on bird brooding. In which Mongolian desert was this fossil found: Gobi, Mojave, Sahara, or Arabian?
Answer: Gobi Desert (the dinosaur died 70 million to 80 million years ago).

24) The birthday of Martin Luther King Jr. was first observed as a federal holiday on the 3rd Monday in January in 1986. Give the Roman numeral for 1986.
Answer: MCMLXXXVI.

25) Identify the labor union that in 1999 elected as president James P. Hoffa, son of its earlier president who mysteriously disappeared in 1975. Its members are involved in the trucking industry, and its name goes back to drivers of teams of harnessed animals.
Answer: Teamsters.

26) Name the SI unit used to measure the loudness of a sound. It is named after Alexander Graham Bell and is abbreviated as dB.
Answer: Decibel (hearing occurs at 0-10 dB and the pain threshold at about 140 dB).

27) What part of speech is *appeal* in the following? In response to the lowest blood supply level in its history, the Red Cross made its first national emergency appeal ever.
Answer: Noun (used as direct object).

28) In which country was composer Franz Shubert born? Two of its cities are Innsbruck and Salzburg.
Answer: Austria.

29) The Equal Rights Amendment passed by the Senate in 1972 was not ratified by the necessary 3/4 of the states. How many states had to approve it for it to become law?
Answer: 38 (the ERA was passed by the Senate on 3/22/1972).

30) Which city is policed by a force founded on September 29, 1829, and popularly referred to as Scotland Yard?
Answer: London.

31) The lost city of Ubar was located in 1992 because of pictures taken from which spacecraft that exploded in 1986?
Answer: *Challenger.*

32) At which Washington, D.C., memorial does a new exhibit commemorate events that have taken place there including Martin Luther King Jr.'s delivery of his 1963 "I Have a Dream" speech? This memorial honors an assassinated President.
Answer: **Lincoln Memorial.**

33) Identify the other state besides South Carolina whose capital is named for Christopher Columbus.
Answer: **Ohio (its capital is Columbus).**

34) What is the largest prime factor of 66?
Answer: **11.**

35) Iraq rejected the U.N.'s demand for cooperation with weapons inspectors. Is a final demand an *invocation*, *referendum*, *subpoena*, or *ultimatum*?
Answer: **Ultimatum.**

36) Name 2 of the 3 tiny bones in the ear that amplify the sounds and carry them across the middle ear. Their names also identify a mallet, a heavy block of iron on which metal is shaped by pounding, and a loop hung on a saddle to hold the rider's foot.
Answer: **Hammer, anvil, and stirrup.**

37) Name Louisa May Alcott's novel about the March sisters— Meg, Amy, Jo, and Beth.
Answer: *Little Women.*

38) Frederic Remington is known for his paintings and sculptures of cowboys and Indians. Spell *sculptures*.
Answer: **S-C-U-L-P-T-U-R-E-S.**

39) What does one call water with something dissolved in it?
Answer: **A solution.**

40) In which year was the United Nations established on October 24, two months after the Japanese surrender in WWII?
Answer: **1945.**

41) Which queen, whose name means "success," ruled for 63 years, making her the longest reigning British monarch?
Answer: **Queen Victoria (she ruled from 1837 to 1901).**

42) Richard Wagner's "Centennial Inaugural March" was first played at the nation's Centennial Exposition in Philadelphia in which year?
Answer: **1876 (Wagner received $5,000 for the march).**

43) Which Midwestern state was represented by Senator John Glenn, who on February 20, 1962, became the first American to orbit the earth? It is nicknamed "The Buckeye State."
Answer: Ohio.

44) If you brush your teeth twice a day, how many times do you brush them during March?
Answer: 62 times.

45) Name the 2 states devastated on September 22, 1989, when Hurricane Hugo tore across them. Both the coastal city of Charleston and the inland city of Charlotte suffered from its force.
Answer: North and South Carolina.

46) Although it has a side effect of permanently turning blue eyes brown, a new drug has been found to fight glaucoma. Is glaucoma a disease of the *eye, heart, lungs,* or *joints*?
Answer: Eye (caused when fluid builds up inside the eyeball).

47) Following South Carolina's secession from the Union, President Buchanan said, "I am the last President of the United States." Spell *secession*.
Answer: S-E-C-E-S-S-I-O-N.

48) In 1992, the first-place Olympic medal was made of crystal with gold trim. Which metals are traditionally used to indicate 2nd and 3rd places?
Answer: Silver (2nd) and bronze (3rd).

49) What is the multiplicative inverse of 5/6?
Answer: 6/5.

50) In which body of water is Grenada, which the U.S. invaded on October 25, 1983, to prevent a Soviet-Cuban takeover?
Answer: Caribbean Sea.

1) Name the Portuguese explorer who in 1520 was the first to sail across the Pacific Ocean. A strait is named for him.
Answer: Ferdinand Magellan.

2) On February 12, 1839, which New England state became involved in a border dispute with the Canadian province of New Brunswick in what is known as the Aroostook War? The name of this state's capital begins and ends with the same vowel.
Answer: Maine (its capital is Augusta).

3) Name the New York canal that opened on October 25, 1825, as the first U.S. man-made waterway. One of the Great Lakes shares its name.
Answer: Erie Canal.

4) The U.S. won a record number of medals in the 1994 Winter Olympics. How many medals did the U.S. win, a number equivalent to 1/6 of 456 less 63?
Answer: 13.

5) On which continent is Sudan, where 10,000 young male refugees were led on a 200-mile trek to a new camp where the Red Cross could more easily provide food and care in 1992?
Answer: Africa.

6) British naturalist Charles Darwin's major work is subtitled *The Preservation of Favoured Races in the Struggle for Life.* What word completes its title: *On the Origin of* _____.
Answer: *Species.*

7) Name King Arthur's sword, which, according to one legend, the Lady of the Lake retrieved from a lake and gave to Arthur.
Answer: Excalibur.

8) Name the artist best known for his seascapes, such as *The Gulf Stream.* His surname is a nickname for a baseball hit that enables the batter to score a run.
Answer: Winslow Homer.

9) If there are 5 1/2 yards in one rod, how many yards would be equal to 4 rods?
Answer: 22.

10) Identify the 3 colors of the Russian flag that replaced the crimson Soviet flag with its golden hammer and sickle.
Answer: Red, white, and blue.

11) Who wrote "The Star-Spangled Banner," which became the national anthem on March 3, 1931?
Answer: Francis Scott Key.

12) Melinda Wagner's 1999 Pulitzer Prize-winning musical composition is called a concerto. Spell *concerto*.
Answer: C-O-N-C-E-R-T-O.

13) The Barents Sea, where a Soviet nuclear submarine collided with a U.S. nuclear sub in 1992, is an arm of which northern ocean?
Answer: Arctic Ocean.

14) What is 100 minus 99 minus 99 minus 99 equal to?
Answer: Negative 197.

15) What word beginning with *K* names an Oriental groundcover planted in the U.S. South in the 1930s to control erosion and now considered a weed because of its rapid growth?
Answer: Kudzu.

16) Name the only 2 planets smaller than Mars.
Answer: Mercury and Pluto.

17) Name 2 of the 4 March daughters in Louisa May Alcott's *Little Women*.
Answer: Amy, Meg, Jo, and Beth.

18) According to author and educator E.D. Hirsch, a first grader should know the artist who painted *Mona Lisa*. Name him.
Answer: Leonardo da Vinci.

19) During a trip, the average speed for the first two hours was 60 mph. The next 6 hours the average speed was reduced to 50 mph. How many miles were traveled on this trip?
Answer: 420 miles.

20) Name the U.S. President who met with Churchill and Stalin in Iran in 1943 to develop a plan to crush Germany.
Answer: Franklin D. Roosevelt.

21) For which invention is New York-born George Pullman known?
Answer: Railway sleeping car.

22) Which fort in San Antonio, Texas, was overrun on March 6, 1836, by an army of Mexicans led by General Santa Anna?
Answer: The Alamo.

23) Azerbaijan and Armenia, two former Soviet republics, have fought over a disputed region in which mountains: the Himalayas, Alps, Andes, or Caucasus?
Answer: Caucasus.

24) What is the weight of 5 tennis balls if 3 tennis balls weigh 15 ounces?
Answer: 25 ounces.

25) Name the former Soviet president who was hired in 1992 to write a column for the *New York Times*.
Answer: Mikhail Gorbachev.

26) Which term is used in geology to designate the central region of the earth?
Answer: Core (consisting of an inner and an outer core).

27) Poet Dylan Thomas was born in Wales in 1914. Give the adjective form of Wales used to designate its natives.
Answer: Welsh.

28) Educator E.D. Hirsch expects a 2nd grader to know the history of the Olympics. By tradition, how often are they held?
Answer: Every 4 years.

29) In 1992, when the Woolworth Company planned to close, sell, or reform 900 of its 6,500 U.S. stores, did the 900 stores represent about 10%, 15%, 20%, or 25% of their stores?
Answer: 15%.

30) From which country did General José de San Martin liberate Argentina, Chile, and Peru in the 19th century?
Answer: Spain.

31) In 1992, which state issued a license plate with the slogan "Heart of Dixie" centered under the state's name?
Answer: Alabama.

32) Whose birthday was first celebrated as a national holiday on the 3rd Monday in January in 1986?
Answer: Martin Luther King Jr.

33) In which Central American country bordered by Honduras on the north did a civil war officially end on February 1, 1992? Its name is Spanish for "the Savior."
Answer: El Salvador.

34) If 2 angles of a triangle measure 50 degrees and 60 degrees, how many degrees are there in the third angle?
Answer: 70 degrees.

35) Name the Baltimore Oriole who broke Lou Gehrig's 56-year-old record on September 6, 1995, by playing in his 2,131st consecutive major league game.
Answer: Cal Ripken Jr.

36) Identify the "third-generation" orbiting Russian space station launched in 1986. Its name means "Peace."
Answer: *Mir*.

37) Massachusetts-born Col. William Prescott allegedly said at the Battle of Bunker Hill in 1775, "Don't fire until you see the whites of their eyes." Spell *Massachusetts*.
Answer: M-A-S-S-A-C-H-U-S-E-T-T-S.

38) Sidney Poitier became the first black to win an Academy Award for a starring role. What are Academy Awards called?
Answer: Oscars.

39) Give the term for the earliest known inhabitants of a region, especially in Australia.
Answer: Aborigines.

40) The Dalai Lama fled Tibet during a 1959 anti-Chinese uprising. Is he a Muslim, Catholic, Hindu, or Buddhist?
Answer: Buddhist (the Dalai Lama fled on 3/19/1959).

41) What marble monument 555 feet tall was dedicated in Washington, D.C., on February 21, 1885?
Answer: Washington Monument (with 898 steps).

42) Which New England state that borders only one other joined the Union as a free state under the Missouri Compromise of 1820?
Answer: Maine.

43) Which desert east of Los Angeles is sometimes the epicenter of earthquakes?
Answer: Mojave Desert.

44) 20 times 64 has the same value as 16 times what number?
Answer: 80 (20 x 4 x 16 = 16 x 80).

45) Against which country did the U.S. launch a ground war, called "The Mother of All Battles," on February 23, 1991?
Answer: Iraq.

46) Which term is used in geology to designate the outermost layer of the earth?
Answer: Crust.

47) Baron von Steuben began drilling General Washington's foot soldiers on February 23, 1778. Are soldiers who fight on foot called *marines, sentries, cavalry,* or *infantry*?
Answer: Infantry.

48) Italian Enrico Caruso earned world-wide fame as a tenor, or singer with the highest male singing voice. Name the highest female singing voice.
Answer: Soprano.

49) If 100 miles on a map is equal to 5 inches, how many inches is 180 miles?
Answer: 9 inches.

50) Which colony settled by Pilgrims did William Bradford serve as governor from 1621 through most of his life?
Answer: Plymouth.

1) Which colorful New Orleans festival ends on the last Tuesday before the beginning of Lent?
Answer: Mardi Gras.

2) In which state was "Stonewall" Jackson accidentally shot by his own troops at Chancellorsville in 1863?
Answer: Virginia.

3) Robert Cavalier, Sieur de la Salle claimed the area drained by the Mississippi and all rivers feeding into it for France. What are such rivers that feed into a larger one called?
Answer: Tributaries (La Salle stopped to build Fort Crèvecoeur on January 15, 1680).

4) What is 10 times 1/2 times 15 times 4?
Answer: 300.

5) In 1994, Aldrich Ames and his wife were arrested for selling to Russia's KGB and its successor the secrets of the U.S.'s federal intelligence agency. Name this agency where he had worked for 31 years.
Answer: CIA (Central Intelligence Agency).

6) Which animal is the 3rd largest member of the cat family of the Eastern Hemisphere? Its coat is either black or a light tan with many black spots.
Answer: Leopard.

7) The space craft *Magellan* sends reports via photographs. Which 2-letter digraph makes the sound "f" as in *pho*togra*ph*?
Answer: "ph."

8) A virus named for Michelangelo, the artist who painted the ceiling of the Sistine Chapel, struck U.S. PCs on his birthday, March 6, in 1992. What is a PC?
Answer: Personal computer.

9) What is 15 percent of 1500?
Answer: 225.

10) The British Parliament's 1765 Stamp Act brought much American protest because it placed a tax on American publications and legal documents. Spell *parliament*.
Answer: P-A-R-L-I-A-M-E-N-T.

11) On which date is St. Patrick's Day celebrated?
Answer: March 17.

12) Name the former 4-term governor of Alabama and 4-time presidential campaigner who died in 1998. He had been wheelchair-bound since an assassination attempt in 1972.
Answer: George Wallace.

13) Which European country, shaped like a boot, did the U.S. hockey team defeat in its first 1992 Olympic match?
Answer: Italy.

14) Which of the following numbers is not divisible by 9 with 0 remainder: *576, 488, 306,* or *792?*
Answer: 488.

15) Supreme Court Justice Harry Blackmun once announced that he could no longer support the death penalty for any crime. Spell the word that completes the term _____ *punishment* to designate the death penalty.
Answer: C-A-P-I-T-A-L (Blackmun was the only one of 9 members totally opposed to it).

16) Identify the branch of medicine dealing with problems of the skin.
Answer: Dermatology.

17) In 1999, athletes from 16 countries gathered in the U.S. to compete in the Women's World Cup Soccer Tournament. Spell *athletes.*
Answer: A-T-H-L-E-T-E-S.

18) Name the large Christian church in Rome for which Michelangelo served as chief architect. It is named for the first pope of the Roman Catholic Church.
Answer: St. Peter's Church (or Basilica).

19) Name the only U.S. President whose name is on a plaque on the moon.
Answer: Richard Nixon.

20) Queen Elizabeth I's accession to the English throne in November 1558 was celebrated as a holiday for more than a century after her death in 1603. Spell *accession,* meaning "the attainment of a new rank or position."
Answer: A-C-C-E-S-S-I-O-N.

21) What kind of aircraft is a chopper?
Answer: Helicopter.

22) Name the 22nd and 24th U.S. President.
    Answer: Grover Cleveland.

23) Name the Appalachian mountain range separating Virginia's Piedmont and Shenandoah Valley.
    Answer: Blue Ridge Mountains.

24) If a VCR sells for $600 and the rate of profit is 20% of the selling price, what did it cost originally?
    Answer: $480.

25) China has deported some Canadian legislators investigating human rights. What 2 languages are spoken in Canada?
    Answer: English and French.

26) Identify the 3 kinds of rock that make up the earth's crust.
    Answer: Igneous, sedimentary, and metamorphic.

27) Which American poet wrote "The Wreck of the Hesperus"? His surname is a compound that might be informally defined as "tall guy."
    Answer: Henry Wadsworth Longfellow.

28) Muslims observe the holy month of Ramadan to mark the revelation of their sacred book to Mohammed. Is this book called the *Koran*, *Odyssey*, *Torah*, or *Thesaurus*?
    Answer: Koran.

29) If in 1992 a Russian scientist's monthly wage of 6500 rubles was the equivalent of $65 U.S. dollars, how many rubles was each U.S. dollar worth at that time?
    Answer: 100 rubles.

30) Who founded the Russian Communist Party: Saddam Hussein, Vladimir Lenin, Nikita Khrushchev, or Mikhail Gorbachev?
    Answer: Vladimir Lenin.

31) If, as predicted, there are 1 billion people 60 years or older in the world in 2020, how many more of these "senior citizens" will there be than the 350 million of 20 years ago?
    Answer: 650 million (actual prediction for 2020 is 1.1 billion).

32) Yale University was founded in Branford, Connecticut, on October 9, 1701, and moved to New Haven in 1716. Identify the climbing vine whose name designates the league to which Yale and other prestigious universities in the Northeast belong.
    Answer: Ivy (League).

33) The Soviets plan to use California's Mojave Desert to test their robot vehicle designed to explore Mars in 1996. What letter makes the *H* sound in the Spanish name *Mojave*?
Answer: "J."

34) Identify the next 2 prime numbers after 13.
Answer: 17 and 19.

35) The *Chronicle of Philanthropy*, a newspaper for charities, reported that charitable donations increased 13% in 1998. Spell both *chronicle*, meaning "a report or historical record," and *philanthropy*, meaning "an effort to serve others by making donations."
Answer: C-H-R-O-N-I-C-L-E and P-H-I-L-A-N-T-H-R-O-P-Y.

36) Which of the following designates a plant that lacks the green pigment chlorophyll and lives by feeding off other animals or plants: *algae, fungi, fern*, or *conifer*?
Answer: Fungi.

37) What is the verb in the *USA Today* headline "Who should police smoking"? This headline was used to report a survey concerning regulation of smoking in public places.
Answer: Should police.

38) Name the page of a newspaper that features essays expressing the opinions of the publishers.
Answer: Editorial page.

39) Give the acronym for "light amplification by stimulated emission of radiation."
Answer: LASER.

40) Name the 2 world leaders who called a formal end to the cold war during a meeting at Camp David in Maryland in 1992.
Answer: George Bush and Boris Yeltsin.

41) What word designates agents who sell stocks and bonds?
Answer: Brokers.

42) Which political party was founded in 1854 by those who opposed the extension of slavery into the territories? Its symbol is the elephant.
Answer: Republican (founded in Ripon, Wisconsin).

43) Name the nation's first national park, created in 1872 and partially inspired by Thomas Moran's huge canvases portraying its natural wonders for Congress.
Answer: Yellowstone National Park.

44) If the sum of 2 consecutive even integers is 18, what is the smaller integer?
Answer: 8.

45) Name the Asian country whose 7-term president, Suharto, resigned in June 1998 after an economic crash led to rioting that left more than 500 dead in Jakarta. It's the 4th most populous country.
Answer: Indonesia (Suharto had been its president since 1968).

46) As the U.S. celebrated the 10th anniversary of its first space shuttle flight on April 12, 1991, whom did the USSR honor as the Columbus of the space age on Cosmonaut Day? He made the first space flight.
Answer: Yuri Gagarin.

47) What part of speech is *since* in the following? *The U.S. has been the world's top tourist destination since 1989.*
Answer: Preposition.

48) John Kagwe of Kenya and Franca Fiacconi of Italy recently won New York City's 26- mile, 385-yard footrace. What is a footrace of this length called?
Answer: Marathon.

49) Find 2 numbers whose sum is 12 and whose difference is 8.
Answer: 10 and 2.

50) By what name is Japan's legislature known in English? The same word designates the food one eats on a regular basis.
Answer: Diet.

1) Name the 4 months that have just 30 days on our calendar.
   Answer: September, April, June, and November.

2) Which war occurred during President William McKinley's administration, 1897-1901: American Revolution, Civil War, Spanish American War, or WWII?
   Answer: Spanish American War.

3) Name the "Palmetto State," whose native son John Calhoun became the first Vice President to resign that office. It is bordered by Georgia and North Carolina.
   Answer: South Carolina.

4) If a dozen baked goods cost 96 cents, what is the average cost per item?
   Answer: 8 cents.

5) Identify the New York airport where government gunmen in 1992 shot nearly 15,000 sea gulls to ward off gull-plane collisions. It is named for the President who established the Peace Corps.
   Answer: John F. Kennedy Airport.

6) Health experts advise those who spend time in the woods to wear protective clothing to avoid contact with which insects known to cause Lyme disease, an infection that often affects the joints?
   Answer: Ticks (disease named for Connecticut town where discovered).

7) The Pritzker Prize is awarded annually for outstanding work in architecture. Spell *architecture.*
   Answer: A-R-C-H-I-T-E-C-T-U-R-E.

8) Leaders of the Methodist Church in Britain warned in 1996 that membership loss had reached a critical point, even in Epworth, birthplace of its founding father, namely which of these: Martin Luther, John Wesley, John Calvin, or Billy Graham?
   Answer: John Wesley.

9) What is the sum of the squares of 5 and 20?
   Answer: 425.

10) Congress appropriated $400 million to help the new Commonwealth of Independent States dismantle its nuclear missiles. Spell *missiles.*
    Answer: M-I-S-S-I-L-E-S.

11) What name is given to the right to print or reproduce a literary or artistic work?
Answer: Copyright (a patent protects an author's rights).

12) In the 1990s, which country opened a theme park for Santa Claus inside a mountain near the Arctic Circle? It shares a long border with Russia, and its northern area is called Lapland.
Answer: Finland.

13) Name the mountains on France's border with Switzerland and Italy.
Answer: Alps.

14) How many is 6 score and 11?
Answer: 131.

15) Identify the former heavyweight boxing champion, whose battle cry was "Float like a butterfly, sting like a bee." He turned 57 in January 1999.
Answer: Muhammad Ali.

16) According to the U.S., China sold missile technology to Syria and Pakistan despite its stated willingness to curb missile exports. Spell *technology*.
Answer: T-E-C-H-N-O-L-O-G-Y.

17) What is the third principal part, or past participle, of the verb *ring*?
Answer: *Rung*.

18) Which profession is said to have been founded by Florence Nightingale, who during the Crimean War in the 19th century became known as the "Lady With the Lamp"?
Answer: Nursing profession.

19) Which Polish astronomer revolutionized scientific thought in the 16th century with his theory that placed the sun at the center of the universe?
Answer: Nicolaus Copernicus.

20) Name the official language of Brazil, which comes from the country of explorer Pedro Alvares Cabral, who is credited with discovering the land on April 22, 1500.
Answer: Portuguese.

21) Spell the title used before a woman's name that makes no reference to whether or not she is married. Gloria Steinem helped found a magazine with this title in 1972.
Answer: Ms. (*Ms.* magazine).

22) E.D. Hirsch's book *What Your 2nd Grader Needs to Know* includes the name of the secret network of people who helped slaves travel to freedom before the Civil War. Name this network, which included Harriet Tubman.
Answer: Underground Railroad.

23) Name the longest river east of the Mississippi River. This river shares its name with a U.S. state.
Answer: Ohio.

24) What number increased by 30% of itself equals 39?
Answer: 30.

25) Which former L.A. Lakers star nicknamed "Magic" personally delivered to President Bush a letter on AIDS which said, "I don't feel you have been there"?
Answer: Earvin "Magic" Johnson.

26) According to the *Journal of the AMA*, caffeinated coffee's contribution to osteoporosis can be negated by consuming which element found in milk?
Answer: Calcium.

27) Identify the literary character whose name today designates "someone hopelessly behind the times." This title character fell asleep for 20 years in a Washington Irving short story.
Answer: Rip Van Winkle.

28) A team from which mountainous island in the South China Sea defeated a California team 11-0 to win its 15th Little League Championship in Williamsport, Pennsylvania, in 1991?
Answer: Taiwan.

29) If carpeting costs $2 per square foot, what will it cost to carpet a room 10 feet by 9 feet in area?
Answer: $180.

30) Name either of the 2 African countries where terrorists bombed U.S. embassies at Nairobi and Dar es Salaam in August 1998, killing 12 Americans and about 250 Africans. Their names begin with the letters *K* and *T* respectively.
Answer: Kenya or Tanzania (formed by a union of Tanganyika and Zanzibar in 1964).

31) In which sport is the Heisman Trophy awarded?
Answer: Football.

32) In which state did James Marshall discover gold while building a sawmill in 1848, prompting the 1849 Gold Rush?
Answer: California (at John Sutter's mill).

33) Is the highest point in Bill Clinton's state of Arkansas in the *Rocky*, *Great Smoky*, *Catskill*, or *Ozark* mountains?
     Answer: Ozark Mountains.

34) How many minutes are there between 4:40 p.m. and 5:30 p.m.?
     Answer: 50.

35) Which state is the site of a bomb shelter built for Congress during the cold war and maintained in case of nuclear attack? It is called the "Mountain State."
     Answer: West Virginia.

36) Name the 2 planets that have just 1 natural satellite each.
     Answer: Earth and Pluto.

37) William Sydney Porter, author of "The Gift of the Magi," allegedly borrowed his pseudonym O. Henry from a prison guard. What does the prefix *pseudo-* mean?
     Answer: False.

38) Which date did the 20th Amendment, ratified on January 23, 1933, establish as the date of the presidential inauguration: Nov. 10, Jan. 20, March 4, or July 4?
     Answer: January 20 (earlier held on March 4).

39) Name the planet whose satellites are Phobos and Deimos.
     Answer: Mars.

40) The 1605 Gunpowder Plot was a plan to blow up King James I and the English legislative body in 1605. Name this body.
     Answer: Parliament (conspirators were convicted on January 27, 1606).

41) Name the state where President Clinton stood beside Narragansett Bay and spoke of a life-long wish of playing his saxophone at its Newport Jazz Festival. It borders Connecticut and Massachusetts.
     Answer: Rhode Island.

42) Name the U.S. legislative body, which is made up of the House of Representatives and the Senate.
     Answer: Congress.

43) Which South American country, known for its problems with rebels, drug traffickers, or other armed groups, has its capital at Bogotá?
     Answer: Colombia.

44) If a town of 100 people gained 30% in population, then lost 30%, how many people were left in the town?
Answer: 91.

45) Which South American country has the largest Catholic population? Pope John Paul II visited it in 1991 to promote Roman Catholicism.
Answer: Brazil.

46) Which English-born physician is called the "Father of Antiseptic Surgery"? A mouthwash is marketed under his name today.
Answer: Joseph Lister.

47) Name the country that was home to poet Robert Burns, who wrote, "The best laid schemes o' mice and men/Gang aft a-gley." It is known for its kilts and bagpipes.
Answer: Scotland.

48) The 1996 Pulitzer Prize for spot news photography was won by Charles Porter, for his image of a fireman cradling the body of 1-year-old Baylee Almon in which city?
Answer: Oklahoma City (she was one of 168 victims of the April 19, 1995, bombing).

49) What is the positive square root of the quantity 18 times 8?
Answer: 12.

50) In 1991, Mikhail Gorbachev resigned as chief of which party that had ruled Soviet life through intimidation and force since 1917?
Answer: Communist Party.

1) What name identifies legendary American lumberjack Paul Bunyan's huge blue ox?
Answer: Babe.

2) W.E.B. Dubois, who was honored on a U.S. postal stamp in 1992, was the first black to earn a Ph.D. from the oldest university in the U.S. Name this Massachusetts school.
Answer: Harvard University (founded in 1636).

3) Which Latin American country is the site of three mountain ranges called the Sierra Madre?
Answer: Mexico.

4) Baltimore-born baseball player Babe Ruth hit 714 career home runs. How many more did Hank Aaron hit with his career record of 755 home runs?
Answer: 41.

5) Complete the title "Operation Uphold _____" used to designate the U.S. military operation in Haiti in 1994 by naming the form of government based on free elections.
Answer: "Democracy."

6) Name the substance that forms the supporting structure for the nose and ears in humans.
Answer: Cartilage.

7) Complete the title of Patricia MacLachlan's Newbery book *Sarah, Plain and ____*, whose story was continued in a *Hallmark Hall of Fame* sequel.
Answer: *Tall*.

8) In 1996, more than 500 performers launched 250 concerts simultaneously in all 50 states featuring which instrument with a keyboard, a pedalboard, and pipes?
Answer: Organ (it was the 100th anniversary of the American Guild of Organists).

9) 124 is what percent of 310?
Answer: 40%.

10) E.D. Hirsch, author of *What Your 2nd Grader Needs to Know*, expects first graders to know the 7 continents arranged according to size. Name the 2 largest.
Answer: Asia (the largest) and Africa.

11) Name the law enforcement group assigned to protect U.S. Presidents.
     Answer: Secret Service.

12) In 1992, former President Gerald Ford called for disclosure of sealed government records related to John Kennedy's assassination. In which Texas city was Kennedy killed?
     Answer: Dallas (Ford served on the Warren Commission).

13) Identify the continent whose southern part consists of a group of islands known as Tierra del Fuego, which means "land of fire."
     Answer: South America.

14) The Congressional Budget Office announced the deficit for 1993 will be $325 billion. What represents 325 in Roman numerals?
     Answer: CCCXXV.

15) Which Australian city, nicknamed "The City of Lights" in 1962 after it lit all its lights when John Glenn orbited the Earth, repeated this illumination for Glenn in 1998? Its name rhymes with the word *birth*.
     Answer: Perth.

16) Andromeda is one of the 3 galaxies beyond our own that can be seen from Earth without a telescope. What is the 2-word name for the galaxy that contains our solar system?
     Answer: Milky Way.

17) Spell *principle* as used in the following: *In a recent meeting with U.S. negotiator Bob Dole in Macedonia, Kosovo's Albanian leaders agreed in principle to sign a peace agreement.*
     Answer: P-R-I-N-C-I-P-L-E.

18) Name Julia Ward Howe's song that was published for the first time in the *Atlantic Monthly* on February 1, 1862, and contains the refrain "His truth is marching on."
     Answer: "Battle Hymn of the Republic."

19) Name 3 of the 4 types of permanent teeth found in adults.
     Answer: Incisors, cuspids (or canines), bicuspids (or premolars), and molars.

20) President Sadat of Egypt was assassinated on October 6, 1981, while reviewing a parade commemorating the country's 1973 war with Israel. Spell *commemorating*.
     Answer: C-O-M-M-E-M-O-R-A-T-I-N-G.

21) The Pope gave what is called a *homily* as part of the Mass in St. Louis. Which of the following best defines *homily*: altar call, blessing, welcome, prayer, or sermon?
Answer: Sermon.

22) The 15th Amendment to the U.S. Constitution states that a voter cannot be denied the right to vote because of his race. What is the paper on which one marks a vote called?
Answer: Ballot.

23) Name the country located in both Europe and Asia whose name designates an animal associated with Thanksgiving.
Answer: Turkey.

24) Two positive numbers are in the ratio of 1 to 3 and their sum is 12. Name either number.
Answer: 3 or 9.

25) In 1992, Israel asked the U.S. for $10 billion in loan guarantees to finance housing for immigrants from the former Soviet Union and Ethiopia. Spell *guarantees*.
Answer: G-U-A-R-A-N-T-E-E-S.

26) Give the word for the study of heredity.
Answer: Genetics.

27) Name Daniel Defoe's fictional character based on sailor Alexander Selkirk, who was rescued from an uninhabited island in the South Pacific on February 1, 1709.
Answer: Robinson Crusoe.

28) In 1992, Algeria arrested the leader of its Islamic party and banned gatherings at Muslim churches. Is a Muslim house of worship a *synagogue*, *mosque*, *cathedral*, or *temple*?
Answer: Mosque.

29) Express 45/75 in lowest terms.
Answer: 3/5.

30) About 2,065 atomic tests have been conducted since the first man-made nuclear explosion in history, at Alamogordo, New Mexico, in July of which year in the 1940s?
Answer: 1945.

31) Some years are called the Year of the Dog on the Chinese lunar calendar. Spell *calendar*.
Answer: C-A-L-E-N-D-A-R.

32) In 1919, which U.S. President collapsed aboard a train after making 40 speeches on behalf of the Treaty of Versailles? Dennis the Menace often irritates a man with the same surname.
Answer: Woodrow Wilson.

33) Which U.S. battleship blew up in 1898 in the harbor of Havana, Cuba, at the start of the Spanish-American War. It was named for the state that borders only one other state.
Answer: U.S.S. *Maine*.

34) What percentage is the equivalent of 3/5?
Answer: 60%.

35) In 1992, Chicago's Mayor Daley fired the transportation commissioner for ignoring a repair memo that could have prevented millions of dollars in flood damage. Spell *commissioner*.
Answer: C-O-M-M-I-S-S-I-O-N-E-R.

36) What term designates any substance able to kill germs in the environment?
Answer: Antiseptic.

37) Give the pen name of Charles Lutwidge Dodgson, who wrote *Alice's Adventures in Wonderland*.
Answer: Lewis Carroll.

38) Name the 2 New York City newspapers that each won 2 Pulitzer Prizes in 1999. One is known for its financial news and includes the name of the city's financial center
Answer: *New York Times* and *Wall Street Journal*.

39) Identify the planet whose 4 large bright satellites Galileo discovered in 1610.
Answer: Jupiter.

40) According to President John Kennedy's defense secretary, which Caribbean country had 36 USSR nuclear warheads in 1962?
Answer: Cuba.

41) Which organization established in the U.S. in 1910 has as its motto "Be Prepared"?
Answer: Boy Scouts (of America).

42) Which inventor formally opened the first U.S. telegraph line on May 24, 1844? The code used in the telegraph is named for him.
Answer: Samuel F.B. Morse (between Baltimore, Maryland, and Washington, D.C.).

43) In the 1990s, Sarajevo, Bosnia's capital, was the site of Europe's bloodiest fighting since WWII. Was Bosnia formerly a part of Yugoslavia, Germany, France, or Brazil?
Answer: Yugoslavia.

44) What percent of the value of a quarter is the value of a nickel?
Answer: 20%.

45) In 1991, *Atlantis*'s astronauts were amazed at the haze over the Earth, which they attributed to the eruption of Mount Pinatubo in which Pacific Ocean island country?
Answer: Philippines.

46) What word names the tube-like organ through which a cephalopod forces out the water it inhales through the gills in its mantle to create a jet effect that sends it surging through the sea? A tornado cloud is also known by this name.
Answer: Funnel (a tornado is known as a *funnel cloud*).

47) Name the character who confronts three ghosts in Charles Dickens' *A Christmas Carol*.
Answer: Ebeneezer Scrooge.

48) In 1998, Britain announced plans to reroute a busy road to recreate the original landscape around a mysterious ring of rocks dating back 5,000 years. Name this famous site.
Answer: Stonehenge.

49) If a sales tax is 6%, what is the tax on $7.50?
Answer: 45 cents.

50) In the 1990s, a French collector paid $5,536 for a lock of hair of the French king beheaded in 1793. Name this king whose number attached to his name is a multiple of 4.
Answer: Louis XVI (a drummer allegedly trapped his head and snipped off the lock).

1) In 1992, in California, a convicted murderer was put to death by a deadly gas. Is a gas that kills described as *pliable, lethal, dense*, or *nocturnal*?
Answer: Lethal.

2) Name the President who on December 2, 1823, set forth a doctrine, now named for him, warning European nations not to interfere with free nations in the New World.
Answer: James Monroe (known as the Monroe Doctrine).

3) Before he was hanged on September 22, 1776, Nathan Hale allegedly said, "I regret that I have but one life to lose for my country." Spell *Connecticut*, the home of this hero.
Answer: C-O-N-N-E-C-T-I-C-U-T.

4) 60% of what number equals 30?
Answer: 50.

5) Kosovo, a small province of Serbia, has an area of 4,200 square miles, or is about the size of which of the following states: Georgia, Maryland, Montana, or Texas?
Answer: Maryland.

6) Which of the following bones is also referred to as the skull: *femur, patella, cranium*, or *pelvis*?
Answer: Cranium.

7) Which prefix meaning "across" begins the full name of TWA, one of the U.S.'s largest airlines?
Answer: *trans-* (Trans-World Airlines).

8) Composer Ludwig van Beethoven conducted his last concert at Vienna in May 1824 with a long piece of music written for a full orchestra. What is such a composition called?
Answer: Symphony.

9) If 80% of the students in a school of 330 are absent the same day, how many students will be present on that day?
Answer: 66.

10) On January 1, Cuba celebrates the anniversary of the day in 1899 when which country gave up its control of the island?
Answer: Spain.

11) Captain William Bligh survived a 47-day voyage after his crew on the HMS *Bounty* revolted and set him adrift in 1789. What term designates a revolt of sailors?
Answer: Mutiny.

12) In which state was Nellie Ross inaugurated as the first woman governor in the U.S., on January 5, 1925? It's the only state west of the Mississippi with a *Y* in its name.
Answer: Wyoming.

13) Which term, Spanish for "steppe," designates the grassy plains in Argentina?
Answer: Pampas.

14) What is 70% of 40% of 100?
Answer: 28.

15) In which New York square did Coca-Cola's Big Bottle, a 4-story high bottle of Coke costing $3 million, make its debut on New Year's Eve in 1991?
Answer: Times Square.

16) What compound is formed when hydrogen is burned?
Answer: Water.

17) What name did Robert Louis Stevenson give to the evil side of his literary character Dr. Jekyll?
Answer: Mr. Hyde.

18) Name the illustrator known for his many cover paintings of American life for the *Saturday Evening Post*. His surname is a compound word naming a mass of stone and a place for pumping water.
Answer: Norman Rockwell.

19) Name the 3 major fossil fuels.
Answer: Natural gas, oil (or petroleum), and coal.

20) Lady Jane Grey was hanged in the Tower of London in 1554 after serving as English queen for only 9 days. Which word beginning with *m* designates a king or queen?
Answer: Monarch.

21) Which U.S. coin pictures Susan B. Anthony, a 19th-century women's rights activist?
Answer: Dollar.

22) According to the 22nd Amendment, ratified on February 27, 1951, how many terms may a U.S. president serve?
Answer: 2 terms.

23) Identify the Parisian tower named for the "Magician of Iron" who built it for an exposition in 1889.
Answer: Eiffel Tower.

24) If you are trying to save 30% of your earnings each week, how much would you save weekly if you earned $290?
Answer: $87.

25) In 1998, the G-7 nations, or 7 richest countries, called for increased cooperation during this time of stock market drops throughout the world. Name any 4 of these G-7 nations.
Answer: Britain, Canada, France, Germany, Italy, U.S., and Japan.

26) What word beginning with the letter T designates the boneless arm-like structures extending from the head of the octopus and other cephalopods?
Answer: Tentacles (*cephalopod* means "headfooted": *cephalo* = "head"; *pod* = "foot").

27) Which award for the most distinguished children's book did Phyllis Reynolds Naylor win for her book *Shiloh*?
Answer: Newbery Medal.

28) Identify the Roman messenger of the gods for whom the Ford line of cars including the Tracer is named.
Answer: Mercury (he wore winged sandals for speedy delivery).

29) In 1991, General Motors eliminated its generous $600 Christmas bonus for about 100,000 employees. About how much did this cut save the company?
Answer: $60 million.

30) From which country did the U.S. acquire the Philippines on December 10, 1898, for $20 million?
Answer: Spain.

31) Give the total of the number of white stripes in the U.S. flag plus the number of colors in the rainbow.
Answer: 13 (6 white stripes plus 7 colors).

32) Name the aviator whose infant son was kidnapped on March 1, 1932, and later killed.
Answer: Charles Lindbergh (case led to a law making kidnapping a federal offense).

33) Mexico, like the U.S., calls its political divisions *states*. What are such divisions like British Columbia and Quebec called in Canada?
Answer: Provinces.

34) Give the square root of the number of squares on a checker-board.
     Answer: 8 (there are 64 squares on a checkerboard).

35) Federal prosecutors once accused one corporation and 9 men, including 2 NASA employees, of bribery and kickback schemes at the space center in Houston. Name the President from Texas for whom this center is named.
     Answer: Lyndon Johnson (Johnson Space Center).

36) Spell *phlegm*, the name for the thick mucus that develops in the lungs during an asthma attack, cold, or other respiratory infection.
     Answer: P-H-L-E-G-M.

37) Since 1949, a stranger has left 3 white roses and a bottle of cognac on the Baltimore grave of which author on the anniversary of his birth, January 19, 1809? He is known for "The Pit and the Pendulum" and other tales of terror.
     Answer: Edgar Allan Poe.

38) What phrase from baseball did President Clinton use at a State of the Union address to describe the mandatory life sentence he favors for 3-time violent felons?
     Answer: "Three strikes (and you're out)."

39) Identify the heavenly bodies whose name in Greek means "wanderers" or "wandering stars."
     Answer: Planets.

40) Identify the late autumn flower of many colors whose name also labels the Japanese throne Hirohito ascended in 1926.
     Answer: Chrysanthemum Throne.

41) What type of bird, a symbol of peace, was not released at opening ceremonies for the 1996 Olympic Games because of animal rights concerns?
     Answer: Dove (the tradition began in 1920 but was not followed in the Games in Norway since the birds became disoriented and were burned when the flame was lit in Seoul in 1988).

42) Complete the name *War on* _____ for the program President Lyndon Johnson launched on January 8, 1964, to give aid to those suffering from lack of financial resources.
     Answer: (War on) Poverty.

43) In which area of Africa does Ethiopia lie: east, west, north or south?
     Answer: East.

44)   The name *Generation X* is being used to designate Americans born after 1960. About how many of the U.S.'s approximate 260 million people fall into this group that makes up about 16% of the total population?
      Answer: 42 million (41.6 million actually).

45)   In December 1991, Mikhail Gorbachev resigned as head of the U.S.S.R. after 6 years and 9 months of service. In which year did he take office?
      Answer: 1985.

46)   During which period of the day are nocturnal animals active?
      Answer: At night.

47)   The 25th Amendment to the U.S. Constitution, ratified in 1967, provides for presidential succession and disability. Spell *amendment*.
      Answer: A-M-E-N-D-M-E-N-T (ratified on 2/10/1967).

48)   Identify the mythological youth who tried to escape from Crete with wings of wax. The asteroid whose orbit brings it closer to the sun than any other is named for him.
      Answer: Icarus.

49)   What power is 10 raised to in the scientific notation form of 1,123,654?
      Answer: Sixth.

50)   What word beginning with *O* completes the name *Eastern _____ Church*, naming Yugoslavia's main religion, which dates to a split in the Roman Catholic Church in 1054?
      Answer: Orthodox (Greek and Russian Orthodox are its major branches).

1) Which civil rights leader and Nobel Peace Prize winner was born in Atlanta on January 15, 1929?
Answer: Martin Luther King Jr.

2) Name the U.S. President who on February 1, 1865, signed the 13th Amendment to the U.S. Constitution, which abolished slavery.
Answer: Abraham Lincoln (the amendment was ratified December 18, 1865).

3) Greece once closed the main trade route to landlocked Macedonia to pressure it to change its name. Albania then offered the former Yugoslav republic the use of a port on which sea: Adriatic, Caribbean, Mediterranean, or Red?
Answer: Adriatic Sea (a Greek province is also named Macedonia).

4) The world's population of about 5.5 billion people is expected to double by 2025. Does the U.S.'s population of about 260 million make up about 1%, 5%, 10%, or 20% of the world's 5.5 billion?
Answer: About 5%.

5) The movie *Teenage Mutant Ninja Turtles*, which opened in 1990, is a movie derived from the pages of a cult comic book. Identify 2 of its 4 pizza-eating turtles named for Renaissance painters.
Answer: Leonardo, Michaelangelo, Donatello, and Raphael.

6) When observed from the Earth, how many degrees per hour does the sun appear to move?
Answer: 15 degrees (15 degrees x 24 hours = 360 degrees).

7) Name the character created by Joel Chandler Harris to narrate tales about Brer Rabbit and Brer Fox.
Answer: Uncle Remus.

8) A sketch for an experimental flying machine was found among the papers of artist Leonardo da Vinci, who died May 2, 1519. Name da Vinci's nationality.
Answer: Italian.

9) What is the width of a rectangular floor 15 feet long with an area of 180 square feet?
Answer: 12.

10) Identify the country whose efforts to add land by diking off the North Sea are clearly shown in 3 decades of satellite images. Rotterdam is its 2nd largest city.
Answer: The Netherlands.

11) In which year—1935, 1945, 1955, or 1965—did President Eisenhower hold TV's first presidential news conference?
Answer: 1955 (on January 19).

12) President Andrew Johnson's impeachment trial began on March 13, 1868, and ended 2 months later when he was found not guilty as charged. Which of the following means "to free from blame": *indict, abscond, abdicate,* or *acquit*?
Answer: Acquit.

13) Northern Ireland and Scotland are part of the country referred to as UK. Identify the UK division, or area, whose name begins with the letter *W*.
Answer: Wales.

14) In 1992, William Aramony resigned as head of the United Way, a charitable organization, after being charged with personal extravagance. With a $463,000-a-year salary, how much did he earn per month, rounded to the nearest thousand?
Answer: $39,000.

15) Name the country once led by Prime Minister Brian Mulroney. Its capital is Ottawa.
Answer: Canada.

16) What word designates both the muscular casing surrounding the internal organs of an octopus or other cephalopod and the layer of rock that surrounds the Earth's core?
Answer: Mantle.

17) The U.S. has raised the tax on goods that China sells to this country. What prefix is used with *port* to make a word for "something brought into one country from another"?
Answer: im- (import).

18) Former Olympic champion Rafer Johnson was the first torchbearer in the 15,280-mile relay that took the Olympic flame from Los Angeles to Atlanta. Name the 10-event competition in which Johnson won a gold medal.
Answer: Decathlon.

19) What name is given to the rain produced by sulfur dioxide and nitrogen oxide, resulting from the combustion of fossil fuels?
Answer: Acid rain.

20) In Japan in 1992, New Year's well-wishers greeted their ruler Akihito with cries of "Banzai," meaning "long life." Is his title *Emir*, *Emperor*, *President*, or *Prime Minister*?
Answer: Emperor.

21) Spell the title for the wife of the Japanese emperor.
Answer: E-M-P-R-E-S-S (Akihito's wife is Empress Michiko).

22) Name 2 of the 3 U.S. government positions with the highest salary except for the presidency.
Answer: Vice Presidency, Speaker of the House, and Chief Justice.

23) In 1992, George Washington's Mount Vernon estate received a $1.75 million Kellogg Foundation grant for a farming exhibit. On which river is Mount Vernon located?
Answer: Potomac River.

24) Find the 2 numbers whose sum is 11 and whose difference is 15.
Answer: 13 and negative 2.

25) Name the British prime minister who called for a general election in April 1992. His surname designates an army rank above a captain and below a lieutenant colonel.
Answer: John Major.

26) Archibald Cox, the Watergate prosecutor dismissed by President Nixon, later withdrew support for the independent counsel law under which Kenneth Starr investigated President Clinton's affairs. Spell *counsel* as used here, meaning "lawyer."
Answer: C-O-U-N-S-E-L.

27) The U.S. secretary of commerce publicly blamed Japan in 1992 for the lingering recession in the U.S. Spell *publicly*.
Answer: P-U-B-L-I-C-L-Y.

28) In 1992, Israel's Philharmonic Orchestra broke its 43-year ban on works by Richard Wagner, a composer admired by Germany's WWII leader. Name this leader.
Answer: Adolf Hitler.

29) What is 5/8 plus 3/5?
Answer: 1 9/40 (accept 49/40).

30) In 1999, which country established the territory of Nunavut to provide a self-governed homeland for its aboriginal people, the Inuits?
Answer: Canada.

31) The acronym ACOG was frequently heard on the news during the summer of 1996, especially during the Olympic Games in late July and early August. What does ACOG stand for?
Answer: Atlanta Committee for the Olympic Games.

32) Name the first chief justice of the Supreme Court. His surname identifies a large blue bird.
Answer: John Jay.

33) In which state did President Bush make his campaign debut on January 15, 1992? By tradition, it holds the nation's first presidential primary, and its capital is Concord.
Answer: New Hampshire.

34) Bill is 4 times as old as John. In 20 years he will be twice as old as John. How old is John now?
Answer: 10 years old.

35) In which country is Rio de Janeiro, where the U.N. sponsored in 1992 what was the world's biggest environmental meeting ever?
Answer: Brazil.

36) German physician Robert Koch discovered the germ that causes tuberculosis. Is tuberculosis a disease of the *intestines*, the *heart*, the *joints*, or the *lungs*?
Answer: Lungs.

37) *Roget's Thesaurus of English Words and Phrases* is a dictionary of words with similar meanings. What term designates a word that shares a meaning with another?
Answer: Synonym.

38) Israel has prevented the sale of books with photographs of some ancient documents from biblical times written on rolls of parchment. What are such rolls called?
Answer: Scrolls (in this case, the Dead Sea Scrolls).

39) In 1992, the Sicilian army was ordered to build barriers to slow the flow from Mount Etna, Europe's most active volcano. Name the hot rock that a volcano sends out.
Answer: Lava.

40) Did the geographer who named America borrow the name form an explorer, an Indian tribe, the Bible, or a king?
Answer: An explorer (from Amerigo Vespucci).

41) Name the oldest signer of both the Declaration of Independence and the Constitution. He is also credited with proving the presence of electricity in lightning.
Answer: Benjamin Franklin.

42) Newt Gingrich served as the Speaker of the House of Representatives for 4 years during the 1990s. How many members does the House have, a number equal to 20 squared plus 35?
Answer: 435 members.

43) In which city, Alaska's largest, does the Iditarod, a 1,159-mile race, begin? It ends in Nome.
Answer: Anchorage.

44) What is the measure of the supplement of a 45-degree angle?
Answer: 135 degrees.

45) Which system of writing developed by a Frenchman in the 19th century was used in 1992 to update McDonald's menus for the visually impaired?
Answer: Braille.

46) Identify 4 of the 7 colors of the spectrum.
Answer: Violet, indigo, blue, green, yellow, orange, and red.

47) The 272 Americans who died in the Gulf War were honored in 1992 in Arlington National Cemetery. Spell *cemetery*.
Answer: C-E-M-E-T-E-R-Y.

48) Identify the large wooden figure from mythology whose name is being used to designate any e-mail attachment that seems harmless but has hiding within it a program that lets another alter your computer files just as the Greeks hid in the figure to invade Troy.
Answer: Trojan horse.

49) What is 50% of 75?
Answer: 37.5 (accept 37 1/2 and 75/2).

50) Name 2 of the ships under Christopher Columbus's command on his voyage to the New World in 1492.
Answer: *Niña, Pinta,* and *Santa María.*

1) What Latin word for "mother" completes the term *alma* _____ designating "the school one has attended"?
Answer: *Mater.*

2) Complete Patrick Henry's famous line from a 1775 speech in support of arming the militia: "I know not what course others may take, but as for me, give me _____ or give me _____."
Answer: "liberty (or give me) death" (given in St. John's Church on March 23, 1775).

3) Lakes Michigan and Ontario once were 95% and 30% frozen, respectively. Name 2 of the 3 Great Lakes that were 100% frozen at that time.
Answer: Lakes Superior, Huron, and Erie.

4) If a worker earns $10 an hour and gets time and a half for every hour over 40 hours, how much will the worker earn in a 60-hour week?
Answer: $700.

5) In a major policy reversal, the FDA once asked Congress for guidance on whether to regulate cigarettes as an addictive drug because of which substance in tobacco?
Answer: Nicotine.

6) Identify the largest flying bird on the North American continent. The last of the 27 living ones was captured in 1987 in an attempt to preserve this species, whose name begins with the letter *C*.
Answer: (California) condor.

7) King Hussein of Jordan designated as his successor his eldest son, Abdullah, rather than his brother, Hassan, who reigned for him while he was in the U.S. for cancer treatment. Spell *reign*, meaning "to rule."
Answer: R-E-I-G-N.

8) Name the fictional London nanny created in 1934 by British author P.L. Travers. The Disney film about her features the song "Supercalifragilisticexpialidocious."
Answer: Mary Poppins (three more Mary Poppins books followed, in 1935, 1944, and 1952).

9) What is the square root of 441?
Answer: 21.

10) February 15 marks the 5th anniversary of the Soviet Union's withdrawal from Afghanistan. What is the silent consonant in the name *Afghanistan*?
Answer: H.

11) Straddling the prime meridian in the observatory at Greenwich, England, places you in which 2 hemispheres at the same time?
Answer: Eastern and Western Hemispheres.

12) Who was the oldest man ever elected U.S. president? He moved to a ranch near Santa Barbara, California, after his presidency.
Answer: Ronald Reagan (at age 73).

13) In 1992, the ice-clogged Winooski River caused flooding in Vermont's capital. Name it.
Answer: Montpelier.

14) 92.7 is 90% of what number?
Answer: 103.

15) In which country did EuroDisney, the 4th in the Disney Park franchise, open in early April near the city known for the Tuileries Gardens and Pompidou Center?
Answer: France (the 3rd Disney park opened in Tokyo in 1983).

16) Give the geologic term for the various mechanical and chemical processes that cause exposed rocks to break up.
Answer: Weathering.

17) Democratic presidential candidate Bill Clinton emerged as his party's front-runner on Super Tuesday in 1992. Spell *candidate*.
Answer: C-A-N-D-I-D-A-T-E.

18) Name the late opera singer honored at a benefit in Harlem chaired honorarily by Hillary Rodham Clinton. She was the first black singer to perform at the White House, and her surname is a variant spelling of that of the author of "The Ugly Duckling."
Answer: Marian Anderson (Hans Christian Andersen wrote "The Ugly Duckling").

19) Which of these accounts for skin color: *pepsin, melanin, pheromone*, or *beta-carotene*?
Answer: Melanin.

20) Complete the title of former British Prime Minister Margaret Thatcher's memoirs *The ____ Street Years* by giving the word for a bird's first soft, fluffy feathers and adding an *-ing*. This *-ing* word names the location of the British prime minister's home.
Answer: Downing (the prime minister's home is at 10 Downing Street).

21) The Bunsen burner used to heat substances in science laboratories is named for Robert Bunsen. Spell *laboratories*.
Answer: L-A-B-O-R-A-T-O-R-I-E-S.

22) Which word meaning "work" identifies the department that President Roosevelt named Frances Perkins to head in 1933, making her the first woman Cabinet member?
Answer: Labor.

23) In which state did John Kennedy initiate the Peace Corps in a campaign speech in Ann Arbor on October 14, 1960? Indiana and Ohio form the state's southern border.
Answer: Michigan (at the U. of Michigan; corps was formally proposed 19 days later).

24) On May 6, 1954, Britain's Roger Bannister became the first man to run the mile in less than how many minutes, the equivalent of 1/15 of an hour?
Answer: Less than 4 minutes.

25) The early mating in 1992 between Ling-Ling and Hsing-Hsing at Washington's National Zoo raised hopes of adding to which dwindling species of bear-like animal?
Answer: Panda.

26) Which childhood disease, almost eliminated after mass immunization began in 1963, staged a comeback in 1989, especially on the East coast?
Answer: Measles.

27) Name the only 4-time winner of the Pulitzer Prize for poetry. This New England poet wrote "The Road Not Taken."
Answer: Robert Lee Frost.

28) The record company of Milli Vanilli had to make partial refunds to about 80,000 fans whom they deceived after she lip-synched her performance at a concert. Is such a deception called *arson, fraud, larceny,* or *perjury*?
Answer: Fraud.

29) Which of the following is the largest: 2/5, 8/16, 3/7, or 1/3?
Answer: 8/16.

30) In 1991, which European country, whose patron saint is St. Patrick, received the most immigrant visas from the U.S.?
Answer: Ireland (Poland, 2nd; Japan, 3rd; Great Britain, 4th).

31) The owners of Times Square, the New York City landmark from which a lighted ball drops to signal the new year, filed for bankruptcy in 1992. Spell *bankruptcy*.
Answer: B-A-N-K-R-U-P-T-C-Y.

32) To which federal position was Sandra Day O'Connor the first woman ever appointed?
Answer: Supreme Court justice.

33) An earthquake in Alaska on March 27, 1964, registered a magnitude of 8.5, the highest ever recorded in North America. On what scale are earthquakes measured?
Answer: Richter scale (the quake killed about 120).

34) Name the 5 consecutive integers whose sum is 85.
Answer: 15, 16, 17, 18, 19.

35) With a record 1 in 10 Americans receiving food stamps in January 1992, about how many of the U.S.'s 250 million citizens were recipients?
Answer: 25 million.

36) Which substance would you add to water to make a saline solution?
Answer: Salt (accept NaCl or sodium chloride).

37) In 1992, some 745 Vietnamese boat people volunteered to leave detention camps in Hong Kong and return to their homeland. What is the verb from which the noun *detention* is made?
Answer: Detain.

38) Name the first evangelist to preach in North Korea. His surname is the middle name of the telephone's inventor.
Answer: Billy Graham.

39) According to doctors, which common illness may be somewhat controlled by making a decoy molecule to fool the invading rhinoviruses that cause half of all of these illnesses?
Answer: The common cold.

40) Which disease is named along with starvation and environmental problems such as water shortage as reasons for likely zero population growth in many African countries in just a few years? It affects the body's immune system.
Answer: AIDS (25% of Zimbabwe's population are carrying the virus).

41) In the 1990s, the U.S. Surgeon General described Latin America as being on the verge of widespread smoking-related disease. What word designates "a disease spread widely throughout a population"?
Answer: Epidemic.

42) Name the only item that has been in the White House since it was built. Dolley Madison saved this item, a portrait, by taking it with her when she fled the house prior to its burning by the British in 1812.
Answer: Portrait of George Washington (by artist Gilbert Stuart).

43) Brazil's top 2 environmental officials were fired in 1992 after feuding over the deforestation of the area surrounding the world's largest river in volume. Name it.
Answer: Amazon River (the world's 2nd longest).

44) Blacks make up about 70% of South Africa's approximately 40 million people. About how many blacks live in South Africa?
Answer: 28 million.

45) A 1992 leak at a nuclear plant brought reminders of the world's worst nuclear plant accident at Chernobyl 6 years earlier. In which former country did the 1986 accident occur?
Answer: Soviet Union (in Ukraine).

46) Identify the imaginary lines 23% 27' north and south of the equator. Their names are also used as signs of the Zodiac.
Answer: Tropic of Cancer and Tropic of Capricorn.

47) The Duchess of York (Fergie) and Prince Andrew separated after 5 years of marriage. Spell *separation*.
Answer: S-E-P-A-R-A-T-I-O-N.

48) Which Atlanta Brave hit his 715th home run on April 8, 1974, breaking Babe Ruth's record set in 1935?
Answer: Henry "Hank" Aaron.

49) What is the simplified form of the square root of 54?
Answer: 3 times the square root of 6.

50) According to a 1977 treaty, Panama gains full control of the Panama Canal on December 31, 1999. Name the Georgia-born President under whom this treaty was ratified.
Answer: Jimmy Carter.

1) In which state did a nuclear accident occur in 1979 at Three Mile Island near the capital of Harrisburg?
Answer: Pennsylvania.

2) Senator Kay Bailey Hutchison of Texas was once acquitted of ethics charges when prosecutors said they could not proceed without a ruling permitting the admission of key evidence. Spell *acquitted*.
Answer: A-C-Q-U-I-T-T-E-D.

3) All 189 people aboard a Boeing 757 were killed when it crashed into the sea off the coast of the Dominican Republic, a country on the island of Hispaniola, located between which sea and which ocean?
Answer: Caribbean Sea and Atlantic Ocean.

4) What is the value of x in the geometric series: 9, x, 81, 243?
Answer: 27.

5) The rampaging Willamette River, at its highest level in 32 years in 1996, stopped just short of a 28-foot seawall in Oregon's largest city. Name this city, an important West Coast port.
Answer: Portland.

6) On March 24, 1882, German scientist Robert Koch announced his discovery of the pathogenic germs of which disease known as TB?
Answer: Tuberculosis.

7) In 1992, Korean President Roh Tae-woo's party conceded defeat in general Parliamentary elections. Spell *conceded*.
Answer: C-O-N-C-E-D-E-D.

8) The new owner of a 70-year-old strength training program says its name "is synonymous with ... the idea of the little guy standing up to the big guy." Complete its name *Charles* _____, the latter part of which also designates a book of maps.
Answer: (Charles) Atlas.

9) Calculate the profit on the sale of 12 sports coats based on the equation $P = n^2 - 6n - 27$, where n is the number of coats sold.
Answer: $45.

10) On which country did the U.S. declare war in 1917 to enter WWI? Its mountainous region called the Black Forest is the setting for many old legends and fairy tales.
Answer: Germany.

11) In 1992, *The New York Times* was awarded 2 Pulitzer Prizes for achievement in journalism. Spell *achievement*.
Answer: A-C-H-I-E-V-E-M-E-N-T.

12) Name the "Volunteer State," in which the Union suffered about 13,000 casualties and the Confederacy about 11,000 in a battle near the Shiloh Church on April 6 and 7, 1862.
Answer: Tennessee.

13) What word beginning with the letter *L* names the 130 miles of embankments built to protect New Orleans from flood waters?
Answer: Levees.

14) What is 5 2/5 minus 2 3/5?
Answer: 2 4/5.

15) Which Washington, D.C., war memorial that includes the names of 58,183 service people who died in a war celebrated its 17th anniversary in 1999?
Answer: Vietnam Veterans Memorial.

16) What is the primary gas in the atmosphere of Venus, which acts like a greenhouse roof to trap the sun's heat, making the rocks on the planet hotter than boiling water?
Answer: Carbon dioxide.

17) How many prepositional phrases are in the following sentence: *Israel was recently cleared by the U.S. of selling Patriot missiles and technology to China?*
Answer: 3 (*by...*, *of...*, and *to...*).

18) Composer John Williams's "Summon the Heroes" was the Official Centennial Olympic Theme of the 1996 Atlanta Summer Games. Spell both *centennial* and *heroes*.
Answer: C-E-N-T-E-N-N-I-A-L and H-E-R-O-E-S.

19) What verb means "to liquefy" or "to make liquid, as by melting"?
Answer: Dissolve.

20) In 1992, South African President de Klerk visited Africa's most populous country. Is this country Nigeria, Hungary, Argentina, or Rumania?
Answer: Nigeria.

21) In 1992, Libyan mobs attacked diplomatic offices of countries supporting U.N. sanctions against their homeland. What are such offices of foreign countries called?
Answer: Embassies.

22) Which state won its independence from Mexico when General Santa Anna was defeated at San Jacinto on April 21, 1836?
Answer: Texas (which was admitted to the U.S. in 1845).

23) Identify the famous city whose name completes the proverb "_____ wasn't built in a day," meaning that anything worthwhile takes time to complete.
Answer: Rome.

24) The largest known prime number, with 227,832 digits, was discovered in 1992 by mathematicians. What is a prime number?
Answer: A number divided evenly only by 1 and itself.

25) What name beginning with *G* identifies the Palestinian-run international airport that opened in late 1998 in a strip of land occupied by Israeli troops from 1967 to 1994?
Answer: Gaza (International Airport; the *Gaza Strip* was occupied by Israeli troops).

26) Which colorless gas 14 times lighter than air is found in coal, oil, and natural gas and is burned in great masses in the Sun, sending light and heat to the Earth?
Answer: Hydrogen.

27) The U.S. Embassy and the Norwegian government traced the ancestry of former U.S. Secretary of State Warren Christopher back to 1747. Spell *genealogy*, meaning "the study of ancestry."
Answer: G-E-N-E-A-L-O-G-Y (Warren Christopher's great-grandfather immigrated to the U.S. from Norway).

28) Italian women claimed 3 of 4 medal positions in pre-Olympic competition in 1996 in the Olympics' only combative sport in which women compete, namely which sport where a scored point is called a touch?
Answer: Fencing (or *touché*, a touch to the opponent's torso with the tip of the foil).

29) What is the area, in square feet, of a rectangle measuring 1 yard by 3 yards?
Answer: 27 square feet.

30) Which battleship was named for the state whose capital is Jefferson City and nicknamed "Mighty Mo"? This ship, which was the site of Japan's formal surrender in 1945, was retired in 1992.
Answer: U.S.S. *Missouri*.

31) Many Japanese return to Iwo Jima each spring in search of fallen relatives from a gruesome WWII battle. Are members of earlier generations of one's family called *descendants, heirs, offspring,* or *ancestors*?
Answer: Ancestors.

32) Which words beginning with *T* and *B* identify the 2 crimes that the U.S. Constitution specifies as grounds for removal from the presidency, as stated in the phrase: for "____, ____ or other high crimes and misdemeanors"?
Answer: Treason and bribery.

33) Name both the "Grand Canyon State" and the "Aloha State," neither of which observes Daylight Savings Time.
Answer: Arizona and Hawaii.

34) If Paul has 3 times as much money as his sister, and he has $12 more than she has, how much money does Paul have?
Answer: $18 (his sister has $6).

35) Name the Illinois manufacturer of earth-moving equipment that sought to replace United Auto Workers on strike at 6 plants before a settlement in 1992. Its name also designates the larva of a moth.
Answer: Caterpillar.

36) Identify the central organ in the nervous system. It is protected by the skull.
Answer: Brain.

37) Spell *site* as used in the following: Cuba's Bay of Pigs was the site of a failed 1961 U.S.-backed invasion.
Answer: S-I-T-E (the invasion was crushed on April 17, 1961).

38) Which Jewish festival celebrates the flight of the Israelites from Egyptian slavery?
Answer: Passover (or Pesach or Pesah).

39) Identify the largest part of the brain, which occupies most of the cranial capacity.
Answer: Cerebrum.

40) What acronym completes the name ____ *package* to designate boxes of food sent to help feed people abroad after WWII by the Cooperative for American Relief Everywhere, a New York-based relief organization that celebrated its 50th anniversary in 1995?
Answer: CARE (an acronym for Cooperative for American Relief Everywhere).

41) Give the anagram used by mistake for the word *United* in *United States* on pens used by senators to pledge justice in the impeachment trial of President Clinton.
Answer: Untied.

42) Name the Native American who will be featured on the new gold-colored one dollar coin to be introduced in 2000. With her baby on her back, she traveled west with the Lewis and Clark expedition, serving as their interpreter.
Answer: Sacajawea.

43) Quezon City, the capital of the Philippines from 1948 to 1976, was named for its first president. What is the present capital of the country?
Answer: Manila.

44) What is the length of the hypotenuse of a right triangle with one leg of length 60 and the other of length 80?
Answer: 100.

45) Name the "Sunflower State," where fed-up taxpayers in 7 Southwest counties once voted to secede.
Answer: Kansas.

46) Did Guglielmo Marconi invent the *telephone*, the *cotton gin*, the *steam engine*, or the *radio*?
Answer: Radio.

47) Senators sometimes call for the President to lift or impose a trade prohibition. Is such a prohibition called an *embargo, quarantine, referendum*, or *siege*?
Answer: Embargo.

48) Composer Andrew Lloyd Webber, known for his Broadway musicals *Cats* and *Phantom of the Opera*, gave his daughter which middle name, meaning "the dawn," and completing the term _____ *borealis*, designating the "northern lights"?
Answer: Aurora (her full name is Isabella Aurora).

49) If a fair die is tossed 3 times, what is the probability that 3 spots will appear face-up on all 3 tosses of the die?
Answer: 1/216.

50) Identify the Venezuelan native whose defeat of the Spanish in 1830 won independence for Venezuela, Colombia, Ecuador, Peru, and Bolivia, which is named for him. In 1998, Venezuela's new president referred to Venezuelan voters as the "people of" this leader.
Answer: Simón Bolívar (Chavez said "people of Simón Bolívar" were "grand people").

1) What name for a burrowing mammal is given to an official inside an intelligence agency who illegally reports to foreign governments?
Answer: Mole.

2) Abraham Lincoln began his first political race on March 9, 1832, when he announced his candidacy for the legislature of which state? It is known as the "Prairie State."
Answer: Illinois.

3) Identify the Australian River that shares its name with the surname of the family of 3 children in James Barrie's *Peter Pan*.
Answer: Darling River.

4) With his total of 18,401 consecutive votes, about how many votes did a Representative Natcher average per year for each of his 40 years in office?
Answer: About 460 per year.

5) To raise money for an inner city project, former President Carter once auctioned signed photos of the 5 ex-Presidents at the 1991 dedication of the library of which President?
Answer: Ronald Reagan.

6) French researchers found the first drug that slows a debilitating, fatal nerve disorder named after Lou Gehrig, who died from it in 1941. Was Gehrig a *politician*, *movie star*, *football player*, or *baseball player*?
Answer: Baseball player (amyotrophic lateral sclerosis is called Lou Gehrig's disease).

7) Which author created Tiny Tim and Ebeneezer Scrooge in his book *A Christmas Carol*?
Answer: Charles Dickens.

8) Which word designates both a group of gorillas and a group of musicians?
Answer: Band.

9) Find the perimeter of a right triangle whose base is 9 inches long and whose hypotenuse is 15 inches.
Answer: 36 inches.

10) In 1994, France enacted a new penal code, or guidelines for punishment for crimes, that overhauls the guidelines set forth by which emperor in 1810?
Answer: Napoleon (Bonaparte).

11) What word containing the word *hot* means "easily angered"?
Answer: Hotheaded (or hot-blooded).

12) In which Georgia city established by James Oglethorpe did Juliette Gordon Low found the Girl Scouts on March 12, 1912?
Answer: Savannah.

13) Identify Italy's largest waterway. Its name sounds like the surname of the author who wrote "The Gold Bug" and is considered the father of the American detective story.
Answer: Po River (in northern Italy; Edgar Allan Poe is the author).

14) What is the value of 27 to the negative 1/3 power?
Answer: 1/3.

15) After the death of a Frenchman was linked to mad cow disease from foreign sources, certain food in French stores began carrying the label *viande française*. Give the English for this French phrase.
Answer: French meat (the home-grown beef bears this label).

16) Scientists reported that the prehistoric ancestor of today's elephant might have outlasted the Ice Age and survived until 2000 B.C. by downsizing from 10 to 6 feet tall. Identify this ancestor, whose name, meaning "huge," also identifies a famous Kentucky cave.
Answer: Mammoth (Mammoth Cave is in the world's longest known cave system).

17) In an action seen as an affront to the rest of Europe, Switzerland once banned foreign trucks from using the nation as a commercial route. Spell *commercial*.
Answer: C-O-M-M-E-R-C-I-A-L (nation is not a member of the European Union).

18) Name the Greek goddess of the rainbow, who was said to have slid down the rainbow to deliver messages to mortals, or name the colored ring surrounding the black center of the eye.
Answer: Iris.

19) At Biosphere 2 (Earth is Biosphere 1), there are samplings of other ecosystems such as an ocean, a desert, a rain forest, a savanna, and a marsh. Which term designates any large-scale ecosystem, like a desert, where plants, insects and people live?
Answer: Biome.

20) A U.S. judge reduced the prison sentence for Manuel Noriega, Panama's former dictator arrested for drug trafficking in 1989, making him eligible for release by 2007. Spell both *trafficking* and *eligible*.
Answer: T-R-A-F-F-I-C-K-I-N-G and E-L-I-G-I-B-L-E.

21) What 2-word term containing the word *cold* and naming a body part means "a snub"?
Answer: Cold shoulder.

22) Identify the U.S. President whose impeachment trial began on March 13, 1868, and ended in an acquittal 2 months later. His surname also identifies President Kennedy's VP.
Answer: Andrew Johnson (Lyndon Johnson was Kennedy's VP).

23) A scene for the movie *Murder in the First* was filmed at a former federal penitentiary on an island in the middle of San Francisco Bay. Name this former prison.
Answer: Alcatraz (it closed in 1963 and is now a tourist attraction).

24) How many items are in two gross, or what is double the square of 12?
Answer: 288.

25) The Brady Act, which took effect February 28, 1994, requires a background check and a waiting period of how long for purchase of a gun?
Answer: 5 days.

26) Identify the Jupiter-bound spacecraft that had the first-ever spacecraft encounter with an asteroid in 1991. It is named for a famous 16th-century astronomer.
Answer: *Galileo* (the asteroid is named Gaspra).

27) Which of the following is a synonym for ancestors: *descendants, heirs, posterity,* or *predecessors*?
Answer: Predecessors.

28) Ulysses S. Grant was appointed as commander of all Union armies on March 9, 1864. Ulysses is the Roman name for which Greek mythological hero who traveled around for 10 years before returning home after the Trojan War?
Answer: Odysseus.

29) If there are a 1000 votes and one of the 2 candidates gets 60% of them, by how many votes does he win?
Answer: 200.

30) On April 27, 1941, the Germans raised the Nazi swastika over the highest point in Athens when they took over which city. What name designates this hill?
Answer: Acropolis.

31) On July 14, France holds Bastille Day, which celebrates the storming of the Bastille in 1789. What was the Bastille?
Answer: A prison.

32) Name the presidential yacht used by U.S. Presidents from 1902 to 1929 to cruise the Chesapeake Bay. It shares its name with the ship that brought the Pilgrims to America in 1620.
Answer: *Mayflower.*

33) Which 2 oceans did Steve Fossett cross in his eastward flight from Argentina to Australia, where he crash-landed on his 4th try to circle the globe in a hot air balloon?
Answer: Atlantic and Indian Oceans (Fossett survived without injury).

34) Give the sum of $14x + 5$ and $-7x - 9$.
Answer: $7x - 4$.

35) The late Melina Mercouri was the first woman ever to hold a senior Cabinet post in which country on a peninsula between the Ionian and Aegean seas?
Answer: Greece.

36) Of the vitamins A, B, D, and K, a deficiency of which one causes night blindness?
Answer: A (retinol).

37) Twain's story "Baker's Blue Jay Yarn" tells of a bird that tries to fill a house with nuts. What 2-word alliterative term designates such a tale that depends on exaggeration for its effect?
Answer: Tall tale.

38) Identify the dance of the gypsies in Spain, characterized by hammering of the heels, and clacking of castanets, accompanied by guitar.
Answer: Flamenco.

39) The ram, or male sheep, is the zodiac sign for Aries, the period from March 21 to April 19. Which word designates a female sheep?
Answer: Ewe.

40) A book by Hugh Thomas gives a dramatic account of Hernando Cortés's overthrow of Montezuma in 1519 in Mexico. Spell the word *conquistador*, which specifically designates any of the Spanish conquerors of Mexico and Peru in the 16th century.
Answer: C-O-N-Q-U-I-S-T-A-D-O-R.

41) A former Bolivian president was sentenced to 30 years in prison for murder, corruption, and betraying his country. What word designates "the betrayal of one's country"?
Answer: Treason.

42) Andrew Johnson served as President during the period called *Reconstruction*, referring to the rebuilding of which of the following: Washington, D.C., after the War of 1812; the U.S. banking system after the stock market crash in 1929; Europe after WWII; or the South after the Civil War?
Answer: South after the Civil War.

43) On which French-controlled island was Napoleon born: Barbados, Corsica, Santa Catalina, or Oahu?
Answer: Corsica.

44) A shop that is closed on Sundays has an average of 50 visitors on weekdays and 150 on Saturdays. How many visitors would they average in a 3-week period?
Answer: 1,200.

45) A computerized traffic light system aimed at easing traffic jams caused chaos in which Thai city with as many cars as in New York but only one-third as many roads?
Answer: Bangkok (capital of Thailand).

46) Identify the planet whose newly discovered moons were named in 1991 for the nymphs Naiad and Galatea; for Poseidon's lovers Thalassa and Larissa; and for Poseidon's son Proteus and his daughter Despoina?
Answer: Neptune (Neptune was Poseidon to ancient Greeks).

47) Is the following a simple, complex, or compound sentence? *On March 2, 1836, Texas declared its independence from Mexico and became a republic.*
Answer: Simple (with a compound verb).

48) The soundtrack from *Aladdin* won 5 Grammys, including song of the year. What word describes a movie featuring drawn figures that move?
Answer: Animated (the song is "A Whole New World: Aladdin's Theme").

49) An 11-year-old Georgia boy climbed Mount Kilimanjaro, Africa's highest peak, making him possibly the youngest ever to do so. How much higher is this 19,340-foot mountain than Mount Elbrus, Europe's highest peak at 18,600 feet?
Answer: 740 feet (Joshua Stewart and his father plan to climb Elbrus next).

50) Name the world leader assassinated on the Ides of March, or March 15, 44 B.C.
Answer: Julius Caesar.

1) Name the blanket-like cloak with a slit in the middle for the head that is part of the traditional gaucho costume in Argentina.
Answer: Poncho.

2) What is the slang term for government funds acquired by a legislator for special local projects as a kind of political favor? It also designates meat that comes from pigs.
Answer: Pork.

3) Which word beginning with *H* completes the name U.S. _____ Memorial Museum opened off the Mall in Washington, D.C., in 1993 to commemorate the persecution of Jews during World War II?
Answer: Holocaust.

4) With 8 pairs of teams playing in each of 4 regions in the NCAA basketball tournament, what is the total number of teams that participate?
Answer: 64.

5) A Japanese vessel sent back the first television pictures of the Marianas Trench, the deepest spot in the world's oceans. In which ocean is this trench near Guam located?
Answer: Pacific Ocean.

6) Of which of the following are stalactites generally made: *quartz, limestone, marble,* or *gypsum*?
Answer: Limestone.

7) On March 4, 1893, President Cleveland was inaugurated for his 2nd, nonconsecutive term of office. Give the total number of syllables in *inaugurated* and *nonconsecutive*.
Answer: 10 (5 each).

8) Scientists have discovered a gene that lets fruit flies live 35% longer than those without it. Identify the biblical figure for whom they named this gene since he is said to have lived 969 years.
Answer: Methuselah.

9) How many quadrants are there in a circle?
Answer: 4.

10) Which country north of England did James VI head when he joined it and England under his reign on March 24, 1603, and took the name James I?
Answer: Scotland.

11) In an effort to showcase American food rather than foreign food, the White House once interviewed new chefs to replace a head chef who specialized in French food. Spell *chef*.
Answer: C-H-E-F.

12) Which New England state was admitted to the Union as the 23rd state on March 15, 1820? President Bush often spent vacations at Kennebunkport on its Atlantic coast.
Answer: Maine (admitted as a free state by the Missouri Compromise).

13) On which river is the Grand Coulee Dam, the U.S.'s largest concrete dam? It forms the border between Washington and Oregon and empties into the Pacific.
Answer: Columbia River (it began producing electricity on March 22, 1941).

14) Which term is used in mathematics to designate any line exactly bisecting a circle?
Answer: Diameter.

15) Name the London residence of the Queen where, for the first time in 1992, women took part in the 155-year-old changing of the guard, as members of a Royal Air Force band.
Answer: Buckingham Palace.

16) What name designates a person or animal lacking the normal pigmentation of skin, hair, or fur?
Answer: Albino.

17) Complete the following proverb, "Don't put the _____ before the horse," meaning "do things in the correct order."
Answer: "cart."

18) Arts educators included the ability to play a musical instrument as one of the national standards recommended to the secretary of education. What word designates both a measure of written music and lawyers as a group?
Answer: Bar.

19) What body organ contains nephrons, which contain microscopic blood vessels and renal tubes used in filtering blood?
Answer: Kidney.

20) In 1998, Queen Elizabeth II opened Parliament by announcing a bill to strip aristocrats of their right to vote in the parliamentary body whose members are not elected but granted seats because of their positions or inherited titles. Complete its name: the House of ___.
Answer: (House of) Lords.

21) Name the traditional dress of women in India consisting of a cloth wrapped to form both a skirt and a drape over the shoulder or head.
Answer: Sari.

22) Which city is the site of Saint John's Episcopal Church where Patrick Henry delivered his "liberty or death" speech? It was also a capital of the Confederacy.
Answer: Richmond (Virginia).

23) Which military fort, now the home of the U.S. Military Academy, did Connecticut-born Revolutionary General Benedict Arnold and John André plan to betray to the British?
Answer: West Point.

24) What is 25% of 3 hours and 20 minutes?
Answer: 5/6 of an hour or 50 minutes.

25) A St. Petersburg, Florida, museum once exhibited 250 works from a museum in the 90-acre walled area housing government offices in Moscow. Is this Moscow government center known as the Acropolis, Louvre, Kremlin, or KGB?
Answer: The Kremlin (the museum is the Florida International Museum).

26) In mixing lights, which 3 colors produce white light and are thus considered the primary colors of light?
Answer: Red, green, and blue (primary pigment colors are yellow, blue, and red).

27) Identify the ancient language whose name is used with *America* to designate the Western Hemisphere countries south of the U.S.
Answer: Latin (America; most of the countries speak languages developed from Latin).

28) Which Hebrew word meaning "praise the Lord" completes the name of the chorus from Handel's *Messiah* that prompted King George II to stand up on March 23, 1743?
Answer: "Hallelujah (Chorus)" (George II thus set a tradition).

29) Represent the decimal .65 in its lowest fractional form.
     Answer: 13/20.

30) Which letter of the alphabet is emblazoned horizontally on
     South Africa's new flag? It is sometimes used to name an inter-
     section at which 2 roads merge to become one.
     **Answer: Y (it symbolizes "yes"; there are 6 distinct col-
     ors on the flag).**

31) What 2-word term is used to designate the cause of death when
     soldiers are killed by their own forces or allies?
     Answer: Friendly fire.

32) On March 25, 1775, George Washington planted at his home
     some pecan trees sent by Thomas Jefferson, who had also
     planted some at his home. Name both Washington's and
     Jefferson's   Virginia   homes,   near   Alexandria   and
     Charlottesville, respectively.
     **Answer: Mount Vernon and Monticello (pecan is
     native to southern N. America).**

33) Name Canada's most populated province, the site of the
     national capital.
     Answer: Ontario.

34) What is the least common multiple of 6 and 8?
     Answer: 24.

35) The Department of Defense, the U.S.'s largest employer, has
     instituted a smoking ban in such areas as offices and vehicles.
     Spell *vehicle*.
     Answer: V-E-H-I-C-L-E.

36) Name both the green pigment found in plants and the red
     pigment found in blood.
     Answer: Chlorophyll and hemoglobin, respectively.

37) In 1998, a fire gutted California's oldest working pier. Give the
     5-letter synonym for *pier* that completes its name: Stearns
     _____?
     Answer: Wharf (it was built in the 19th century).

38) A 1994 French recording of composer Ravel's works includes
     which extremely repetitive piece of music that bears the same
     name as a short jacket worn open in the front with tight pants
     in Mexico?
     **Answer: *Boléro* (recording by Semyon Bychkov and
     L'Orchestre de Paris).**

39) Bonnie is halving the recipe for a cake since she wants only one layer. If the original recipe calls for 3/4 cup of butter, how much butter will she need for half a recipe?
Answer: 3/8 of a cup.

40) On May 9, 1926, which American became the first to fly over the North Pole? His surname is a homophone for a word designating an animal that is kept in an aviary.
Answer: Richard Evelyn Byrd (accompanied by Floyd Bennett).

41) Centenarian George Burns was buried with his sheet music, 3 cigars, and his hairpiece. Which of the following designates a hairpiece worn to cover a bald spot: *kimono, cummerbund, poncho*, or *toupee*?
Answer: Toupee.

42) Which U.S. President had to flee from Washington, D.C., when the British invaded it and burned the White House in 1814? His surname contains a word for "angry."
Answer: James Madison (he was born in Virginia on 3/16/1751).

43) According to the Census Bureau, by the year 2020 both Texas and Florida will overtake which state that is now the U.S.'s second most populous? It's called the "Empire State."
Answer: New York (now outranked only by California).

44) What is your cost if you buy an $800 television at a 20% discount?
Answer: $640.

45) In 1999, which country marked the 50th year of the reign of its Prince Rainier? It is known for its gambling casino at Monte Carlo.
Answer: Monaco.

46) Some 300 rare gorillas were once left to fend for themselves against poachers after scientists fled war-torn Rwanda's Volcano National Park. Are gorillas classified as *amphibians, canines, mollusks* or *primates*?
Answer: Primates (the gorillas were featured in the film *Gorillas in the Mist*).

47) Henry David Thoreau accidentally set fire to the woods near Concord, Massachusetts, on April 30, 1844, burning 300 acres. Spell *accidentally*.
Answer: A-C-C-I-D-E-N-T-A-L-L-Y.

48) The only abstract painting in the White House is on loan from artist Willem de Kooning. What is the name for the chalk-like crayons used to create some of his works?
Answer: Pastels (the painting in the White House is *Untitled XXXIX*).

49) If the Holocaust Museum in D.C. has about 4,000 visitors daily, how many can be expected to visit it in December, excluding Christmas Day?
Answer: 120,000.

50) Japanese Emperor Hirohito, father of today's emperor, Akihito, ascended what is called the Chrysanthemum Throne in 1926. Spell *ascend*, in this case meaning "to take over."
Answer: A-S-C-E-N-D.

1) Give either the French or Spanish word for "farewell" or "good-bye."
Answer: *Adieu* **or** *adios*, **respectively.**

2) Which U.S. President ironically stated in a famous speech, "The world will little note, nor long remember what we say here"? He did so in his Gettysburg Address.
Answer: **Abraham Lincoln.**

3) The nation's largest river restoration project at Florida's Kissimmee River is the first step in a plan to save which national park, the second largest in the continental U.S.?
Answer: **Everglades National Park.**

4) The 16th Amendment to the Constitution, ratified on February 3, 1913, grants Congress the power to levy taxes on income. If a flat tax rate of 17% were passed, how much income tax would a person earning $30,000 annually owe?
Answer: **$5,100.**

5) With a current population of about 5.6 billion and a 25 year increase of about 40%, is the population in 2020 expected to be about 6 billion, 8 billion, 10 billion, or 12 billion?
Answer: **8 billion.**

6) Because of 1994's cool summer with its plentiful foliage and increase in aphids on which ladybugs feed, droves of ladybugs invaded the Seattle area. Spell *foliage*, meaning "leaves."
Answer: **F-O-L-I-A-G-E.**

7) French-born author Marie Henri Beyle used the pseudonym Stendhal. Spell *pseudonym*, meaning "false name."
Answer: **P-S-E-U-D-O-N-Y-M.**

8) Is Leonardo da Vinci's *Mona Lisa* known for her snake-like hair, wrinkled brow, calm half-smile, or brocade gown?
Answer: **Calm half-smile.**

9) The International Monetary Fund, known as IMF, once approved a loan of $1.5 billion to Russia. Is one billion represented by 10^3, 10^5, 10^7, or 10^9?
Answer: 10^9.

10) Saudi Arabian officials have warned repeatedly that political demonstrations by Iranian Muslims headed to the birthplace of Muhammad will not be tolerated. In which of the following was the prophet Muhammad born: Bethlehem, Jerusalem, Mecca, or Riyadh?
Answer: Mecca.

11) In which state did President Clinton throw out the first ball when the Indians opened the American League season at their home stadium, Jacobs Field?
Answer: Ohio (in Cleveland).

12) Which word beginning with *P* designates any location where people go to vote in the U.S.?
Answer: Poll.

13) Name the country whose official language is Hindi, the world's 3rd most commonly spoken language.
Answer: India.

14) The Senate Finance Committee once proposed raising the minimum earnings on which social security taxes must be paid for a nanny or domestic worker to $630 a year. Does an annual salary of $630 amount to about $30, $50, $70, or $90 a month?
Answer: About $50 a month.

15) In which Asian country was the leader of a doomsday cult arrested in 1995 for the nerve gas attack that killed 12 and injured more than 5,000 on a subway?
Answer: Japan (in Tokyo; Shoko Asahara was arrested).

16) Which of the following designates a scientist who studies insects: *cardiologist, entomologist, orthodontist*, or *physicist*?
Answer: Entomologist.

17) In the 1990s, comedian Steve Martin published a collection of 23 short pieces giving his personal thoughts on such subjects as memory failures after age 50. What 5-letter word beginning with *E* names a brief piece of writing expressing one's own thoughts?
Answer: Essay.

18) A man with a guilty conscience once returned 2 Van Gogh paintings stolen from a museum in the Netherlands. What word designates the nationality of Van Gogh and other natives of the Netherlands?
Answer: Dutch.

19) What name is given to the measure of a place's height in relation to the level of the sea?
Answer: Altitude.

20) Great Britain, the U.S., and Russia were called the Allies in their WWII fight against Germany, Italy, and Japan. Spell *Allies*, meaning "those joined together in the same cause."
Answer: A-L-L-I-E-S.

21) A 3-million-year-old complete skull, possibly that of humanity's earliest known ancestor, was found in Ethiopia in 1994. On which continent is Ethiopia?
Answer: Africa.

22) Richard Nixon, the 37th president of the U.S., was buried on the grounds of the Richard Nixon Library and Birthplace in the town of Yorba Linda in which state?
Answer: California.

23) Name the state in the continental U.S. with the highest average altitude. It meets 3 other states at a point called "Four Corners" and is the site of Mesa Verde National Park.
Answer: Colorado.

24) The prime-rate of interest once rose from 6% to 6¼%. What is the decimal equivalent of 6¼%?
Answer: .0625.

25) Musician Al Hirt, who had more than 50 Grammy nominations during his 50-year career, died in 1999. Complete his nickname "King of the ____" by identifying the brass wind instrument whose name also designates the resounding call of the elephant.
Answer: Trumpet.

26) The late French geneticist Jerome Lejeune is credited with discovering the genetic cause of the mental and physical handicaps of Down Syndrome. Are the thread-like structures that carry the genetic material of heredity called *corpuscles, chromosomes, hormones,* or *platelets*?
Answer: Chromosomes (those with Down Syndrome have an extra chromosome).

27) On April 14, 1865, President Lincoln was assassinated at Ford's Theater in Washington, D.C., by John Wilkes Booth, whose family were famous thespians. Is a thespian an *astronomer, actor, diplomat,* or *explorer*?
Answer: Actor (*thespian* comes from Thespis, the alleged founder of Greek tragedy).

28) Name the New York City center of professional theater nick-named "The Great White Way."
Answer; Broadway.

29) The cost of 3 shirts and 2 sweaters is $89. If each shirt cost $15, how much did each of the 2 equally priced sweaters cost?
Answer: $22.

30) In an effort to increase tourism in Egypt, 11 royal mummies, including Ramses II, were put on display. What word designates an ancient Egyptian king such as Ramses II?
Answer: Pharaoh.

31) Which of the following is the Spanish word for "an afternoon nap": *desperado*, *hacienda*, *machismo*, or *siesta*?
Answer: *Siesta*.

32) A Dutch colonizer landed on Manhattan Island on May 4, 1626, an island he later bought from the Indians. Which of the following French words, meaning "midnight," designates this person: *midi*, *chapeau*, *cravate*, or *minuit*?
Answer: Minuit (Peter Minuit was the Dutchman).

33) Is New York City called the *Bay City*, *Big Apple*, *Mile-High City*, or *Windy City*?
Answer: The Big Apple.

34) What is the greatest common factor of 36 and 117?
Answer: 9.

35) Congressional term limit laws, enacted by 23 states since 1990, were struck down by the Supreme Court in 1995. What is the length of a single term in both the House and the Senate?
Answer: 2 years (House) or 6 years (Senate).

36) According to a Johns Hopkins University study, a compound in the green vegetable once scorned by Presidential Bush protected rats against breast cancer. Identify this vegetable with 2 *C*'s in its name.
Answer: Broccoli.

37) What word beginning with *G* designates sex and completes the rule specifying that a pronoun must agree with its antecedent in person, number, and _____?
Answer: Gender.

38) Is an Alpine home with a sloping roof known as an *adobe*, a *chalet*, a *citadel*, or a *monastery*?
Answer: Chalet.

39) What is the acronym for "sound navigation ranging," the name for a system using reflected sound waves to locate objects under water?
Answer: Sonar (*sound navigation ranging*).

40) Captain William Bligh survived a 47-day voyage of 3,600 miles after being set adrift following a mutiny aboard the HMS *Bounty* on April 28, 1789. What do the initials *HMS* before a ship's name stand for?
Answer: Her (His) Majesty's Ship.

41) If an 18-carat gold ring weighs one ounce and pure gold is 24-carat, what is the weight of the pure gold in the ring?
Answer: 3/4 ounce or .75 ounce.

42) Name the awards announced annually by Columbia University for excellence in literature and journalism.
Answer: Pulitzer Prizes.

43) In 1994, a New England state became the first to require that milk from cows treated with a hormone to increase milk production be so labeled. Identify this state which lies on New Hampshire's western border.
Answer: Vermont.

44) What number when squared completes the following equation: $3^2 + 8^2 = 48 +$ ___ ?
Answer: 5 (9 + 64 = 48 + 25).

45) From which spacecraft did Jim Lovell and 2 others safely return to Earth in 1970 after its oxygen tank exploded? In July 1995, Lovell received the Congressional Space Medal of Honor as Tom Hanks, star of the hit summer movie about the mission, stood by.
Answer: *Apollo 13*.

46) In 1960, Theodore Maiman of the U.S. became the first to build and operate which device that amplifies light into a powerful beam of the kind now used for delicate surgery?
Answer: Laser (acronym for *light amplification by stimulated emission of radiation*).

47) What word completes the phrase *standing* _____ used to designate the form of applause the Gridiron Club once gave Bill and Hillary Clinton for their spoof of the "Harry and Louise" TV ads opposing Clintons' health-reform plan?
Answer: Ovation.

48) Melinda Wagner recently won the 1999 Pulitzer Prize for music with a composition she wrote for flute, strings, and percussion. Which of the following is a percussion instrument: *cello, harp, trombone,* or *xylophone*?
Answer: Xylophone.

49) What's the U.S. tooth fairy's average gift based on a Gallup poll reporting an average of $5.02 in the West; $3.25 in the South; $2.25 in the East; and $2.90 in the Midwest?
Answer: $3.36.

50) Although Watergate led him to become the only President to resign his position, the late Richard Nixon is also remembered for reopening relations with which Communist country that he visited in 1972?
Answer: China.

1) Name the movie based on the 19th-century Hans Christian Andersen tale about a girl who springs magically from the center of a flower.
Answer: *Thumbelina.*

2) Identify the May 5, 1864, battle in Virginia that was the first major battle between Robert E. Lee and Ulysses S. Grant by giving the word meaning "a wild, overgrown or heavily forested tract of land."
Answer: **Wilderness (Battle of the Wilderness).**

3) Do the Galapagos Islands, where several rare mammoth turtles once died in a raging land fire, lie off the coast of Africa, Australia, Canada, or South America?
Answer: **South America (off the coast of Ecuador on South America's west coast).**

4) The White House revealed that Hillary Clinton invested $1,000 on the commodities market in the 1970s and earned almost $100,000 in profits. About how much did she gain for each $1 invested?
Answer: **About $100.**

5) Which of the following physicians specializes in treatment of the heart: *ophthalmologist, cardiologist, neurologist,* or *orthopedist*?
Answer: **Cardiologist.**

6) Scientists have found what they think is the last of 12 subatomic particles from which everything is made. Are these particles called *electrons, neutrons, protons,* or *quarks*?
Answer: **Quarks (new one is smaller than a trillionth of the thickness of a hair).**

7) What word beginning with *D* names the category in which Margaret Edson's play *Wit* won a Pulitzer Prize in 1999?
Answer: **Drama (Michael Cunningham's *The Hours* won the Pulitzer in fiction).**

8) Unlike Lyndon Johnson, Richard Nixon chose not to have his coffin placed for public view in which domed room of the Capitol before burial?
Answer: **Rotunda.**

9) With a total of 148 points scored in a NCAA men's basketball championship game, how many points did the University of Arkansas score to beat Duke by 4 points?
Answer: 76 points (final score 76-72).

10) Hong Kong reverted to Chinese rule in 1997. Which European country ruled this territory prior to its return to China?
Answer: Great Britain.

11) What fairly recently coined term means "stealing a car from its occupants by force"?
Answer: Carjacking.

12) Name the huge memorial near Custer, South Dakota, that celebrated its 50th birthday in May 1998. It honors the Sioux chief who defeated Custer and his cavalry in 1876.
Answer: Crazy Horse (Memorial; begun by K. Ziolkowski, continued by his widow).

13) According to a survey, gasoline is least expensive in oil-rich countries, with a price equivalent to 21 cents a gallon in Caracas and 33 cents in Riyadh. Name either of the countries whose capitals are Caracas and Riyadh, respectively.
Answer: Venezuela or Saudi Arabia.

14) What is the diameter of a circular floor with an area of 64 *pi* square feet?
Answer: 16 feet.

15) Are the leaders of Great Britain and Canada, such as John Major and Brian Mulroney, called *monarchs, czars, presidents,* or *prime ministers*?
Answer: Prime ministers.

16) What is the name for particles of matter with a fixed, orderly pattern and smooth, flat surfaces, such as salt and sugar?
Answer: Crystals.

17) The University of Connecticut defeated Gonzaga to win a spot in the NCAA Final Four. Spell the name of the Canadian territory that is a homophone for Connecticut's nick-name UConn.
Answer: Y-U-K-O-N.

18) Which silent consonant ends the name of the French artist Monet and the word *chalet*?
Answer: *T* (C-H-A-L-E-T).

19) Which of the following designates an inflammation of the liver: *anorexia, hemophilia, hepatitis,* or *meningitis*?
Answer: Hepatitis.

20) On May 7, 399 B.C., in which European city did philosopher Socrates carry out his own death sentence by drinking hemlock after being convicted of corrupting the youth?
Answer: Athens.

21) A company reportedly coordinated illegal jumps made from the Golden Gate Bridge while attached to an elasticized cord. What is such a cord called?
Answer: Bungee.

22) Name the New England state whose town of Springfield is the site of the Basketball Hall of Fame.
Answer: Massachusetts.

23) Name the mercantile company chartered by the British on May 2, 1670, to establish a fur trade in what is now Canada, or name the large bay in northeastern Canada.
Answer: Hudson's Bay Company or Hudson Bay.

24) In an interview, Joseph Heller once said he tries to produce each day 3 handwritten pages, or the equivalent of one typed page. At this rate, how many handwritten pages and how many days did it take him to produce *Closing Time*, his 466-page novel?
Answer: 1,398 handwritten pages and 466 days.

25) Is a person who lives in Iraq called an *Iranian*, *Iraqi*, *Iraqian*, or *Iraqivite*?
Answer: Iraqi.

26) Which of the 9 planets has an atmospheric makeup of approximately 78% nitrogen, 21% oxygen, and 1% argon with small amounts of other gases?
Answer: Earth.

27) A Singapore government-controlled newspaper once ran a detailed description of caning to prove that it is not the barbaric attack described in U.S. media. Which of the following means "to counter or disprove": *reciprocate*, *refute*, *reminisce*, or *renovate*?
Answer: Refute.

28) After U.S. attacks in 1998, Sudanese Muslims stormed the empty U.S. Embassy in Khartoum, shouting "Down, Down USA!" and in Arabic "God is Great." Which of the following is the Muslim's name for God: *Allah*, *Buddha*, *Mecca*, or *Ayatollah*?
Answer: Allah (*Allahu Akbar* means "God is Great")

29) If the total surface area of a cube is 24 square inches, how long is any one of its edges?
Answer: 2.

30) Nelson Mandela became the 2nd foreign leader ever to address Congress twice. Which former British prime minister, whose name includes a synonym for *tabernacle*, also addressed the group twice?
Answer: Winston Churchill (he served as prime minister 1940-45 and 1951-55).

31) A museum near Rome's Trevi Fountain is devoted to which national food made from sliced dough that goes by such names as linguini and spaghetti depending on its cut?
Answer: Pasta.

32) Name 4 of the 5 U.S. Presidents who attended President Nixon's funeral in Yorba Linda, California.
Answer: Gerald Ford, Jimmy Carter, Ronald Reagan, George Bush, and Bill Clinton.

33) What island lies between Jamaica and the U.S.?
Answer: Cuba.

34) Women once ran for governor in 10 states, or, in lowest terms, in what fraction of the U.S. states?
Answer: 1/5.

35) What letter of the alphabet represents the *y* sound in the name *Sarajevo*, the capital of Bosnia and Herzegovina?
Answer: *J*.

36) What 2-word term designates the loud sound that results when an airplane goes faster than the speed of sound?
Answer: Sonic boom.

37) To promote public awareness of nutrition labels, the FDA's mascot for public service announcements was once which fictional monkey from children's books?
Answer: Curious George (in the series by H.A. Rey).

38) In recent years, Russia's Hermitage Museum exhibited a Van Gogh work hidden since Soviet troops took it and about 80 others from Germany in 1945. Complete its title *The _____ at Night* by naming the U.S. building once called the Presidential Palace.
Answer: White House (*The White House at Night*), painted 6 weeks before his death).

39) The 5 excretory organs of the body are represented by the mnemonic device SKILL. Which 2 organs, one of which is the body's largest gland, do the 2 *L*'s stand for?
Answer: Liver and lungs (skin, kidneys, and intestines are the other 3).

40) On October 17, 1945, in which South American country did Colonel Juan Perón seize power to become that nation's absolute dictator? Its capital is Buenos Aires.
Answer: Argentina (named from *argentum*, the Latin for "silver").

41) A music publisher once filed a lawsuit alleging illegal copying of his work in the "I Love You" song sung by which children's character representing which kind of animal?
Answer: Barney, the dinosaur.

42) Benjamin Franklin created the first newspaper cartoon, the "Join or Die" drawing published on May 9, 1754. Identify the state whose name completes the newspaper's title: _____ *Gazette.*
Answer: *Pennsylvania.*

43) An environmentalist group has listed the Anacostia River among the nation's 10 most endangered. In which major city does the Anacostia meet the Potomac River?
Answer: Washington, D.C.

44) What is the value of the 8 in the decimal number .2728?
Answer: 8 ten thousandths.

45) Name the mid-Atlantic island and popular vacation spot where voters rejected in 1995 a proposal to become independent from Britain. Its name identifies a kind of short pants.
Answer: Bermuda (*Bermuda shorts* end just above the knee).

46) Engineer Henry Bessemer patented his process for making which product from molten pig iron on October 17, 1855? It's used in building ships, buildings, and autos.
Answer: Steel (in 1855).

47) Robert Louis Stevenson's *Child's Garden of Verses* was recently reissued. What word completes the following lines from one of its best known poems: "I have a little _____ that goes in and out with me.../He is very, very like me from the heels up to the head;/And I see him jump before me, when I jump into my bed"?
Answer: Shadow (April is National Poetry Month).

48)   The New York Metropolitan Opera once staged *Idomeneo* by which composer, whose given name is Wolfgang Amadeus?
      Answer: Wolfgang Amadeus Mozart.

49)   In cubic inches what is the capacity of a backpack measuring 15 inches high by 12 inches wide by 5 inches deep?
      Answer: 900 (cubic inches).

50)   In 1999, crowds gathered at the mausoleum of former Iranian leader Ruhollah Khomeini to mark the 20th anniversary of the Islamic revolution. Which of the following designates the title he held as a spiritual leader: *rabbi, mahatma, Dalai Lama,* or *ayatollah?*
      Answer: Ayatollah (a Persian word meaning "reflection, or sign, of Allah").

1) What 4-letter word names the unit of money formally introduced at midnight on December 31, 1998, as the monetary unit
of the European Union?
Answer: Euro.

2) In a 1998 survey of 600 teens, 74% knew TV character Bart
Simpson's hometown, but only 12% knew where Abraham
Lincoln lived and practiced law. Name this latter city.
**Answer: Springfield (Illinois; Bart Simpson's home is
also Springfield).**

3) Archaeologists believe that 16th-century artifacts and a moat
found in 1994 are from a fort that protected which Florida city,
the first successful European colony in the U.S.?
Answer: St. Augustine.

4) How many decimal places will there be in the product of
7.28 ÷ 1.3?
Answer: 3.

5) In 1995, Vietnam marked the 50th anniversary of the day
when which leader declared its independence from France? Its
largest city is named for him.
Answer: Ho Chi Minh.

6) Scientists say the discovery of 2 new dinosaur species in Africa
that resemble dinosaurs found on other continents implies
they may have spread worldwide when there was only a single
supercontinent. Is that supercontinent called *Andromeda*,
Pangea (păn jēə), *Okeechobee*, or *Siberia*?
Answer: Pangea (also Pangaea).

7) The 103rd Congress's only major environmental protection bill
preserved 6.6 million acres of desert and created 3 parks in
California. Spell *environment*.
Answer: E-N-V-I-R-O-N-M-E-N-T.

8) A monument, placed between the Lincoln and Jefferson memorials in Washington, D.C., honors the President who learned to
walk with leg braces and a cane after polio paralyzed his legs.
Name him.
Answer: Franklin Delano Roosevelt.

9) A huge can in the shape of a right circular cylinder has radius
6 meters and height 5 meters. What is the exact volume of the
can in cubic meters?
Answer: 180 *pi* (cubic meters).

10) With 15 buildings set afire and one man killed by mob action in Haiti, President Aristide called for an end to vengeance. Spell *vengeance*.
Answer: V-E-N-G-E-A-N-C-E.

11) Identify the first U.S. woman to travel in space. Her surname means "to travel by horse, car, or other vehicle."
Answer: Sally Ride (she traveled in space on June 18, 1983).

12) Give the 3-word Latin motto on U.S. coins meaning "out of one, many."
Answer: *E pluribus unum*.

13) On which sea is Latvia located: Bering, Baltic, Mediterranean, or Red?
Answer: Baltic Sea.

14) Round 25.88 to greatest place value.
Answer: 30.

15) Once a flotilla on its way to Cuba to protest Castro's policies returned to Key West because of storms. Is a flotilla a *barge*, a *protest group*, a *group of boats*, or *an airplane that lands on the water*?
Answer: A group of boats.

16) Name the highly enriched radioactive element stored in the Oak Ridge, Tennessee, disarmament plant shut down in the 1990s because of safety violations. Its symbol is U.
Answer: Uranium (the plant was the U.S.'s only repository for this kind of uranium).

17) Stephen King entitled one of his books *Insomnia*. Does *insomnia* mean "difficulty in digestion," "lack of conscience," "inability to sleep," or "subject to nightmares"?
Answer: Inability to sleep.

18) What was the nationality of sculptor Frédéric Auguste Bartholdi, who sculpted the Statue of Liberty, which was dedicated on October 28, 1886, in New York Harbor?
Answer: French (the statue's full name is *Liberty Enlightening the World*).

19) Rounded to the nearest thousand, how many miles per second does light travel?
Answer: 186,000 (186,282 miles per second).

20) In 1994, Finland was endorsed for membership in the European Union. Of Northern, Southern, Eastern, and Western, in which 2 hemispheres is Finland located?
Answer: Northern and Eastern (Eastern includes Europe, Asia, Africa, and Australia).

21) What word designates the kind of reference book originally issued annually to give farmers weather forecasts and tables of other information?
Answer: Almanac.

22) By federal election law, how much money can candidates accept from any source other than themselves? The dollar amount is symbolized by the letter k.
Answer: $1,000.

23) What color identifies the Vermont mountains for which the troops headed by Revolutionary War hero Ethan Allen were nicknamed?
Answer: Green (Ethan Allen headed the "Green Mountain Boys").

24) Olympics' rules specify that each gold medal must contain at least 6 grams of pure gold. If this amount of gold is worth $75, what is the value of a gram of pure gold?
Answer: $12.50 (rules also specify medal size: 60 mm in diameter and 3 mm thick).

25) In 1995, Jerusalem held the first of many celebrations to mark the 3,000th anniversary of its conquest by which biblical king known for his friendship with Jonathan? This king was Saul's successor.
Answer: King David.

26) Which term derived from the Latin word for "cow" designates the injection of a substance into the body to produce immunity to a disease?
Answer: Vaccination.

27) Excluding the articles *a*, *an*, and *the*, how many adjectives are in the following: *The chancellor of Germany won a fourth term by an extremely narrow margin*?
Answer: 2 (*fourth* and *narrow*; Helmut Kohl is the chancellor).

28) The principal cellist at a California symphony orchestra quit in protest of a performance of which 1936 Prokofiev work she said encourages the killing of wolves?
Answer: *Peter and the Wolf.*

29) Six is what percent of 8?
Answer: 75%.

30) At the request of his children, Charles Shelton was declared dead in 1996 after 27 years of being listed as a POW. He was the last American prisoner of which war?
Answer: Vietnam War.

31) A British canine club once announced its concern about Walt Disney Corporation's call for dogs with spots to make a live-action movie of which cartoon featuring these dogs?
Answer: *101 Dalmations*.

32) A U.S. judge in California ruled the gas chamber an unconstitutional form of punishment because it produces an "air hunger" similar to drowning. Which word for "out of the ordinary" completes the 8th Amendment phrase "cruel and ____" to describe prohibited punishments?
Answer: "unusual."

33) In 1904, which city on the Mississippi hosted the first Olympic Games held in the U.S.? It is named for a French king.
Answer: St. Louis (Missouri).

34) Give the remainder of 57 divided by 6 as both a decimal and a fraction in lowest terms.
Answer: .5 and 1/2.

35) Name the Senate committee that voted unanimously to recommend Oregon Senator Bob Packwood's expulsion for sexual and official misconduct in 1995. The word used to name it begins with the letter E and means "standards of behavior or moral conduct."
Answer: Ethics Committee (Packwood resigned after its vote).

36) Name the disease for which Edward Jenner made the first vaccination, on James Phipps on May 14, 1796.
Answer: Smallpox (also known as *variola*).

37) Identify the direct object in the following: *Jonas Salk, who was born on October 28, 1914, developed a vaccine for the disease known as polio.*
Answer: Vaccine.

38) Who is the patron saint of doctors and artists? This physician and painter, who died about A.D. 68, wrote the third Gospel and the Acts of the Apostles.
Answer: St. Luke (his feast day is October 18).

39) What word is used to describe twins that begin life from 2 eggs?
Answer: Fraternal.

40) Queen Elizabeth II made the first-ever visit to Russia by a British monarch. Spell *monarch*.
Answer: M-O-N-A-R-C-H.

41) Is Russia's monetary unit a *peso, franc, pound*, or *ruble*?
Answer: Ruble.

42) Identify the Indian princess whose burial site and statue at St. George's Church in Gravesend, a Thames River town about 20 miles southeast of London, has become a popular tourist site. She was buried there on March 21, 1617.
Answer: Pocahontas (her Christian name is Rebecca; she married John Rolfe).

43) Coconut Harry, a golden retriever swept overboard at sea, showed up safely 8 days later at Monkey Island in which island chain, site of the U.S.'s southernmost point?
Answer: Florida Keys.

44) Which of the following numbers is divisible by 3: *387*; *526*; *892*; or *431*?
Answer: 387.

45) In 1994, Jamie Whitten, of Mississippi, retired from the House of Representatives after 53 years of service. In which year did he begin his first term?
Answer: 1941.

46) A Georgia girl once advanced to the 2nd round of the National Spelling Bee by correctly spelling *larynx*. Spell *larynx*, the term for the "voice box" in the human body.
Answer: L-A-R-Y-N-X.

47) Spell the correct form of the verb *swim* to complete the following: He had not _____ a stroke before he became interested in the triathlon 10 years ago.
Answer: S-W-U-M.

48) An *album* is a recording of different musical pieces. Which of the following designates a collection of stories or other writings: *menagerie, medley, anthology,* or *bibliography*?
Answer: Anthology.

49) Give the 5 different positive prime numbers that sum to 28.
Answer: 2, 3, 5, 7, and 11.

50) Which English soldier established a colony at Roanoke Island in Pamlico Sound in what is now North Carolina in 1585? The capital of North Carolina is named for him.
Answer: Sir Walter Raleigh (he was executed October 29, 1618 ,for attempting to dethrone James I).

1) In which city was the first section of a subway system that was to become the largest in the country opened on October 27, 1904?
Answer: New York City.

2) Name the 2 Englishmen who with their 1767 survey to settle a land dispute between Maryland and Pennsylvania established the line that came to be the boundary between slave and free states. The surname of one also identifies a kind of jar used in canning.
Answer: Charles Mason and Jeremiah Dixon (Mason-Dixon Line).

3) Which river connecting Lake Erie with Lake Ontario is known for its great falls on the U.S.-Canadian boundary?
Answer: Niagara River.

4) Customers don't have to pay New York City's 8.25% tax on food at the coffee shop in the United Nations Headquarters because it is considered international territory. How much will a person save by not having to pay an 8% tax on a food bill of $15.00?
Answer: $1.20.

5) According to an Amnesty International report, on which continent consisting of a single country are Aborigines, its earliest natives, jailed at 27 times the rate of other citizens?
Answer: Australia.

6) What terms designate respectively a mass of ice that moves on the land and a mass of ice that travels on water?
Answer: Glacier (moves on land) and iceberg (moves on water).

7) R.L. Stine, author of the new adult novel *Superstitious*, has written over 100 children's books. Complete the titles of these 2 Stine series: ____ *Street* and ____*bumps*.
Answer: *Fear Street* and *Goosebumps*.

8) What term, also used in Kentucky's nickname, designates the kind of country music Allison Krauss sings? She once won 4 Country Music Association awards.
Answer: Bluegrass (a kind of Southern folk music with rapid tempos; Kentucky is the "Bluegrass State").

9) Round 754.5739 to the nearest hundredth.
Answer: 754.57.

10) At a 1995 New York festival, a choral oratorio was combined with the showing of a 1927 silent film about which French martyr who was burned at the stake for her beliefs?
Answer: Joan of Arc.

11) Lawrence Livermore Laboratory has created a portable laser that uses photoacoustic stress waves to obliterate the messages and drawings that people carve or write on walls in public areas. By what name are such markings known?
Answer: Graffiti (the lasers cost about $250,000 each).

12) Which African-American educator did President Theodore Roosevelt invite to the White House for dinner in 1901, causing criticism from some Southern newspapers?
Answer: Booker T. Washington.

13) In which rectangularly shaped state is Yellowstone National Park primarily located? It was established by Congress on March 1, 1872, as the nation's first national park?
Answer: Wyoming.

14) A mile is the equivalent of 5,280 feet, and the fathom, a measure used for depth of an ocean, is equivalent to 6 feet. How many fathoms are in a mile?
Answer: 880 fathoms.

15) Jerry Lewis has raised millions with his Labor Day television show to fight muscular dystrophy. What word designates a long TV show to raise money for charity?
Answer: Telethon.

16) A rainbow results when light is refracted by water drops. What word beginning with *B* is a synonym for *refract*?
Answer: Bend.

17) The U.N. observes International Literacy Day on September 8. Show your literacy by identifying the word without a double consonant in the following group: *slippery, illegal, beginning,* or *sloping*.
Answer: Sloping.

18) Which of the following designates the shape of the 555-foot-tall Washington Monument in Washington, D.C.: *pyramid, colonnade, obelisk,* or *rotunda*?
Answer: Obelisk (a tall 4-sided structure that rises to a point).

19) On which planet did the spacecraft *Magellan* photograph a channel longer than any river on Earth? It is named for the Roman goddess of love.
Answer: Venus.

20) Did the U.N., which was formally established in San Francisco after WWII, celebrate its 33rd, 43rd, 53rd, or 63rd anniversary on October 24, 1998?
Answer: 53rd (it was founded on October 24, 1945).

21) A high school football team won a game 23 to 10 by scoring 2 touchdowns, 2 extra points, and how many field goals?
Answer: 3 (for 9 points).

22) At which Virginia site with *town* in its name did British leader Lord Cornwallis surrender more than 7,000 soldiers to George Washington on October 19, 1781?
Answer: Yorktown.

23) Which Communist country on the Indochinese Peninsula greeted Cuban President Fidel Castro warmly during his 1995 visit to demonstrate Communist unity? Its capital is Hanoi.
Answer: Vietnam.

24) By how many feet was the elevation of Mount St. Helens reduced in its May 18, 1980, eruption? It measured 9, 677 feet before the eruption and 8,363 feet afterwards.
Answer: 1,314 feet.

25) What word designates both the Marshall Island atoll, or coral island, that scuba divers were permitted to use as a base as of January 1, 1996, and a skimpy 2-piece bathing suit? The U.S. used the atoll for nuclear tests after WWII.
Answer: Bikini.

26) Name the process that accounts for a lowering of the water level in a container of water left open to the air for 24 hours.
Answer: Evaporation.

27) Which word beginning with *V* and meaning "aspects of good-ness" completes the title of William Bennett's 1993 best seller, *The Book of* _____? He is a former secretary of education.
Answer: *Virtues (The Book of Virtues).*

28) Complete the title of John Philip Sousa's famous march "The _____ and _____ Forever," which was first publicly performed on May 14, 1897.
Answer: "Stars" and "Stripes."

29) Which of the following numbers is the largest and which is the smallest: 5.1, 5.08, 5.297, 5.013?
Answer: 5.297 is the largest and 5.013 is the smallest.

30) What is the term for the picture writing on the 3,000-year-old bronze seal found in 1995 in Turkey and viewed as evidence that the citizens of ancient Troy could write?
Answer: Hieroglyphics.

31) Identify the oldest public building in Washington, D.C., whose cornerstone was laid on October 12, 1792. It is known for its Green Room, Red Room, and Blue Room.
Answer: White House.

32) Name the airplane aboard which President Clinton and former Presidents Jimmy Carter and George Bush traveled to the funeral of Yitzhak Rabin in 1995.
Answer: *Air Force One.*

33) What word designates a green area in a desert where plants can grow because of underground springs or wells?
Answer: Oasis.

34) What integer does $2^4 + 4^2$ [READ: 2 to the 4th power plus 4 squared] equal?
Answer: 32.

35) Name the recently unified country that won the most medals awarded to a single team at the 1992 Winter Olympics.
Answer: Germany (it won 26 medals; 63 teams participated).

36) Which word beginning with *D* is used in science to complete the following: *A boat floats because it _____ enough water based on its size to keep it atop the water?*
Answer: "displaces."

37) Identify the Clinton administration's first secretary of state. This person's surname is the same as the first name of Winnie the Pooh's human friend.
Answer: Warren Christopher (Christopher Robin is Winnie the Pooh's friend).

38) A 1995 album features lesser known works by the songwriter who wrote "God Bless America." Identify this composer whose surname also designates Germany's capital.
Answer: Irving Berlin (he died at age 101 in 1989).

39) What scientific name beginning with *C* did the brainy character of the comic strip *Tiger* use to identify the dense, white, fluffy cloud his less sophisticated friends described as an elephant and a fat man?
Answer: Cumulus.

40) A memorial was built in Washington D.C. across the Reflecting Pool from the Vietnam Veterans Memorial to honor veterans of the 1950-1953 war. Name this war.
Answer: Korean War.

41) Orville Redenbacher is best known for popcorn? What is within a kernel of corn to make the kernel pop when heated?
     Answer: Moisture, or water (which turns to steam and makes the kernel pop).

42) The world's first nuclear-powered submarine, the *Nautilus*, was launched 10 years following WWII. In which year was it launched?
     Answer: 1955 (christened on January 21, 1954).

43) In which state was the last battle of the Civil War fought near the mouth of the Rio Grande River? It was readmitted to the Union on March 30, 1870.
     Answer: Texas.

44) Jan wants to buy a computer game that costs $20. What fraction of her $10 a week allowance must she save for each of 4 weeks in order to purchase it?
     Answer: 1/2 (the equivalent of $5 a week).

45) Name the South African leader who spent 18 of his 27 years of imprisonment in an island prison near Cape Town that has been opened to tourists.
     Answer: Nelson Mandela (Robben Island is the prison).

46) At 5:00 p.m. the temperature was 16% F. By how many degrees had it dropped when at midnight it reached –3%?
     Answer: 19%.

47) Name the fictional teenage girl who leaves River Heights with friends Bess and George to attend college in a continuation of the detective series begun in 1930.
     Answer: Nancy Drew (the new series is *Nancy Drew on Campus*).

48) Jose Carreras, Placido Domingo, and Luciano Pavarotti reunited for a 5-city tour in 1996. What is the term for their singing voice, the highest natural adult male voice?
     Answer: Tenor.

49) What simple fraction is equivalent to 4/5 – 2/6?
     Answer: 7/15.

50) What name meaning "Truce Day" did Woodrow Wilson give to the November 11 holiday he established in 1919 to remind Americans of the tragedies of war? Its name was changed to Veterans Day in 1954 to honor all U.S. veterans.
     Answer: Armistice Day (armistice ending WWI was signed on November 11, 1918).

2501) Richard Wagner's "Centennial Inaugural March" was first played at the U.S.'s Centennial Exposition in Philadelphia in 1876. How old will the U.S. be in 2501?

Answer: 725.

INDEX

Aaron, Hank, 202, 221
Abacus, 30
Aborigines, 256
Accordion, 167
Account of a Visit from St. Nicholas, An, 25
Achilles, 156
Acid rain, 213
Acoustics, 183
Acronyms/Initialisms
  ABA, 95
  ACOG, 215
  AIDS, 1, 131, 220
  AMA, 70
  CARE, 225
  CFCs, 126
  CIA, 1, 192
  DNA, 25, 158
  DST, 144
  EPA, 49
  ERA, 184
  FBI, 1
  FEMA, 178
  GATT, 131
  GOP, 99
  HAL, 163
  HDR, 110
  HUD, 56, 100
  ICC, 155
  IQ, 75
  LASER, 195, 243
  MADD, 23
  MIA, 67
  NAACP, 71
  NAFTA, 126
  NASA, 82, 129
  NATO, 26, 145
  NOAA, 182
  NRA, 151
  OMB, 49
  PC, 192
  PLO, 2, 100
  POW, 67
  Sonar, 243
  START, 48
  UNICEF, 40
  U.S.S.R., 102
  WHO, 32, 126
Acropolis, 85, 230
Adams, John, 43
Adriatic Sea, 83, 212
Adventures of Tom Sawyer, The, 110, 119
Adventures of Huckleberry Finn, The, 38
Aesop, 170
Afghanistan, 112
Africa, 6, 123, 131, 145, 202, 241
Air Force One, 259
Alabama, 10, 69, 94, 127, 189
Aladdin, 232
Alamo, The, 72, 124, 189
Alamogordo (New Mexico), 204
Alaska, 7, 110, 143, 170, 216
Alberta (Canada), 156

Albino, 234
Albright, Madeleine, 56
Alcatraz, 86, 229
Alchemy, 136
Alcott, Louisa May, 185, 188
Algeria, 132
Ali, Muhammad, 198
Alice's Adventures in Wonderland, 133, 205
Allen, Ethan, 90, 253
Allies, 157
Alloy, 12
Alps, 198
Altitude, 241
Amazon.com, 118
Amazon River, 159, 221
America, 215
"America the Beautiful," 118, 129
American Bar Association, 95
American eagle, 9
American Medical Association, 70
American Revolution, 29, 54, 116
Ampere, André, 49
Amphibians, 57
Amphibious, 5
Amsterdam, 58
Amtrak, 61
Anacostia River, 249
Ancestors, 224
Anchorage (Alaska), 216
And to Think I Saw It on Mulberry Street, 53
Andersen, Hans Christian, 38, 47, 101, 152, 218, 245
Anderson, Marian, 64, 91, 101, 218
Andersonville prison, 33
Andes Mountains, 44, 102
Andorra, 77
André, John, 22
Anesthetic, 145
Angelou, Maya, 48, 60
Anglican Church, 34
Anna and the King of Siam, 170
Annapolis (Maryland), 15
Anne of Green Gables, 60
Annunciation, 69
"Ant and the Grasshopper, The," 170
Antarctica, 156
Anthony, Susan B., 208
Antoinette, Marie, 112
Aorta, 146
Apollo 13, 243
Appalachian Trail, 128
Apple computer, 107
Appomattox Court House, 92
Aquarium, 111
Arabian Nights' Entertainments, The, 75
Arabian Sea, 75
Arabic, 172
Arafat, Yasir, 2, 100
Arctic Ocean, 90, 188
Argentina, 58, 249
Aristotle, 31
Arizona, 16, 67, 70, 75, 130, 163, 178, 225

Arkansas, 40, 200
Arlington National Cemetery, 61
Armistice Day, 260
Arnold, Benedict, 22, 235
Around the World in Eighty Days, 177
Artificial heart, 34
Ash Wednesday, 139
Ashe, Arthur, 3
Asia, 131, 144, 202
Aspirin, 9
Astronomy, 21
Athens (Greece), 85, 247
Atlanta (Georgia), 50, 109
Atlanta Committee for the Olympic Games, 215
Atlantic Ocean, 52, 222
Atlas, Charles, 222
Atom, 13
Atomic bomb, 11, 72, 181
Atomic tests, 204
Attorney general, 51, 153
Audubon, John James, 63
Aurora borealis, 1, 226
Australia, 71, 81, 127, 134, 256
Austria, 128, 180, 184
Autobiography, 48
Autry, Gene, 130
Aves, 139
Axle, 161
Babe, 202
Bacon, Nathaniel, 20
Badger, 78
Baker III, James A., 17
Bald eagle, 156
Ball and socket joints, 151
Ballet dancer, 55
Baltic republics, 74
Baltic Sea, 22, 172, 252
Baltimore (Maryland), 20, 92
Bangkok (Thailand), 231
Bannister, Roger, 219
Banting, Frederick Grant, 12
Barcelona (Spain), 1, 50
Barents Sea, 188
Barney, 249
Barrie, J.M., 92
Barrow (Alaska), 90
Bartholdi, Frédéric Auguste, 109, 252
Bartlett's Familiar Quotations, 31
Basketball, 118, 176
Basketball Hall of Fame, 247
Bastille, 230
Bates, Katherine Lee, 118
Bats, 169
"Battle Hymn of the Republic, The," 24, 119, 203
Battle of Antietam, 164
Battle of Gettysburg, 111
Battle of Monmouth, 141
Battle of San Jacinto, 16
Battle of Saratoga, 159
Battle of Shiloh, 223
Battle of the Thames, 107
Battle of the Wilderness, 245
Battle of Trafalgar, 17
Baum, L. Frank, 51, 155
Beans, 110
Beatles, The, 113
Beauty and the Beast, 141

Beethoven, Ludwig van, 8
Bell, Alexander Graham, 50, 184
Bennett, William, 258
Bering Sea, 104
Berlin (Germany), 111
Berlin, Irving, 259
Berlin Wall, 15, 91, 151, 155
Bermuda, 249
Bermuda Triangle, 45
Bessemer, Henry, 4, 249
Bethlehem, 175
Bhopal (India), 168
Bikini, 258
Bill of Rights, 131
Biome, 229
Birds of America, 63
Bituminous coal, 72
Black Death, 124
Black Forest, 222
Black Hills, 119
Black Sea, 18
Bligh, William, 76
Blue Ridge Mountains, 194
Bluegrass music, 256
Blues, 142
Blume, Judy, 30
Bohr, Niels, 168
Boiling point, 14
Boléro, 236
Bolívar, Simón, 226
Bolivia, 44
Bolsheviks, 36
Bolshoi Ballet, 140
Bombay (India), 75
Book of Virtues, The, 258
Boone, Daniel, 35
Booth, John Wilkes, 68
Boston (Massachusetts), 12, 50, 124
Boston Tea Party, 145
Botany Bay, 127
Boutros-Ghali, Boutros, 25
Boy Scouts, 205
Boycott, Charles C., 167
Boys Town, 126
Bradford, William, 191
Brady Act (Bill), 162, 229
Braille, 216
Brain, 225
Brass, 150
Brazil, 3, 85, 99, 105, 198, 201, 215
Broadway, 242
Broccoli, 242
Bronco Buster, 27
Bronze, 27
Brown, Jesse Leroy, 56
Brown, John, 179
Brown, Margaret Wise, 179
Buchanan, James, 155
Buckingham Palace, 130, 234
Budapest (Hungary), 167
Buddhist, 190
Buffalo (New York), 98
Bug's Life, A, 170
Burnett, Frances Hodgson, 98
Burns, Robert, 201
Burnside, Ambrose, 130
Burundi, 145

Bush, Barbara, 180
Bush, George, 24, 55, 195, 248
Byrd, Richard Evelyn, 44, 237
Cabral, Pedro Alvares, 85, 198
Caesar, Julius, 70, 232
Caffeine, 169
Cairo (Egypt), 162
Calcium, 199
Calendar, 197
California, 35, 102, 146, 190, 199, 241
California condor, 217
Calvert, Philip, 146
Cambodia, 169
Camp David, 143, 180
Campbell, Ben Nighthorse, 38
Canada, 23, 60, 97, 102, 109, 180, 194, 209, 213, 214
Canadian flag, 16
Cape Hatteras, 48
Cape Horn, 80
Capillaries, 110
Capital punishment, 121
Captain Nemo, 129
Caracas (Venezuela), 246
Carat, 89
Carbohydrates, 127
Carbon, 126
Carbon dioxide, 90, 165, 223
Carbon monoxide, 168
Carburetor, 180
Cardinal, 76
Caribbean Sea, 52, 186, 222
Carlsbad Caverns National Park, 8
Carnegie, Andrew, 53
Carroll, Lewis, 133, 139, 205
Carson, Kit, 125
Carter, Jimmy, 70, 159, 221, 248
Carter, Rosalyn, 104, 180
Cartilage, 202
Cascade Mountains, 79, 84
Caspian Sea, 151
Castro, Fidel, 3
Cat in the Hat, The, 104
Caterpillar, 225
Cathedral of Notre Dame, 130
Catskill Mountains, 16
Caucasus Mountains, 189
Cavendish, Henry, 4
Caxton, William, 178
"Celebrated Jumping Frog of Calaveras County, The," 25
Cells, 164
Celsius, 34, 153, 177
Census Bureau, 51, 169, 237
Centennial Exposition, 185
Centennial Park, 8
Centigrade, 14
Central Intelligence Agency, 1, 192
Centrifugal force, 55
Century, 55
Cerebrum, 225
Cervantes, Miguel de, 146
Challenger, 19, 185
Chancellor, 22
Chancellorsville, 192
Chanukah, 182
Chavez, Cesar, 95
Chemotherapy, 140

Chernobyl, 113, 221
Cherokee, 37
Chesapeake Bay, 54
Chess, 2
Chicago (Illinois), 153, 168
Chicago fire, 40
Chief Joseph, 106
Chief Justice of the U.S., 32, 214
Child's Garden of Verses, 249
China, 69, 95, 174, 244
Chisholm, Shirley, 125
Chlorine, 126
Chloroflurocarbons, 126
Chlorophyll, 36, 236
Christian Coalition, 161
Christian Scientists, 179
Christmas, 154
Christmas Carol, A, 206, 227
Christopher Robin, 259
Christopher, Warren, 259
Chromosomes, 241
Chrysanthemum Throne, 95, 210
Churchill, Winston, 61, 87, 152, 248
Cirrhosis, 88
Civil War, 48, 122
Clark, Dr. Barney, 34
Clark, William, 36
Clay, Henry, 5
Clemenceau, Georges, 163
Cleveland, Grover, 71, 194
Clinton, Bill, 24, 32, 40, 60, 125, 150, 248
Clinton, Chelsea, 43, 178
Clinton, Hillary Rodham, 106, 180
Cold-blooded animal, 75
Colombia, 120, 129
Colorado, 24, 36, 38, 241
Columbia, 113, 200
Columbia (South Carolina), 66
Columbia River, 76, 234
Columbus (Ohio), 185
Columbus, Christopher, 22, 43, 92, 128, 175, 216
Comet, 25, 141, 156
Common cold, 220
Commonwealth, 134
Communist Party, 201
Compass, 29
Confederacy, 90
Congruent, 91
Cooperative for American Relief Everywhere, 225
Copernicus, Nicolaus, 198
Coral, 146
Core, 189
Corn, 99
Cornwallis, Lord, 23
Corsica, 231
Cotton, 95
Cotton gin, 43, 130
Cousteau, Jacques, 133
Crayola, 127
Crazy Horse Memorial, 246
Crockett, Davy, 124
Crystals, 246
Cuba, 3, 10, 39, 55, 113, 148, 205, 207, 248
Cumulus cloud, 259
Cupid, 25
Curfew, 105
Curie, Marie, 117

Curious George, 248
Cy Young awards, 173
Czar, 49
Czechoslovakia, 51, 174
D-Day, 4
da Vinci, Leonardo, 80, 188, 212, 239
Dag Hammarskjöld Plaza, 117
Dallas, 203
Dan Quayle Center, 114
Dane, 30
Danube River, 143
Darling River, 227
Darwin, Charles, 187
Davis, Jefferson, 58, 80, 141
Daylight-saving time, 144
de Balboa, Vasco Núñez, 9, 78
de Klerk, F.W., 64, 111
de León, Juan Ponce, 80
De Soto, Hernando, 124
Dead Sea, 69, 111
Dead Sea Scrolls, 215
Death Valley, 63
Decade, 54
Decibel, 184
Deciduous teeth, 173
Declaration of Independence, 57, 109
Defoe, Daniel, 2, 204
Delaware, 42, 150
Delmarva Peninsula, 146
Denmark, 2, 92
Density, 24
Denver (Colorado), 20, 98
Deoxyribonucleic acid, 158
Department of Housing and Urban Development, 56
Depression, Great, 112
Dermatology, 193
Des Moines (Iowa), 91
Desalination, 119, 172
Detroit (Michigan), 163
Dewey Decimal system, 147
Diabetes, 12
Diameter, 234
Diamond, 17
Dickens, Charles, 206, 227
Diesel engine, 19
Diet, 196
DiMaggio, Joe, 157
Dinosaur, 156
Discovery Day, 43
Displaces, 259
District of Columbia, 79
"Dixie," 117
DNA, 25
Dr. Jekyll, 208
Doctor of Philosophy, 178
Dodge, Mary Mapes, 37
Dollar, 253
Dominican Republic, 145, 222
Don Quixote, 146
Don't Look Back, 148
Doppler radar, 151
Dove, 210
Dow Jones Industrial Average, 135
Downing Street Years, The, 219
Doyle, Arthur Conan, 1, 180
Drake, Sir Francis, 27, 40

Drama, 245
Dust Bowl, 158
Dynamite, 175
$E = mc^2$, 120
Ear, 185
Earhart, Amelia, 138
Earth, 157, 200, 212, 247
Earthquake, 143
East Germany, 41
Easter Parade, 25
Eastern Hemisphere, 218
Eastern Orthodox Church, 211
Ebeneezer Scrooge, 206
Ecology, 122
Ecuador, 121
Edison Company, 84
Edison, Thomas, 6, 183
Editorial page, 195
Egypt, 12, 85, 87, 88, 93, 138
Eiffel Tower, 209
Einstein, Albert, 23, 86, 120
Eisenhower, Dwight David, 28, 34, 55, 85, 89, 213
El Paso, 133
El-Sadat, Anwar, 12
El Salvador, 47, 100, 189
Election Day, 118
Electric current, 49
Electrons, 132
Elizabeth II, 83
Ellis Island, 51
Emancipation Proclamation, 46
Embryo, 116
Emmett, Daniel Decatur, 117
Emmy, 162
Emperor, 214
Emperor Akihito, 12, 214
Emperor Hirohito, 210
England, 34
English, 194
English Channel, 114
Enlist, 33
Environmental Protection Agency, 49
Epiphany, 135
Equal Rights Amendment, 184
Erie Canal, 187
Eriksson, Leif, 14, 158
Esophagus, 109
Espy, Mike, 48
Estonia, 74
Ethics Committee, 254
Ethiopia, 71, 94, 210, 241
Euro, 251
EuroDisney, 218
Evacuation, 72
Evaporation, 258
Everglades (National Park), 27, 126, 239
Ewe, 231
Excalibur, 187
Exponent, 90
Eye, 178, 186
Fahrenheit scale, 138, 154
Faneuil Hall, 12
Farewell Address, 12
Fathom, 257
Fault, 10
Fear Street, 256
Federal Bureau of Investigation, 1

Federal Emergency Management Agency, 178
Fencing, 224
Ferraro, Geraldine, 78
Ferris Wheel, 64
Fiddler crab, 159
Fidelio, 8
Filibuster, 81
Finland, 19, 182, 198, 252
First Ladies, 180
Flag Day, 6
Flamenco, 231
Flanagan, Father Edward, 126
"Flight of the Bumblebee, The," 83
Florida, 27, 31, 65, 70, 80, 119, 126, 239
Florida, University of, 69
Florida Keys, 255
Florida State University, 175
Fluoride, 25
Folger Library, 57
Food pyramid, 134
Fools of Chelm and Their History, The, 143
Football, 118, 199
Ford, Betty, 180
Ford, Gerald, 140, 248
Fort Ticonderoga, 90
Fossett, Steve, 230
Fossil fuels, 208
Foster, Stephen Collins, 152
Four Corners, 241
France, 4, 70, 118, 180, 218, 230
Franco, Francisco, 81
Frank, Anne, 168
Franklin, Benjamin, 49, 93, 215, 249
French, 194
French and Indian War, The, 62
French meat, 228
Friction, 162
Frost, Robert Lee, 219
Fudge, 30
Fugitive, The, 77
Fulcrum, 64
Funnel, 206
Fusion, 102
G-7 nations, 209
Gabon, 177
Gabriel, 69
Gagarin, Yuri, 196
Gaggle, 114
Galahad, Sir, 183
Galapagos Islands, 87, 175, 245
Galaxy, 117
Galileo, 33, 46, 77, 229
Gambia, The, 177
Garfield, James, 21
Gas, 24, 152
Gateway Arch, 11, 74, 75
Gaza International Airport, 224
Gaza Strip, 110
Gehrig, Lou, 157, 227
Geisel, Theodor Seuss, 104
Gene, 165, 233
General Agreement on Tariff and Trade, 131
Genetics, 204
George VI, 86
George III, 116
George Washington Bridge, 113
Georgia, 17, 33, 79, 138, 140, 175

Germany, 15, 22, 29, 74, 88, 171, 182, 222, 259
Gettysburg (Pennsylvania), 28, 115
Gettysburg Address, 239
Ghana, 177
Gibraltar, 50
Gifted children, 119
Girl Scout pledge, 116
Girl Scouts of America, 31, 66, 228
Glacier, 85, 256
Glacier National Park, 167
Glaucoma, 186
Glenn, John, 36, 186, 203
Glidden, Joseph, 39
Gobi Desert, 121, 184
"God Bless America," 259
"Gold Bug, The," 228
Gold, frankincense, and myrrh, 137
Gold rush, 35, 199
Golden anniversary, 171
Golden Fleece, 62
Goldwater, Barry, 142
Goodnight Moon, 179
Goosebumps, 256
Gorbachev, Mikhail, 59, 156, 189, 211
Gorgas, William C., 55
Gorge, 62
Gorillas, 237
Graham, Billy, 220
Graham, Martha, 99
Grammar, 10, 17, 18, 24, 26, 28, 32, 34, 45, 58, 66, 72, 85, 103, 112, 113, 134, 142, 150, 176, 181, 184, 195, 196, 198, 223, 232, 242, 253, 254, 255
Grand Canyon (National Park), 16, 67, 130
Grand Old Party, 99
Grand Coulee Dam, 234
Granite, 174
Grant, Ulysses S., 85, 92
Graphite, 92
Gravity, 54, 102
Gray, Robert, 86
Gray wolf, 22
Great aunt, 97
Great Barrier Reef, 81
Great Lakes, 11, 13, 14, 217
Great Salt Lake, 32
Great Seal of the U.S., 9
Great Smoky Mountains, 155
Great Sphinx, 138
Great Wall of China, 141
Greece, 230
Green card, 81
Green Mountain Boys, 253
Greenhouse effect, 105
Greenwich (England), 159
Gregorian calendar, 4, 180
Grenada, 186
Groundhog, 69
Guam, 21
Guinea, 177
Guinea-Bissau, 177
Guinness Book of World Records, The, 32
Gulf of Mexico, 94, 105
Gulf of Tonkin Resolution, 97
Gulliver's Travels, 95
Hague, The, 53
Haiti, 202
Hale, Nathan, 207

Haley, Alex, 26
"Hallelujah Chorus," 235
Halley, Edmund, 11
Halley's comet, 41, 115
Hamilton, Alexander, 67
Hancock, John, 57
Handel, Gregor, 235
Hanoi (Vietnam), 82
Hans Brinker, 37
Harlem, 169
Harper's Ferry (West Virginia), 179
Harpers Ferry National Park, 106
Harris, Joel Chandler, 43, 212
Harrison, William Henry, 63
Harvard University, 202
Hawaii, 225
Health-care system, 106
Heisman Trophy, 199
Helium, 40, 105
Hemisphere, 37
Hemoglobin, 236
Henry, Patrick, 76, 217, 235
Hepatitis, 246
Her (His) Majesty's Ship, 243
Hercules, 21, 145
Hermit crab, 158
Hermitage, The, 108
Hieroglyphics, 258
Himalayas, 43, 77
Hindi, 240
Hinduism, 107
Hiroshima (Japan), 23
Hirt, Al, 241
Hispaniola, 124, 222
Hitler, Adolf, 214
Ho Chi Minh (Vietnam), 251
Hoffa, James P., 184
Holland Tunnel, 34, 165
Holmes, Sherlock, 1
Holocaust, 45
Hologram, 26
"Home on the Range," 172
Homer, Winslow, 187
Homo sapiens, 137
Honduras, 164
Hong Kong, 93, 137, 246
Honshu, 183
Hoover, Herbert, 39
Hope (Arkansas), 40
Hot air balloon, 230
House of Lords, 235
Housing and Urban Development, 100
Houston, Sam, 16, 116
Howe, Julia Ward, 24, 119, 203
Hsing-Hsing, 50
Hubble Space Telescope, 31, 142
Hudson Bay, 4, 247
Hudson River, 34, 113, 161
Hudson's Bay Company, 247
Huggins, Miller, 157
Hughes, Langston, 169
Humanitarian Daily Ration, 110
Hunchback of Notre Dame, The, 36
Hungary, 18, 108, 166
Huntsville (Alabama), 10
Hurricane, 157
Hurricane Hugo, 186

Hussein, Saddam, 21, 106
Hydrogen, 4, 105, 224
Hypertension, 135
I Know Why The Caged Bird Sings, 48
Iberian Peninsula, 51
Icarus, 211
Iceland, 153
Idaho, 28, 46
Ides of March, 70
Iditarod Trail Sled Dog Race, 170, 216
Igneous rock, 194
Illinois, 227
In the Night Kitchen, 106
Inauguration Day, 56, 200
Incisors, 15
Income tax, 70
Incumbent, 19
India, 92, 95, 103, 107, 168, 183, 240
Indian Ocean, 32, 84, 183
Indiana, 114
Indonesia, 196
Insects, 104
International Date Line, 32, 83
Interstate Commerce Commission, 155
Iowa, 40
Iran, 20, 140
Iraq, 21, 97, 169, 190, 247
Ireland, 9, 72, 95, 220
Iris, 228
Iron, 61, 151, 161
Irving, Washington, 82, 128, 199
Istanbul (Turkey), 87
Italy, 65, 83, 86, 125, 193
Ivan the Terrible, 49
Ivory Coast, 153
Ivy League, 194
"Jabberwocky," 139
Jackson (Mississippi), 99
Jackson, Andrew, 51, 99, 108, 147
Jackson, Jesse, 5, 180
Jackson, "Stonewall," 192
Jacobs Field, 240
James I, 234
Jamestown (Virginia), 20, 133
Japan, 95, 96, 108, 164, 181, 183, 196, 210, 240
Japanese-Americans, 65
Jason, 62
Jay, John, 215
Jefferson, Thomas, 3, 29, 31, 42, 43, 75
Jenner, Edward, 254
Jericho, 99
Jerusalem (Israel), 147
Joan of Arc, 257
Johns Hopkins University, 31
Johnson, Andrew, 102, 229, 231
Johnson, Earvin "Magic," 199
Johnson, Lady Bird, 180
Johnson, Lyndon, 4, 97, 210
Jones, John Paul, 67, 176
Jordan, 7, 180
Jordan, Michael, 110
Jordan River, 67, 69
Joseph, 127
Joseph and the Amazing Technicolor Dreamcoat, 127
Joseph Katz and His Coat of Many Colors, 170
Judaism, 78, 182

Julian calendar, 3
Jupiter, 46, 62, 205
Jurassic Park, 50
Jutland Peninsula, 2, 92
Kansas, 32, 226
Keene, Carolyn, 80
Kennebunkport (Maine), 135
Kennedy Airport, John F., 197
Kennedy, Jacqueline, 148
Kennedy, John, 10, 11, 29, 33, 61, 74, 123, 203, 219
Kentucky, 5, 64
Kenya, 199
Key, Francis Scott, 188
Keys, 65
Khrushchev, Nikita, 89, 91
Kidney, 234
Killer Angels, The, 111
Kilowatt, 27
King Amenhotep III , 85
King Arthur, 187
King David, 253
King George II, 235
King George III, 103
King Haakon VII, 128
King Herod, 49
King Hussein, 7
King John, 176
King Kong, 137
King Jr., Martin Luther, 27, 55, 57, 79, 93, 161, 179, 185, 189, 212
Koch, Robert, 68
Koran, 194
Korea, 34, 56, 131
Korean War, 7, 8, 178
Korean War Memorial, 259
Kosovo, 136, 207
Kremlin, 235
Kudzu, 188
Kuwait, 55, 163, 169
Kwajalein, 83
Kwanzaa, 182
L'Engle, Madeleine, 168
La Niña, 150
Labor, 219
Laënnec, Théophile, 58
Lake Havasu City (Arizona), 5
Lake Michigan, 82, 157, 169
Lake Ontario, 14
Lama, Dalai, 190
Lapland, 198
Larynx, 163
Laser, 195, 243
Lassie Come Home, 28
Latin America, 235
Latvia, 74, 252
Lava, 215
Lead, 9, 134
Leap year, 8, 98, 180
Lebanon, 154, 180
Lee, Robert E., 92
Legend of Sleepy Hollow, The, 82
Lenin, Vladimir, 194
Lent, 139
Leopard, 131, 192
Levees, 223
Lewis, C.S., 105
Lewis, Meriwether, 36

Lewis and Clark expedition, 159, 226
Lexington (Massachusetts), 52
Liberty Bell, 91
Liberty Enlightening the World, 26
Library of Congress, 148
Libya, 20, 92, 171
Life on the Mississippi, 138
Ligament, 148
Light, 235
Light amplification by stimulated emission of radiation, 195, 243,
Light year, 142
Lilliputians, 96
Lima (Peru), 66
Limestone, 87, 233
Lincoln, Abraham, 13, 29, 44, 46, 67, 84, 90, 100, 113, 168, 212, 227, 239, 251
Lincoln Memorial, 91, 185
Lindbergh, Charles A., 96, 165, 209
Ling-Ling, 50
Lion, the Witch, and the Wardrobe, The, 105
Lipizzaner horses, 39
Lister, Joseph, 201
Liszt, Franz, 7, 111
Lithuania, 22, 74
Little Bighorn Battlefield National Monument, 37
Little House on the Prairie, 116
Little League baseball, 35, 97, 199
Little Women, 185, 188
Liver, 46, 88, 249
Loch Ness monster, 3
Loire, 70
London, 184, 234
London Bridge, 5
London, Jack, 127
Longfellow, Henry Wadsworth, 81, 89, 194
Louis XVI, 206
Louisiana, 101
Louisiana Purchase, 3, 132
Louvre, 59, 136
Low, Juliette Gordon, 66, 228
Lungs, 68, 215, 249
Luther, Martin, 23
Luxor, 87
Lyme disease, 197
Mach, 45
MacLachlan, Patricia, 202
Madison, Dolley, 221
Madison, James, 31, 68, 237
Madrid (Spain), 67
Magellan, Ferdinand, 187
Magna Carta, 176
Maiden name, 42
Maine, 187, 190, 234
Major, John, 214
Malcolm X, 184
Mall, The, 35
Mammals, 57
Mammoth, 228
Mammoth Cave National Park, 64
Mandela, Nelson, 64, 111, 260
Manhattan Island, 95
Manila (Philippines), 226
Mantle, 213
Mantle, Mickey, 157
Maple leaf, 16
Marathon, 196

Marble, 173
March, 112
Marconi, Guglielmo, 226
Mardi Gras, 139, 192
Marianas Trench, 233
Mars, 15, 54, 97, 200
Marshall, James, 199
Marshall, Thurgood, 60, 62
Martha's Vineyard, 100
Martin, José de San, 189
Mary Lennox, 98, 103
Maryland, 54, 77, 79, 143, 146, 164, 180, 207
Mason-Dixon Line, 34, 110, 256
Massachusetts, 61, 247
Massachusetts Bay colony, 37
Masters Golf tournament, 79, 149
Mauna Loa, 56
Maya Indians, 183
Mayflower, 230
Mayflower Compact, 37
Mayo Clinic, 100
McAuliffe, Christa, 19
McKinley, William, 98
Measles, 219
Mecca, 240
Medal of Honor, 48
Mediterranean Sea, 18, 92, 93, 132
Melanin, 218
Memorial Day, 169
Memphis (Tennessee), 55
Mendel, Gregor, 63
Mercury (metal), 43
Mercury (planet), 52, 70, 118, 188
Mercury (mythology), 43, 65, 209
Mesabi Range, 20
Messiah, 235
Metamorphic rock, 73, 133, 194
Meteorology, 31
Methodist Church, 197
Methuselah, 233
Metropolis, 137
Metropolitan Opera Company, 64
Mexico, 56, 89, 183, 202
Michelangelo, 164
Michigan, 11, 14, 52, 147, 219
Mile run, 219
Military-industrial complex, 55
Milky Way, 203
Milne, A.A., 52, 56
Minnesota, 70, 88, 100, 122
Mint, 79
Minuit, 242
Minuit, Peter, 95
Mir, 190
Missing In Action, 67
Mississippi, 48, 70
Mississippi River, 124
Missouri, 17, 40, 142
Missouri Compromise, 190, 234
Missouri River, 137
Mr. Hyde, 208
Mrs. O'Leary's cow, 168
Mitchell, Margaret, 109
Mohammed, 13
Mojave Desert, 190
Mona Lisa, 188, 239
Monaco, 237

Monarch butterfly, 91
Monday, 41
Mongolia, 184
Monitor, The, 48
Monroe, James, 31, 207
Monroe, Marilyn, 169
Monsoon, 97
Montana, 37, 46, 167
Montgomery, Lucy Maud, 60
Monticello, 42, 236
Montpelier (Vermont), 218
Montreal (Canada), 139
Montserrat, 115
Moon, 72, 125
Moore, Clement, 25, 144
Moose, 115
Mormons, 17, 176
Morse code, 94
Morse, Samuel F.B., 205
Moscow (Russia), 42, 101, 140
Mosquito, 55
Mothers Against Drunk Driving, 23
Mount Erebus, 40
Mount Everest, 1, 77
Mount of Olives, 131
Mount Pinatubo, 4, 206
Mount Rainier, 84
Mount Rainier National Park, 71
Mount Rushmore, 27, 29
Mount St. Helens, 79
Mount Vernon, 59, 214, 236
Mount Vesuvius, 125
Mountains, 179
Mozambique, 183
Mozart, Wolfgang Amadeus, 56, 250
Ms. magazine, 198
Mudd, Dr. Samuel, 68
Muhammad, 240
Muir Woods, 102, 146
Mulroney, Brian, 60
Munich (Germany), 29
Muscovites, 42
Muslim, 13, 73
Mussolini, Benito, 86
My Lai massacre, 72
My Story, 19
Myrrh, 137
NaCl, 19
Nagasaki (Japan), 23
Naismith, James, 176
Nancy Drew, 80, 260
Napoleon, 6, 33, 228
Narragansett Bay, 200
Nashville (Tennessee), 174
National Aeronautics and Space Administration, 82, 129
National Association for the Advancement of Colored People, 71
National Civil Rights Museum, 55
National Oceanic and Atmospheric Administration, 182
National Rifle Association, 151
National Zoo, 50
Nautilus, 260
Nazi Party, 20
Nebraska, 126
Nehru, Jawaharlal, 183

Nelson, Horatio, 17, 78
Nepal, 115
Neptune, 84, 231
Netherlands, The, 53, 213
Nevada, 30, 40, 112
Never-Never-Land, 92
New Hampshire, 215
New Haven (Connecticut), 107
New Jersey, 141, 183
New Mexico, 8, 72, 152, 181
New Orleans (Louisiana), 87
New York, 13, 90, 94, 237
New York City, 25, 33, 73, 208, 242, 256
New York Times, 205
New Zealand, 97, 134
Newbery Medal, 65, 209
Newfoundland, 78
Newspaper, 195
Newton, 107
Niagara River, 256
Nicotine, 217
Nigeria, 150, 223
Nightingale, Florence, 73, 198
Nippon, 173
Nixon, Richard, 11, 170, 193, 244, 248
Nixon Library, Richard, 241
Noah, 182
Nobel, Alfred, 14, 175
Nobel Peace Prize, 23, 117, 179, 212
Nobel Prizes, 14, 22, 46, 57
Noriega, Manuel, 68
Normandy, 4
Norse, 128
North American Free Trade Agreement, 126
North Atlantic Treaty Organization, 26
North Carolina, 48, 57, 101, 155, 186
North Church, 50
North Dakota, 90
North Korea, 129
North Star, 77
Norway, 177
Norwegian, 128
Nova Scotia, 109
Nunavut, 214
Nureyev, Rudolf, 55
Nursing, 198
"O Captain, My Captain," 84
O'Connor, Sandra Day, 220
Oakley, Annie, 62
Oasis, 259
Octagon, 54, 122
Octopus, 62
Odysseus, 230
Office of Management and Budget, 49
Oglethorpe, James, 1, 228
Ohio, 180, 185, 186, 240
Ohio River, 199
Oklahoma, 39
Oklahoma City, 201
Old Faithful, 85
Olympic medal, 186
Olympics, 1, 7, 50, 69, 105, 179, 181, 189, 210, 224, 254, 259
On the Origin of Species, 187
101 Dalmations, 254
180th meridian of longitude, 32
Ontario, 236

Opera, 8
Orbit, 22
Orchard, 100
Ore, 20
Organ, 202
Oriole Park at Camden Yards, 92
Orpheus, 163
Oscars, 190
Oslo (Norway), 57
Oswald, Lee Harvey, 2, 74
Ottawa (Canada), 124
Outer Banks, 101
Oval Office, 59
Owens, Jesse, 30
Owl, 60
Ozark Mountains, 200
Ozone layer, 171
Pacemaker, 75
Pacific Ocean, 18, 21, 78, 83, 117, 129, 233
Paderewski, Ignace, 15
Paganini, Niccolò, 142
Paige, Satchel, 148
Pakistan, 23
Palestine, 164
Palestine Liberation Organization, 2, 100
Palm Sunday, 77
Pampas, 208
Panama, 26, 36, 54, 68, 97, 120
Panda, 50, 219
Pandora's box, 40
Pangea, 251
Panmunjom (North Korea), 7
Paper money, 67
Parallelogram, 64, 78
Paris (France), 59, 136
Parker, John, 52
Parks, Rosa, 19, 110
Parliament, 74, 200, 235
Passover, 225
Paul Bunyan, 69, 70, 202
"Paul Revere's Ride," 81, 89
Pauling, Linus, 158
Pea plants, 63
Peace Corps, 29, 219
Peace Palace, 53
Pearl, 144, 146
Pearl Harbor (Hawaii), 24
Pegasus, 85
Penn, William, 110
Pennsylvania, 68, 69, 110, 111, 115, 134, 222
Pennsylvania Avenue, 1600, 96
Pennsylvania Gazette, 249
Pentagon, 52
Pentathlon, 111
Percussion, 168
Perkins, Frances, 219
Perón, Juan, 58
Perpendicular, 79
Perseus, 96
Persian Gulf, 31, 53
Personal computer, 192
Perth, 203
Peru, 18
Peter and the Wolf, 253
Peter Pan, 92
Peter Rabbit, 91
Petersburg National Battlefield Park, 102

Ph.D., 178
Philadelphia (Pennsylvania), 91, 185
Philippines, 4, 32, 35, 148, 206, 209
Philippine Islands, 137
Phrases
  ABC's of, The, 63
  Alma mater, 217
  Cold shoulder, 229
  Dust Bowl, 158
  Friendly fire, 236
  Generation X, 211
  Green with envy, 163
  Intelligence Quotient, 75
  John Hancock, 57
  Military-industrial complex, 55
  Nest egg, 165
  P's and Q's, 63
  Purple with rage, 163
  Red tape, 153
  Solid as the Rock of Gibraltar, 50
  Standing ovation, 243
  Tall tale, 230
  White collar, 5
Physics, 168
Piano, 21, 169
Piano, grand, 34
Pikes Peak, 36, 118
Pilgrims, 37, 61, 135, 191
Pioneer 12, 18
Pistons, 180
Pitcher, Molly, 141
Pixar Animation Studios, 147
Pizarro, Francisco, 66
Plains of Abraham, 180
Planets, 210
Plasma, 124
"Pledge of Allegiance," 22
Pluto, 59, 65, 140, 188, 200
Plutonium, 157
Plymouth (Massachusetts), 61, 135, 191
Po River, 228
Pocahontas, 173, 255
Poe, Edgar Allan, 61, 210, 228
Poet laureate, 16
Poinsettia, 143
Poland, 15, 113
Polaris, 77
Polio, 69, 95, 106
Polk, James, 35
Polygon, 53
Poncho, 233
Pony Express, 142
Poor Richard's Almanac, 49
Popcorn, 260
Pope, 61
Poppins, Mary, 217
Population, world, 239
Pork, 233
Portland, 222
Portugal, 51
Portuguese, 198
Potomac River, 59, 89, 214
Potter, Beatrix, 11, 91
Pound, 3
Presidents' Day, 183
Presley, Elvis, 169
Primary colors, 235

Primary election, 173
Primates, 237
Prime meridian, 62
Prime Minister, 46
Prince Charles, 44, 103
Prince Edward Island, 60
Prince Hakon, 177
Prince Rainier, 237
"Princess and the Pea, The," 38
Princess Diana, 44
Princess Kristin, 177
Prisoner of War, 67
Pro-am, 129
Prokofiev, Sergei, 253
Prometheus, 138
Promised Land, 67
Protein(s), 67, 127
Protons, 86
Proverb, 224
Provinces, 209
Puerto Rico, 43, 58, 113, 123, 126
Puget Sound, 146
Pulitzer Prize, 3, 243, 245
Pullman, George, 188
Purple Heart, 25
Quakers, 52, 158
Quarks, 245
Quasimodo, 36
Quebec, 17
Queen Elizabeth II, 38, 96, 130, 182
Queen Victoria, 185
Quotations/Slogans/Mottoes
  "All we ask is to be left alone," 141
  "Be Prepared," 205
  "Don't put the cart before the horse," 234
  "Early to bed, early to rise," 49
  E pluribus unum, 252
  "Even God Almighty has only 10 points," 163
  "Free at last," 57
  "From where the sun now stands," 106
  "I am the last President of the United States," 155
  "I have a dream," 27, 161, 185
  "I have not yet begun to fight," 176
  "I know not what course others may take," 76, 217
  "I regret that I have but one life to lose for my country," 207
  "I'd rather be right than be president," 5
  In God We Trust, 177
  "It takes two to tango," 132
  "Iron Curtain," 61
  "Liberty and Union, now and forever," 59
  "Main work of my life is done, The," 159
  "May the force be with you," 31
  "Me want cookie," 31
  "Oh, give me a home where the buffalo roam," 172
  "Remember the Alamo," 72
  "So this is the little lady who made the big war," 44
  "Speak softly and carry a big stick," 117
  "Stand your ground," 52
  "This will be over soon, and then I can go home to Tara," 174
  "Three men in a tub," 17
  "Three strikes and you're out," 210

"'Tis our true policy to steer clear of permanent alliances," 12
"Watson come here. I want you," 50
"We hold these Truths to be self-evident," 109
"World must be made safe for Democracy, The," 142
"World will little note, The," 239
Radar, 29
Radio, 226
Radon, 74
Railway sleeping car, 188
Rainbow, 32, 209
Rainey, Ma, 142
Raleigh, Sir Walter, 255
Ramses the Great, 88
Ravel, Maurice, 236
"Raven, The," 61
Ray, James Earl, 79,
Reagan, Nancy, 180
Reagan, Ronald, 60, 66, 218, 227, 248
Reconstruction, 231
Rectangle, 75
Red Sea, 42, 53, 93, 96
"Red Shoes, The," 38
Red Square, 101
Redwoods, 146
Rehnquist, William, 32
Remington, Frederic, 27
Republican, 99
Republican Party, 195
Revelation, 157
Revels, Hiram, 70
Revere, Paul, 50
Revolution, 156
Revolutionary War, 28, 148, 159
Reyes Syndrome, 9
Rhinoceros, 49
Rhode Island, 200
Rhombus, 64
Rice, 108
Richmond (Virginia), 80, 235
Richter scale, 178, 220
Ride, Sally, 252
Rimsky-Korsakov, Nicolai, 83
Rio Grande, 96, 133
Rip Van Winkle, 128, 199
Ripken Jr., Cal, 190
Riyadh (Saudi Arabia), 246
"Road Not Taken, The," 219
Robinson Crusoe, 2, 204
Rock, 194
Rockwell, Norman, 208
Rolfe, John, 133
Roman numerals, 20, 23, 24, 27, 39, 45, 70, 96, 109, 163, 179, 184, 203
Rome (Italy), 144, 165
Romeo and Juliet, 84
Romulus, 144
Roosevelt, Eleanor, 104
Roosevelt, Franklin D., 5, 14, 65, 75, 106, 123, 152, 175, 188, 251
Roosevelt, (Teddy) Theodore, 8, 29, 30, 46, 59, 85, 116, 117, 257
Roots, 26
Rosh Hashanah, 78
Ross, Nellie, 208
Rotunda, 245
Ruble, 254
Ruby, Jack, 74
"Rudolph, the Red-Nosed Reindeer," 130
Russia, 36, 89, 132, 143, 254
Russian flag, 188
Russian Revolution, 116, 178
Ruth, Babe, 157, 174, 202
Rwanda, 145
Sabin, Albert, 95
Sacajawea, 226
Sacramento (California), 80
St. Augustine, 251
St. Louis (Missouri), 11, 254
St. Luke, 254
Saint Nicholas, 39, 181
St. Patrick, 72, 220
St. Patrick's Day, 193
St. Peter's Church, 193
St. Petersburg (Russia), 138, 178
Salem (Massachusetts), 137
Salem (Oregon), 80
Salk, Dr. Jonas, 69, 72
Salt, 220
San Andreas Fault, 127
San Antonio (Texas), 189
San Diego (California), 22
San Francisco (California), 98, 147
San Jacinto, 224
Sand, 172
Santa Ana winds, 121
Santa Anna, 72, 224
Santa Claus, 181
Sarah, Plain and Tall, 202
Saturday Evening Post, 208
Saturn, 62
Saudi Arabia, 53
Savannah (Georgia), 1, 31, 228
Saxophone, 60, 183
Scarlett O'Hara, 174
Score, 106
Scotland, 3, 201, 234
Scotland Yard, 93, 184
Sears Tower, 153
Seattle (Washington), 77, 84, 146
Sebaceous glands, 147
Secret Garden, The, 98, 103
Secret Service, 203
Sedimentary rock, 2, 170, 194
Seize, 50
Senate Minority Leader, 38
Sendak, Maurice, 106
Seton, Elizabeth, 6
Seuss, Dr., 53, 104, 170
Seward, William, 143
Shakespeare, William, 2, 57, 84
Shepard Jr., Alan B., 94
Sherlock Holmes, 180
Sherman, William T., 38, 66
Shoemaker-Levy 9, 156
Shubert, Franz, 184
Sierra Club, 2
Sierra Madre, 202
Sierra Nevada, 2, 154
Similar, 172
Singer, Isaac Bashevis, 143
Skin, 147
Smallpox, 254

Smithsonian Institution, 29, 177
Smithsonian's Museum of Natural History, 104
Smog, 115
Smokey the Bear, 141
Soccer, 132, 170
Social Security (Act), 75, 111
Socrates, 247
Sodium chloride, 19
Solution, 185
Solzhenitsyn, Alexander, 22
Somalia, 30
Sonic boom, 248
Sound of Music, The, 128
Sonar, 243
Sousa, John Philip, 18, 107, 258
Sousaphone, 107, 161
South Africa, 64, 111, 236
South America, 71, 103, 159, 203
South Carolina, 155, 186, 197
South Dakota, 27, 119, 246
Soviet Union, 11, 181, 221
Spain, 7, 77, 81, 189, 207
Spanish, 36, 58
Spanish American War, 82, 197, 205
Speaker of the House, 139, 214
Spectrum, 29, 35, 216
Spelling
    Accession, 193
    Accidentally, 237
    Achievement, 223
    Acknowledged, 26
    Acquired, 77
    Acquitted, 222
    Afghanistan, 218
    Allegedly, 108
    Allies, 241
    Amateur, 35
    Ambassador, 56
    Amendment, 211
    Antarctica, 8
    Appalachian, 118
    Appointee, 78
    Appropriations, 86
    Archaeologists, 10
    Architect, 6
    Architecture, 197
    Artificial, 56
    Ascend, 238
    Assassination, 11
    Assess, 167
    Assistant, 89
    Asylum, 63
    Athletes, 193
    Attorney, 71
    Avalanche, 33
    Bankruptcy, 220
    Bidding, 120
    Boulders, 165
    Calendar, 204
    Calvary, 147
    Camouflage, 171
    Campaigning, 4
    Candidate, 218
    Capital, 193
    Capitol, 90
    Caribbean, 121
    Cavalry, 16

Cease, 110
Cease-fire, 16
Ceded, 46
Cemetery, 216
Censorship, 27
Centennial, 223
Chalet, 28, 246
Chateau, 28
Chauffeur, 116
Chef, 234
Choreography, 82
Chronicle, 195
Civilians, 95
Colonel, 89
Commemorate, 54
Commemorating, 203
Commencement, 107
Commercial, 228
Commissioner, 205
Committed, 98
Conceded, 222
Concerto, 188
Condemning, 33
Connecticut, 107, 207
Conqueror, 107
Conquistador, 231
Copyright, 120
Corps, 29
Council, 106
Counsel, 214
Counterfeiter, 81
Coup, 25, 161
Cuisine, 92
Debris, 70, 165
Debt, 100
Debut, 39
Deceased, 140
Dinosaurs, 2
Disastrous, 52
Discoverer, 19
Discriminate, 122
Drought, 43
Effectively, 105
Eligible, 229
Empress, 214
Environment, 251
Environmental, 37
Epitaph, 111
Extinction, 113
Foliage, 239
Foreign, 104
Formally, 112
Genealogy, 224
Genetically, 156
Ghetto, 79
Guaranteed, 74
Guarantees, 204
Gubernatorial, 126, 154
Haiti, 108
Harassment, 123
Hawaii, 155
Hawaiian, 23
Heir, 59
Hemisphere, 83
Heroes, 223
Immigration, 51
Inaccurately, 133

Inaugurated, 7, 233
Inauguration, 109
Indivisible, 22
Initial, 94
Initiated, 48
Inoculation, 123
Inseparable, 59
Iridescent, 175
Kamikaze, 97
Kennedy, 122
Kindergarten, 167
Laboratories, 219
Laboratory, 132
Larynx, 255
League, 101
Leisure, 147
Libraries, 43
Loosened, 135
Lying, 94
Lynching, 159
Martyr, 139
Massachusetts, 190
Massacred, 136
Mathematician, 49
Medal, 173
Meddle, 173
Medieval, 87
Mediterranean, 35
Memphis, 81
Millennium, 174
Minnesota, 182
Missiles, 197
Mission, 122
Mojave, 195
Monarch, 254
Mosque, 48
Mutual, 114
Negotiate, 160
Negotiating, 99
Negotiations, 57
Nighttime, 122
Nominee, 64
Nonconsecutive, 233
Officially, 67
Opposition, 149
Oppressors, 157
Originally, 125
Pamphlet, 170
Parachutist, 120
Paralysis, 112
Pare, 73
Parliament, 192
Passed, 125
Pennsylvania, 115
Permanently, 100
Perseverance, 137
Personnel, 115
Philanthropy, 195
Philippines, 5, 101
Phlegm, 210
Physician, 52
Plague, 153
Plaque, 55
Playwright, 60
Pneumonia, 80
Preceded, 58
Predecessor, 59

Prejudice, 159
Principle, 203
Privilege, 18
Procedure, 45
Proclaim, 13
Prosecutor, 27
Pseudonym, 239
Publicly, 214
Puerto Rico, 125
Recommend, 88
Recommendation, 118
Refugees, 8
Reign, 217
Renaissance, 18
Renowned, 66
Resuscitate, 87
Rhythm, 14
Sarajevo, 248
Satellite, 15
Scarves, 162
Scheduling, 131
Scholarship, 132
Sculptures, 185
Secede, 172
Secession, 186
Secretary, 29
Seize, 110
Seizure, 11
Seizures, 53
Separation, 221
Shuttle, 122
Site, 225
Sloping, 257
Sophomores, 76
Strait, 91
Studios, 12
Succeed, 117
Succession, 9
Successor, 20
Superintendent, 66
Surgeon, 135
Survey, 34
Surveyor, 107
Susceptible, 61
Symphony, 178
Technology, 198
Tennessee, 67
Tentative, 96
Tentatively, 134
Terrorists, 102
Thailand, 65
Toll, 158
Tomb, 47
Trafficking, 229
Unanimous, 139
Unprecedented, 93
Vaccination, 130
Vaccine, 72
Varying, 138
Vehicle, 236
Vengeance, 252
Versailles, 38, 107
Wrestling, 62
Yugoslavia, 82
Yukon, 246
Spielberg, Steven, 50
Spring training, 70

Springfield (Illinois), 251
Springfield (Massachusetts), 247
Sputnik, 64
Square, 73
Sri Lanka, 84
Stalin, Joseph, 137, 181
Stamp Act, 117
"Star-Spangled Banner, The," 20, 65, 188
"Stars and Stripes," 136
"Stars and Stripes Forever, The," 258
State of the Union, 153
States of matter, 152
Statuary Hall, 122
Statue of Liberty, 26, 109, 252
Steel, 151, 249
Stethoscope, 58
Stevenson, Robert Louis, 36, 83, 124, 208, 249
Stine, R.L., 256
Stockholm (Sweden), 57
Stone, Lucy, 42
Stonehenge, 206
Stowe, Harriet Beecher, 44
Strait, 98
Strategic Arms Reduction Treaty, 48
Straus, Oscar, 116
Stuart, Gilbert, 221
Sudan, 187
Suez Canal, 42, 181
Suffrage, 82
Sugar Bowl, 69
Sun Devil Stadium, 163
Sun, 141
Superfudge, 30
Supreme Court, 4, 8, 98, 144, 220
Supreme Court Cases
   Brown v. Board of Education, 32, 62
   Miranda v. Arizona, 28
   Roe v. Wade, 165
Supreme Court votes, 98
Sweden, 14
Swift, Jonathan, 95
Switzerland, 45
Sydney (Australia), 105
Symphony, 207
Symphony orchestra, 131
Syria, 180
Table salt, 19
Tadpoles, 171
Taiwan, 7, 199
Tale of Peter Rabbit, The, 12
Tales of a Fourth Grade Nothing, 30
Tanzania, 199
Tariff, 54
Tarrytown (New York), 128
Tasman Sea, 141
Tasman, Abel, 134
Teamsters, 184
Tecumseh, 107
Teenage Mutant Ninja Turtles, 212
Teeth, 15, 203
Tennessee, 155, 223
Tennis, 71
Tennyson, Alfred Lord, 16
Tentacles, 209
Texas, 16, 29, 124, 224, 260
Thailand, 170
Thatcher, Margaret, 59, 219

38th parallel, 131
Thomas, Clarence, 162
Thomas, Doubting, 162
Thorpe, Jim, 111
Three Bears, The, 121
Three Mile Island, 222
Thumbelina, 245
Tiber River, 106, 176
Ticks, 197
Tierra del Fuego, 203
Tigger, 56
Time zones, 7, 42, 76
Times Square, 73, 208
Titanic, 21
Tobacco, 133
Tornado Alley, 123
Toronto Blue Jays, 12
Tortoise, 80
Tower of Pisa, 65
Toy Story, 147
Trachea, 125
Transcontinental railroad, 89
Trapezoid, 106
Treason, 61
Treasure Island, 36, 83, 124
Treaty of Guadalupe Hidalgo, 56
Treaty of Paris, 54, 62
Trench, 179
Trial jury, 21
Tributary, 133
Trojan horse, 216
Tropic of Cancer, 221
Tropic of Capricorn, 221
Troubling A Star, 168
Truman, Harry S, 178
Tuberculosis, 68, 215, 222
Turkey, 13, 18, 204
Tuskegee (Alabama), 127
Tutu, Desmond, 175
Twain, Mark, 25, 38, 41, 138
'Twas the Night Before Christmas, 144
Twenty Thousand Leagues Under the Sea, 101, 129
2001: A Space Odyssey, 163
Typhoon, 37
Tyrannosaurus rex, 38
"Ugly Duckling, The," 38, 47
U.N. secretary-general, 25
U.N. Security Council, 10
U.S. Air Force Academy, 140
U.S. Congress, 44, 114, 200, 242
U.S. Constitution, 101
U.S. Constitutional Amendments
   8th Amendment, 254
   13th Amendment, 45, 212
   17th Amendment, 82
   18th Amendment, 167
   19th Amendment, 156
   21st Amendment, 167
   22nd Amendment, 208
   23rd Amendment, 24
   26th Amendment, 125
U.S. flag, 124, 209
U.S. Holocaust Memorial Museum, 233
U.S. House of Representatives, 70, 127, 216, 255
U.S. Military Academy, 140, 161, 235
U.S. Naval Academy, 15, 140
U.S. population, 150

U.S. Post Office, 81
U.S. Senate, 254
U.s. senator, 108
U.S. Space and Rocket Center, 10
U.S. Virgin Islands, 52
U.S.S. *Constitution*, 161
U.S.S. *Maine*, 205
U.S.S. *Missouri*, 224
Ukraine, 78, 113
Umbra, 148
Uncle Remus, 43, 212
Underground Railroad, 199
Underlining, 26
Union, 90
Union of Soviet Socialist Republics, 102
United Kingdom, 79, 120
United Nations, 13, 185, 258
United Nations Charter, 98
United Nations International Children's Emergency Fund, 40
Upper Peninsula, 147
Uranium, 252
Uranus, 65, 104, 105, 182
USSR, 57
Utah, 32,
Vacuum, 30
Valley Forge, 69
Van Gogh, Vincent, 240
Vatican, The, 20
Venezuela, 151
Venus, 53, 84, 103, 105, 223, 257
Vermont, 9, 243
Verne, Jules, 101, 177
Versailles Peace Conference, 107
Vespucci, Amerigo, 215
Veterans Day, 121
Vice Presidency, 214
Vietnam, 72, 97, 127, 136, 154, 258
Vietnam Veterans Memorial, 29, 223
Vietnam War, 253
Vietnam War museum, 183
Vineyard, 100
Violin, 142
Virginia, 13, 23, 79, 92, 102, 124, 192, 194
Vitamin C, 158, 170
Vitamin D, 8
Vitamins, 230
Vocabulary
  Abolitionists, 145
  Aborigines, 190
  Ace, 152
  Acquit, 213
  Acronym, 56
  Aeronautics, 129
  Aggression, 161
  Allah, 247
  Almanac, 253
  Ambassador, 13
  Amnesty, 136
  Amphibious, 155
  Anagrams, 119, 225
  Anarchy, 76
  Anesthetic, 145
  Angiogram, 39
  Animated, 232
  Ante-, 104
  Anthology, 255

Antiseptic, 205
Aquatic, 3
Aqueduct, 172
Arbitration, 144
Archaeologist, 6
Archbishop, 175
Arid, 119
Arsenal, 179
Artifact, 33
Atrium, 1
Aurora borealis, 226
Autobiography, 48
Ayatollah, 250
Azure, 24
Bail, 119
Ballot, 204
Band, 227
Bankrupt, 42
Bar, 234
Bibliography, 148
Bicentennial, 171
Bigamy, 93
Bikini, 258
Bilateral, 150
Biography, 21, 164
Biotechnology, 181
Bipartisan, 114
Blitzkrieg, 65
Boycott, 167
Brackish, 175
Bribery, 225
Brokers, 195
Bungee, 247
Canal, 9
Canonized, 6
Canyon, 130
Carat, 89
Cardi-, 66
Cardiologist, 245
Carjacking, 246
Carnivorous, 138
Cathedral, 174
Centennial, 8
Chalet, 167, 242
Chapeau, 105
Charismatic, 55
Choreographer, 109
Circum-, 91
Cobbler, 156
Commence, 6
Convent, 86
Copyright, 198
Corporation, 80
Cosmonaut, 74
Coup, 146
Cranium, 207
Crust, 191
Curator, 134
Cyberspace, 109
Debut, 115
Decathlon, 213
Deceased, 124
Den, 136
Deport, 35
Detain, 220
Digraph, 192
Dismantle, 115

Dissolve, 223
Draft, 120
Ellipse, 144
Elliptical, 142
Embargo, 122
Embassies, 223
Embezzlement, 64
Entomologist, 240
Epidemic, 221
Equestrian, 31
Essay, 240
Etching, 180
Eulogy, 150
Evacuate, 158
Extraterrestrial, 78
Facsimile, 67
Famine, 14
Feline, 132
Felony, 116
Fiancée, 86
Flotilla, 252
Fraternal, 254
Fraud, 219
Fungi, 195
Genealogy, 68
Graffiti, 257
Guerrillas, 123
Guillotine, 112
Harvest, 159
Hawk, 71
Helicopter, 193
Holocaust, 233
Homicide, 121
Homily, 204
Homograph, 87
Homophones, 55
Horticulturist, 60
Hotheaded, 228
Hyper-, 135
Ignite, 176
Impeach, 45, 102
Import, 213
Inauguration, 151
Indict, 108
Infantry, 191
Insomnia, 252
Interned, 14
Invocation, 49
Jabber, 139
Kosher, 117
Lent, 139
Lethal, 207
Lilliputian, 96
Lunar, 128
Mall, 35
Maritime, 69
Mesa, 10
Metropolis, 137
Metropolitan, 64
Micro-, 46
Mole, 227
Monarch, 208
Monopoly, 100
Mont, 115
Mosque, 204
Murals, 88
Mutiny, 76, 208

Narcotics, 153
Neo-Nazi, 173
Nocturnal, 211
Obelisk, 257
Obituary, 68
Octogenarian, 81
Orator, 126
Pasta, 248
Pastels, 238
Patent, 4
Perk, 99
Pharaoh, 242
Phil-, 9
Philanthropist, 171
Pioneer, 18
Poll, 240
Pontoon, 152
Porcine, 159
Pork, 75, 233
Portrait, 130
Predecessors, 229
Prime ministers, 246
Pseudo-, 200
Quincentennial, 171
Ransom, 141
Ratify, 174
Refract, 257
Refute, 247
Rendezvous, 142
Retaliate, 153
Rookie, 121
Royalty, 145
Sari, 235
Scrolls, 215
Septuplets, 120
Sequel, 44
Shark, 166
Sí, 151
Sideburns, 130
Siesta, 242
Soprano, 191
Spelunkers, 162
Stalking, 76
Stallion, 39
Subpoena, 114
Suffix, 50
Suffrage, 82
Suicide, 85
Summit, 129
Symphony, 207
Synonym, 215
Tariff, 131
Tele-, 44
Telethon, 257
Tenor, 260
Thespian, 241
Toupee, 237
Trans-, 207
Treason, 225, 231
Tributaries, 192
Trumpet, 241
Ultimatum, 185
Unanimous, 102
Urban, 100
Vaccination, 253
Veto, 129
Virtues, 258

Warranty, 140
Wharf, 236
Voting Rights Act, 4
Vulcan, 181
Wagner, Richard, 185
Wales, 189, 213
Walker, Mary Edwards, 48
Wall Street Journal, 205
Wallace, George, 193
War on Poverty, 210
War of the Worlds, The, 29, 54
War of 1812, 51, 107
Warm Springs (Georgia), 14
Warren Commission, 2
Washington, 71, 79, 84, 164
Washington, Booker T., 127, 257
Washington, D.C., 26, 29, 50, 91, 223, 249
Washington, George, 12, 25, 29, 31, 44, 59, 88, 94, 221
Washington Monument, 190
Water, 208
Waterloo, 6
Weathering, 218
Weaver, Robert, 56
Webster, Noah, 33
Weekly Reader, 19
Welles, Orson, 29, 54
Wells, H.G., 29
Welsh, 189
Wesley, John, 197
West Germany, 41
West Point, 22, 235
West Virginia, 15, 106, 152, 200
Western Hemisphere, 218
Whale, 92, 135, 139
White blood cells, 150
White collar, 5
White Fang, 127
White House, 96, 152, 177, 248, 259
Whitman, Walt, 84
Whitney, Eli, 43, 130
Wilder, Laura Ingalls, 29, 116
Wilderness, 245
Wilderness Road, 35
William I (the Conqueror), 19, 107
Wilson, Woodrow, 142, 205, 260
Winnie-the-Pooh, 52, 56
Wirz, Henry, 33
Wisconsin, 168
Witch trials, 137
Women's Hall of Fame, 110
Wonderful Wizard of Oz, The, 32, 51, 155
Woodwinds, 168
World Cup soccer, 105, 132
World Health Organization, 32, 126
World Trade Center, 73
World War II, 171
World's Fair, 1962, 84
"Wreck of the Hesperus, The," 194
Wren, Christopher, 6
Wright, Frank Lloyd, 173
Wrinkle in Time, A, 168
WWI, 88
Wynken, Blynken, and Nod, 132
Wyoming, 46, 136, 208, 257
Xylophone, 244
Yale University, 107, 194

Yankee Stadium, 157
Yeager, Charles E., 45
Yellowstone National Park, 22, 46, 85, 195, 257
Yeltsin, Boris, 99, 105, 170, 195
Yemen, 144
Yiddish, 141
Yorba Linda (California), 241, 248
Yorktown (Virginia), 23, 258
Yosemite National Park, 102
Young, Brigham, 17, 176
Young, Denton T. "Cy," 94
Yucatan Peninsula, 105
Yugoslavia, 136, 206
Zaire, 123
Zodiac, 221, 231